CANADIANS UNDER FIRE

CANADIANS
UNDER FIRE

Infantry Effectiveness in the Second World War

ROBERT ENGEN

McGILL-QUEEN'S UNIVERSITY PRESS

Montreal & Kingston · London · Ithaca

ISBN 978-0-7735-3626-5

Legal deposit fourth quarter 2009
Bibliothèque nationale du Québec

Printed in Canada on acid-free paper that is 100% ancient forest free (100% post-consumer recycled), processed chlorine free.

This book has been published with the help of a grant from the Canadian Federation for the Humanities and Social Sciences, through the Aid to Scholarly Publications Programme, using funds provided by the ·Social Sciences and Humanities Research Council of Canada. Funding has also been provided by the Canadian Defence Academy of the Department of National Defence.

McGill-Queen's University Press acknowledges the support of the Canada Council for the Arts for our publishing program. We also acknowledge the financial support of the Government of Canada through the Book Publishing Industry Development Program (BPIDP) for our publishing activities.

Library and Archives Canada Cataloguing in Publication

Engen, Robert C. (Robert Charles)
Canadians under fire : infantry effectiveness in the Second World War / Robert C. Engen.

Includes bibliographical references and index.
ISBN 978-0-7735-3626-5

1. Canada. Canadian Army–Infantry–Operational readiness. 2. Canada. Canadian Army–History–World War, 1939–1945. 3. Marshall, S.L.A. (Samuel Lyman Atwood), 1900–1977. I. Title.

D768.15.E545 2009   940.540971   C2009-903662-2

This book was designed and typeset by studio oneonone in Garamond 11/14

For my partner, Claire.
… in perpetuity.

CONTENTS

ACKNOWLEDGMENTS

Writing *Canadians Under Fire*, my first book, has been a challenging, sobering, and delightful experience, and has been made possible by the assistance of a number of individuals to whom I owe a great deal.

This book has its origins as a graduate thesis at Queen's University, Kingston, and I owe thanks to all the members of my defence committee: Dr Jeffrey McNairn, Dr Jeffrey Brison, Dr Randall Wakelam, and Dr Alan Okros. Their suggestions for improvement and revision of the text were vital in rewriting it as a manuscript. My supervisor at Queen's, Dr Allan English, deserves all the credit and gratitude in the world, as it was his encouragement and insistence upon the merit of this project that initially gave me the impetus to seek publication and has kept me working toward this goal ever since. I also need to thank two of my fellow PhD candidates at Queen's, Howard Coombs and Matthew Trudgen, for, respectively, originally informing me about the existence of the battle experience questionnaire collection, and for hospitality during my many trips to Ottawa. My good friend Shen-wei Mark Lim also did a masterful job of tabulating my research into an incredibly convenient spreadsheet, something I know I could not have done myself. The History Department at Queen's University has provided a welcoming and intellectually stimulating environment for my research from the beginning. And, most importantly, my partner, Claire Cookson-Hills, has been both an inspiration and a tireless editor, reader, and commentator on my work.

I owe Major-General Daniel Gosselin and the staff at the Canadian Defence Academy a great deal of thanks and gratitude for their generous financial contribution to this project, as I do the Canadian Federation of Humanities and Social Sciences for their support through the Aid to Scholarly Publications Program.

The editors and staff at McGill-Queen's University Press have been exceptionally helpful and tolerant of this nervous first-time author, and have taken much of the anxiety and trepidation out of the publication process. I owe special thanks to Kyla Madden, my editor in Kingston, and Joan McGilvray, the coordinating editor in Montreal, for their hard work, encouragement, and belief in this project. Jane McWhinney in Toronto also did an excellent job copyediting the manuscript and transforming it into something worth releasing to the public.

On a personal note, I have too many people to thank to list them all: friends and family in Calgary and the United States, and friends, colleagues, and peers in Kingston. Thank you all for your love and support throughout my writing of this book.

CANADIANS UNDER FIRE

INTRODUCTION

A fascination with the quality and effectiveness of military power runs deep in the roots of Western culture. Homeric verse captures the essence of battlefield effectiveness in ancient Greece in the concept of *aristeia*, the prowess and qualitative excellence of the warrior in combat. In the dramatic conventions of heroic poetry like the *Iliad*, a scene of *aristeia* was one in which the hero was inspired to offensive action of such power and excellence that it would usually result in the death or defeat of any foes standing in the hero's way, mortals or gods alike.[1] While the time of the heroic warfare of the *Iliad* has long passed, and disciplined mechanized armies have taken the place of the individual warrior striving for battlefield glory, the assumption has remained that victorious armies possess a certain quality or collection of qualities that elevates them above the defeated.

In more recent reckoning, "combat effectiveness" has been the subject of considerable scholarly debate, and while there exists no consensus, an acceptable definition for the term is that it encompasses the ability of a military force to carry out its assigned mission successfully and ultimately prevail in combat.[2] "Combat effectiveness" is a function of a number of factors, including highly subjective criteria such as troop cohesion, leadership quality, resilience, and soldiers' willingness to fight and "impose their will" upon an enemy. It also includes more objective elements such as the material and technical capabilities and operational readiness of a military unit.3 Some analysts describe combat effectiveness as the process by which armed forces convert their resources into fighting power, and such arguments categorize combat motivation, leadership, and *esprit de corps* as quantifiable "resources."4 Ultimately, the effectiveness of a given military force can best be judged by its performance on the battlefield, but that performance is at the same time a function of the combat effectiveness of a unit. *Aristeia* remains a good term to envelope the different aspects of the concept; combat effectiveness is what constitutes the "winning" qualities in a victorious force, or, by default, the "losing" qualities in a defeated one.

Efforts to identify the *aristeia* of contemporary armies and assign an empirical, quantifiable value to combat effectiveness have preoccupied some military historians and operational analysts since the end of the Second World War. Despite the inherent subjectivity of many core elements of combat effectiveness, which would better qualify it as a form of "art" rather than a science, attempts to quantify effectiveness empirically are widespread. This is not surprising: explaining the "why" and "how" of an army's performance in battle makes for interesting military history, while attempting to gather such data for use in predicting the performance of future military forces makes for lucrative analytical prognostication. It is fundamentally easier to rely upon supposedly quantified, objective criteria, since empirical data are easier to collect, measure, and analyse than more subjective sociological, psychological, and political phenomena.5 Branches of operations research have applied mathematical and statistical models to the experience of war to try to determine the combat effectiveness of a given unit or army. "Cost per kill," the number of friendly soldiers lost as casualties per enemy soldier killed or wounded, was an undeniably empirical measure of effectiveness, and it provides a popular numerical assessment of effectiveness to this day.6 By such calculations, for example, since the German soldier of the Second World War regularly inflicted three casualties upon the Allies for every two casualties sustained, the *Wehrmacht* was considered more combat-effective than the Allied armies, in spite of its ultimate defeat.7

Another popular way of quantifying military effectiveness is the concept of the "divisional slice." Also known as the "teeth-to-tail ratio," the divisional slice is the proportion of support personnel to combat soldiers. According to Canadian historian John English, during the Second World War seven noncombatant men were needed in the divisions of the Western Allies (the United States, Britain, and Canada) to keep one man fighting, whereas in the Soviet Red Army the same ratio was lower than two to one.[8] In this view, the army that is best able to weed out inefficient bureaucracy and redundancy from its organization will best be able to capitalize on its own resources and fighting power, and will thus be the most combat-effective – although this calculation downplays the benefits of a strong logistical and support infrastructure. Furthermore, elaborate computational frameworks have been built, using a number of input variables to produce statistical values of "fighting effectiveness." These were most famously employed by Colonel Trevor Dupuy. According to Dupuy's computational analysis of tactical combat on the western European theatres of operation in the Second World War, the *Wehrmacht* held a 20 percent "fighting effectiveness" advantage over the Allies, regardless of all other circumstances.[9]

The Second World War has been the most-studied of all conflicts in terms of assessing and attempting to quantify combat effectiveness. This attention may be due to a popular perception among both scholars and laymen that the war's results were incongruous. Many believe that the armed forces of Nazi Germany represented the pinnacle of modern military effectiveness, and that the *Wehrmacht* and *Waffen-SS* divisions displayed unparalleled organizational and fighting qualities from 1939 to 1945, only to be overwhelmed by numbers and Allied material resources in the end.[10] For much of the past sixty years the view has been perpetuated that the land forces of the Allied countries – particularly Britain, the United States, and Canada – performed poorly in comparison to the Germans, and that their eventual triumph had little if anything to do with the combat effectiveness and fighting skill of their own soldiers. Many of the aforementioned studies attempted to explain Germany's superiority and the Allies' shortcomings by quantification in support of their conclusions. However, no attempt at quantifying the effectiveness of soldiers in battle comes close to being as influential as the work of American journalist S.L.A. Marshall on what he termed the "ratio of fire."

Samuel Lyman Atwood Marshall, (whose name is almost always written as S.L.A. Marshall, or SLAM) was not one to adhere to established patterns of military thinking. An American journalist, battlefield observer, and military writer from the First World War to Vietnam, Marshall, through his voluminous writings, helped to define the study of human behaviour in combat during the second half of the twentieth century.

Never shy about overturning an established idea if he believed it to be faulty, Marshall made a successful career and name for himself through examining, critiquing, and attempting to reform American military policy. His 1947 book *Men Against Fire* is still considered the definitive monograph on infantry combat and the high water mark for measuring combat effectiveness, in that it brings quantification to a very subjective, psychological element of warfare – combat motivation. Results from Marshall's interviews with American soldiers during the Second World War, which will be discussed in more depth in later chapters, showed that only 15 to 25 percent of front-line combat riflemen ever fired their weapons. The great majority of soldiers, the remaining 75 to 85 percent, not only made no effort to kill the enemy in battle, but did not so much as fire their rifles to miss, intimidate, or suppress.[11] Marshall believed that an army's relative combat effectiveness could be measured at the tactical level as a function of how many infantrymen fired their weapons at the enemy, as he was utterly convinced of the supremacy of small-unit firepower in the course of battle. An army in which even elite rifle companies could expect no more than a quarter of their riflemen to make any use of their weapons could not be considered an effective war-fighting institution. Even in Marshall's U.S. Army in the European Theatre of Operations, the infantry carried the brunt of the fighting and sustained the worst of the war's casualties; over 85 percent of all combat casualties were suffered by infantry divisions.[12] If, throughout the army, only a handful of soldiers in any given squad could be counted upon to do any actual fighting, Marshall estimated, then the empirical measurement of this ratio could function as a new quantitative measure for combat effectiveness. An army in which 100 percent of front-line riflemen took part in the fighting could be considered fully combat-effective; conversely, the lower the ratio of men firing their weapons, the more difficulties with combat motivation the unit had, and hence the lower its effectiveness. When compared to the problem of soldiers not fighting at all, most other measurements of combat effectiveness seemed like foolishness to Marshall.

This makes a certain sense, since Marshall's ratio of fire properly locates the essence of combat effectiveness in unit cohesion and soldiers' willingness to resist and engage the enemy. But it was through the precise quantification of this ratio, from data supposedly gathered in post-combat group interviews with infantry units, that S.L.A. Marshall established this new means of measuring combat effectiveness and solidified his reputation as a military theorist. Although few scholars have attempted to take their own measurements of firing ratios, Marshall's work has nonetheless come to be regarded as one of the pivotal historical analyses not only of the U.S. Army in the Second World War but also more generally of human behaviour in warfare.[13] *Men Against Fire* remains one of the most-cited books in the literature on combat effectiveness and the human elements of battle.

This present study has two purposes. The first is to examine accounts of Canadian infantry soldiers' experience in combat during the Second World War, with the aim of assessing those soldiers' effectiveness in battle. New primary source evidence, provided by a series of previously unanalysed battle experience questionnaires taken by Canadian officers before the end of the war, gives historians a fresh look at the tactical realities of combat at the section, platoon, and company level. The second purpose of this study is to use this new evidence to directly address the ratio of fire claims made by S.L.A. Marshall's book *Men Against Fire*, which for sixty years has conveyed the impression that Allied infantrymen in the Second World War were profoundly ineffective combatants. Although scholars have challenged Marshall's credibility before, documented historical evidence has never before been available either to validate or to disprove his contentions. The original impetus for this study was the search for primary source documentation that could address in some way Marshall's claims regarding ratio of fire – whether to corroborate, challenge, or merely problematize them. The newly examined battle experience questionnaires, in addition to offering commentary on infantry tactical effectiveness during the war, provide new evidence on the ratio of fire from a Canadian perspective.

The questionnaire results, when compiled and analysed, demonstrate that the tactical combat effectiveness of Canadian infantry in the Second World War was much greater than has sometimes been allowed in the historical literature. Canadian soldiers displayed initiative and imagination in battle and proved to be capable warriors, frequently out-fighting their enemies in close combat. Despite the fact that the Canadian Army suffered from a number of operational, command, and doctrinal problems, and from 1943 to 1945 fought on extremely difficult terrain and against a dug-in German opponent, Canadians managed to fight extremely well on the tactical level, and the infantry proved itself both competent and effective. This effectiveness – their *aristeia*, if you will – fluctuated frequently according to factors such as terrain, weather, numbers of casualties, the introduction of untried "green" replacements, and the general friction of war. Performance in battle was not a constant for any side of the conflict. But the responses and commentaries within the Canadian battle experience questionnaires indicate that Canadian infantrymen were, generally speaking very effective combatants.

Just as important, the evidence from the questionnaires provides, possibly for the first time, a direct refutation of Marshall's observations of a highly ineffective ratio of fire in Allied troops. Not a single questionnaire respondent wrote about problems resulting from too few riflemen firing their weapons – and the officers filling out the questionnaires would have been in a position to know. Indeed, these surveys show that it was *too much* fire, rather than not enough, that presented a major problem on the battlefields of the Second World War. Controlled, disciplined fire was considered a virtue; firing to excess was not. Similarly, no mention was made in the questionnaires troops' lack of participation in the fighting being a problem, serious or otherwise. This should come as no surprise, as such findings are very much in line with what military psychology has been telling us for some time about the behaviour of soldiers in battle. Documentary historical evidence, however, now stands against Marshall's interpretation of combat, rather than with it. For Canadian soldiers in the Second World War, the ratio-of-fire theory is inapplicable.

In the first chapter of this book I examine the historiography relating to the issue of infantry effectiveness, with particular emphasis on the influence of S.L.A. Marshall and the fierce scholarly debates over his credibility and reliability. Although Marshall was considered an authoritative source from the time *Men Against Fire* was published, his work began to come under critical scrutiny in the late 1980s. His support has never died out in parts of the scholarly community, however, and despite the eventual discrediting of Marshall as an authoritative source, his ratio-of-fire numbers have become, thanks to recent writing, more popular and widespread than ever before.

My second chapter presents a detailed examination of the Canadian battle experience questionnaires as a source, detailing their origin, contemporary application, and validity as evidence for this study. I also reflect briefly upon the process of survey creation to help situate the questionnaires as historical artifacts in their own right, and to discuss some of the strengths, weaknesses, and potential problems created by employing them here as my major resource. Although these surveys represent one of the best-documented sources on tactical combat during the war, they need to be critically scrutinized, and not merely taken at face value, for their evidence to be considered more credible than, for example, Marshall's observations on the subject.

In the third chapter I take a look at the survey respondents themselves: that is, at the Canadian infantry officers who engaged in combat in the Mediterranean and Northwest Europe theatres of war between 1943 and 1945. Rather than treat the officers as faceless points of data, I have tried to situate the subjects historically, briefly examining their cultural background in cases where it would have impacted their perceptions of war. I also examine and explain the officers' duties and responsibilities in the field, and address one of the potential criticisms that Marshall's work suggests – that officers were not aware of what their troops were doing in battle.

In the fourth chapter, my analysis of the questionnaire data begins in earnest, with an examination of the role – and, indeed, the supreme importance – of Canadian infantry as part of the combined-arms team that included armour, artillery, and tactical air power. Many accounts of Second World War combat portray these mechanized arms of the army as the decisive instruments on the modern battlefield. The battle experience questionnaires, however, alongside assessments of doctrine and the combat experiences of the First World War, show that armour and artillery both suffered from several critical shortcomings in battle, and that, at least for Canadians, these shortcomings prevented them from being the proverbial "arms of decision" in and of themselves. Infantry in the Second World War remained the "sledgehammer" of combat, and battles turned on the ability of infantry to achieve its objectives successfully. Although combined-arms tactics were a necessity on the modern battlefield, the infantry was unquestionably the senior member of that partnership throughout the war.

In my final chapter I offer a detailed analysis of Canadian infantry combat using the battle experience questionnaires as evidence, and show precisely why infantry soldiers remained the arm of decision despite the increasing mechanization of the battlefield. I address in detail several under-appreciated elements of infantry fighting between 1943 and 1945, including bite-and-hold tactics, fire and movement, patrol and raiding actions, and nighttime fighting. There are elements of truth to accusations that the Canadian Army suffered from "tactical arthritis" during the war – a lack of fine tactical control and flexibility in favour of broad sweeping strokes against the enemy. Evidence from the questionnaires shows, however, that whatever operational or command problems the army faced, the infantrymen fighting at the sharp end were typically skilled, innovative combatants capable of independent tactical action. Although the set-piece doctrine they often used in attack could be rigid, individual soldiers and units displayed great initiative in other aspects of combat. In addition, this chapter presents evidence from the questionnaires on infantry small-arms use and participation in battle, evidence that stands in opposition to the ratio-of-fire findings of Marshall's classic *Men Against Fire* and casts grave doubt upon the universal applicability of ratio-of-fire observations.

Attempts to quantify combat effectiveness, which reduce the fighting capabilities of soldiers to points of data on a grid or to simplistic percentiles, are extremely popular but may miss the important point that combat is not reducible to numeric values. Battle is too complex, especially in land warfare, and is grounded in too many intangible elements such as fear, courage, and group cohesion ever to be accurately summed up through generalized quantified representations. The Canadian battle experience questionnaires demonstrate the need for military historians to peer into the complicated, confusing, often contradictory realities of personal combat at the tactical level to get a true feel for combat effectiveness, particularly for the infantry. The discipline of history must be able to look beyond simple, consensus-driven answers and remain dedicated to the pursuit of the best evidence-based analyses available.

CHAPTER ONE

HISTORY AGAINST FIRE

Although elemental to the experience of every fighting soldier, what takes place on the battlefield at the personal levels of warfare is very difficult for historians to evaluate. Despite – and because of – the millions of soldiers who have fought in the past hundred years, discerning what took place at "the sharp end," at the level of individual soldiers and their immediate comrades, can be a daunting task. The problem is as much logistical as it is conceptual: even if all soldiers kept written accounts of their experiences – and many do not – the task of collecting, organizing, and forging individual accounts into a cohesive narrative would be Herculean even for a single engagement in a war. The Duke of Wellington once cynically commented that writing the history of a battle was similar to trying to write the history of a dress party: "Some individuals may recollect all the little events of which the great result is the battle lost or won; but no individual can recollect the order in which, or the exact moment at which they occurred, which makes all the difference as to their value or importance."[1] Reconstructing what occurred on the battlefield therefore inevitably takes on an anecdotal quality. Opinions and recollections can be found for almost any event in war, but can one such testimony, or even ten, constitute a representative view of what took place? Given the chaos of battle and the recalcitrant nature of memory, battlefield knowledge has always retained a certain unknowable quality.

When analysing battles and warfare, most historians have kept to the higher ground of operational- and strategic-level narratives, preferring to detail the movements and collective actions undertaken by formations of soldiers. Such narratives rarely delve beneath the company level of about a hundred soldiers, and when they do it is often solely to collect a scattering of anecdotal tactical detail at the individual or squad level before surfacing again. Speaking of groups in this manner allows the historian to adhere to a narrative of the battle, as the actions of a large group of soldiers can more easily be constructed in line with an ultimate "progress" and "outcome" than can the tasks of every individual participant. Individual soldiers are also hardly ever aware of the broader picture behind their actions, and, owing to a lack of communication and the intensely local focus needed to stay alive in battle, few would be able to meaningfully relate their own experiences to the overall progress or outcome.[2] War only becomes comprehensible in its scope at the higher echelons: while keeping accounts of the collective actions of a dozen companies in an engagement may be possible, doing the same thing for each of the 1,200 soldiers who constitute those fighting units would drive their chronicler mad, particularly if significant time had passed since the original event transpired. And even then one could not account for the experiences of the dead, or of those who did not wish to revisit what they had gone through.

The descriptions of even the most skillfully rendered battle narrative often bears only a distant and fragmented resemblance to what physically happened to the soldier on the ground. War at the "sharp end" is chaotic and terrifying, frequently nonsensical, and breathtakingly dangerous – all the more so in the modern era, when death in battle has become a mechanized process. The infantry rifleman in particular, having a lower profile in combat than tanks, artillery, or aircraft but still fighting and dying in the greatest numbers, remains a largely unknown quantity. Individual accounts and isolated stories may be recounted in battle narratives to graphically illustrate certain points, but analysis occurs primarily at the level where men move as "companies," "units," or "formations." These are levels of considerable abstraction, since such entities exist only to the extent that the soldiers that compose them do. While it is relatively easy to analyse and compare the tactics of a company, a squad, or even a section on the basis of the way they were written down as doctrine, discovering how that doctrine was actually applied by soldiers is a less obvious task. Historical analyses thus tend to be similarly abstracted from the realities of tactical combat. While this level of abstraction is understandable, the difficulty of assembling enough personal accounts to generalize meaningfully on the tactical level of war tends to leave such narratives and analyses wanting.

There is, it is true, a limited tradition, particularly in Anglo-American countries, of historians attempting to pierce the fog of war and find another perspective on what has become known colloquially as the "face of battle": how war-fighting looks to its participants on the front lines. One of the first examples, and still one of the best, is the work of British historian John Keegan, who in the 1970s opened up the field of military history to deeper inquiry than the classic "battle piece," studying the direct experience of individual combatants in terms of their emotions, motives, and physical conditions.[3] More recently, an international group of historians associated with the Historial de la Grande Guerre Museum in Péronne, France, including Jay Winter, Annette Becker, and Stéphane Audoin-Rouzeau, have begun to study *cultures de guerre* as potential windows to the passions, hatreds, and cultural contradictions that accompany the mass violence and killing of war.[4] As Audoin-Rouzeau and Becker point out in their collaborative book *14–18: Understanding the Great War*: "If the aim of historians is to start with people, and to undertake a 'history from the bottom up,' as the *Annales* school believed, who can deny that for the men who have lived through wars and survived them, wars and their violence have been the most important experiences of their lives?"[5]

These trends aside, however, it can be difficult for military historians to actively seek out details about combatants' battle experiences. What's more, doing so for every encounter in every battle would slow the narrative to a crawl, and histories concerned with major operations and battles need their accounts to move along briskly, rather than becoming mired in tactical minutiae and personal experience. A wider perspective is also useful; there could be no social history, for example, if historians were obliged to trip over every individual's experience *en route* to discussing the peculiarities of an entire population. For the most part it is simply a matter of where one's research interests lie.

However, historians who have felt compelled to speak to the experience of the common soldier despite the inherent difficulties of doing so normally fall back upon an established military and academic literature relating to combat. A small number of "authoritative" works contribute disproportionately to this body of literature. Such is the nature of historiography, but it means that in the search for the sharp end of land warfare, particularly in the Second World War, certain personalities and ideas have dominated and, over the years, become authoritative due to the consensus that has accrued around their work. This is the case with the historiography of infantry combat in the Second World War, which has, for the past sixty years, been profoundly influenced by the work of an American writer named S.L.A. Marshall.

Samuel Lyman Atwood Marshall was, until the late 1980s, one of the most respected American military writers of the twentieth century. He claimed to have "seen" combat in every war that the United States had been engaged in between 1917 and 1975, although he had served as a soldier only in the First World War. His reputation as a combat observer was established during the Second World War with his work for the U.S. Army's G-2 Historical Branch, a fledgling entity that he helped to spearhead despite having no formal historical training.[6] In his memoirs Marshall described his wartime assignment as being "to search for some new system of battle reporting that would clear away all of the confusions of the fire fight."[7] This he found in his famous "mass interview" oral history techniques, which involved interviewing large groups of American infantrymen fresh from the battlefield, to piece together, for the sake of Historical Section research, the details of the action in which they had participated. Marshall at one time stated that he performed over five hundred interviews in the Pacific and Northwest Europe during the Second World War, and in the process became an authority on the tactical and personal experiences of the American soldier in battle.[8]

Having personally recorded the collective accounts of thousands of soldiers, Marshall had the sympathetic ear of the U.S. military establishment for the rest of his life, and in subsequent years applied his same oral history techniques in Korea, Vietnam, and Israel's Six-Day War. He wrote thirty books before his death in 1977, almost all of which dealt with aspects of the U.S. Army through four decades of conflict, typically recounting observations on the plight of the infantryman, or combat narratives to much the same effect. One of Marshall's books, *Pork Chop Hill: The American Fighting Man in Action*, was subsequently made into a popular war movie, and, as Marshall told it, the official historical records of the U.S. Airborne divisions in Normandy were copied from his own field notes, which that became a book entitled *Night Drop*.[9]

The work for which Marshall probably remains best known, however, is a slim volume printed in 1947, his first book after the Second World War, entitled *Men Against Fire: The Problem of Battle Command in Future War*. Marshall considered himself to be a great humanist and wrote *Men Against Fire* with the intention of uncovering previously unknown truths about what the "common American soldier" experienced in the Second World War. Certainly his innovative data-collection method and unprecedented first-hand contact with the mass of soldiers he was studying placed him in the unique position of having access to precisely the kind of evidence needed to examine thoroughly the sharp end of war, and to help improve the lot of the combat soldier. However, as historian and critic Roger Spiller was to point out after Marshall's death, "the centrepiece of *Men Against Fire* had less to do with Marshall's sympathetic and humanistic interpretation of modern combat."[10] The crux of the book, and the source of the controversy that has come to surround it, is an oft-quoted (and frequently misquoted) observation of Marshall's, supposedly derived from the "hard data" of hundreds of mass interviews with American infantrymen during the war:

> Later when the companies were interviewed at a full assembly and the men spoke as witnesses in the presence of the commander and their junior leaders, we found that on an average not more than 15 per cent of the men had actually fired at the enemy positions or personnel with rifles, carbines, grenades, bazookas, [automatic rifles], or machine guns during the course of an entire engagement. Even allowing for the dead and wounded, and assuming that in their numbers there would be the same proportion of active firers as among the living, the figure did not rise above 20 to 25 per cent of the total for any action. The best showing that could be made by the most spirited and aggressive companies was that one man in four had made at least some use of his fire power.[11]

Marshall was not implying that only a quarter of U.S. infantrymen were using their weapons effectively; he was arguing that less than a quarter made any use of them whatsoever. "I do not mean to say," Marshall continued in *Men Against Fire*, "that throughout an engagement, the average company maintained fire with an average of 15 per cent of its weapons … if [the soldier] had so much as fired a rifle once or twice, though not aiming it at anything in particular, or lobbed a grenade roughly in the direction of the enemy, he was scored on the positive side."[12] Marshall claimed that during the Second World War only a very small percentage of combat soldiers ever shot at the enemy, given any opportunity or provocation, even in the face of death. And this percentage did not include support personnel – a key distinction, since only a tiny fraction of U.S. Army personnel participated in battle – but was specific to front-line infantry riflemen.[13] Any close-combat killing that was being done on the battlefield, according to Marshall, was being done either by a tiny minority of the men or else by heavy weapons such as artillery and bombers. Non-firing soldiers were not necessarily cowards, nor, as *Men Against Fire* made explicit, would they break and run when confronted with a firefight: "They did not shirk the final risk of battle ... they were there to be killed if the enemy fire searched and found them."[14] But ultimately they still would not fire their weapons.

Marshall maintained that this lack of fire had little or nothing to do with the training or discipline of the troops. Indeed, he believed quite the opposite: "Company by company we found in our work that there were men who had been consistently bad actors in the training period, marked by the faults of laziness, unruliness, and disorderliness, who just as consistently became lions on the battlefield ... They could fight like hell but they couldn't soldier."[15] Instead, Marshall theorized that the cause for their reluctance to fire was more fundamental to the human condition, and particularly to the American national condition, since civilization had cultivated in most people a "fear of aggression" so strongly absorbed that it became "part of the normal man's emotional make-up."[16] He wrote in *Men Against Fire*:

> It is therefore reasonable to believe that the average and normally healthy individual – the man who can endure the mental and physical stresses of combat – still has such an inner and usually unrealized resistance toward killing a fellow man that he will not of his own volition take life if it is possible to turn away from that responsibility. Though it is improbable that he may ever analyse his own feelings so searchingly as to know what is stopping his own hand, his hand is nonetheless stopped. At the vital point, he becomes a conscientious objector, unknowing.[17]

Speculating on a previously undocumented aspect of human behaviour, Marshall went beyond simple observations about the Second World War to postulate a revolutionary idea that he considered applicable to the entire scope of human warfare. Soldiers were failing to fire their weapons not because of training deficiencies, but because human beings in general, and Americans especially, possessed an inner resistance to killing one another. Despite the claims of his academic advocates to the contrary,[18] Marshall was providing more than a "snapshot" of the American GI from 1943 to 1945; he was making the case that this resistance to killing was a normal aspect of human nature and warfare. His implication was that, as a universal principle of war, the ratio of fire of only 15 to 20 percent of soldiers firing applied to all armies at all times. He extended his hypothesis even further in *Men Against Fire*: "Why the subject of fire ratios under combat conditions has not been long and searchingly explored, I don't know [but] I suspect that it is because in earlier wars there had never existed the opportunity for systematic collection of data."[19] The proof for Marshall's surprising revelation about the disinclination of human beings to kill one another in war was to be found in the hard data collected during his group interviews.

It was this "systematic" data collection and analysis within Marshall's work that fixed his reputation as an expert on infantry combat, as if the appeal to rigorous empirical methods conferred an absolute authority upon his findings.[20] Although *Men Against Fire* chronicles many of Marshall's other observations on combat – it contains some of the early discussions on small group cohesion that British historian Hew Strachan would much later claim had made Marshall the "high priest of the small group" in military circles – it was the precise calculation of the ratio of infantry fire that truly consummated the book's argument.[21] Marshall's claim, based on the supposition that the main cause of military failure was the inability to bring sufficient infantry fire to bear in combat, was that the art of tactics could be reduced to "how much fire can be brought to bear" by the maximum number of troops.[22] Infantry small arms (and crew-served) firepower, applied at the correct place at the correct time by the greatest possible number of men, was what would win battles and, ultimately, wars. The implications of the ratio of fire, which suffuse *Men Against Fire*, became his best-known argument, carrying through his other work so that Marshall's reputation endured for the remainder of his life.

Marshall claimed to have first observed this ratio of fire phenomenon in the Pacific War in 1943, and later concluded that the same observations held true in all particulars for the land war in northwest Europe during 1944 and 1945.[23] Never one for modesty, Marshall declared that he had broken new ground as the first person to observe and empirically document this phenomenon. This was a claim from which he never backed down. As Spiller comments: "Marshall regarded himself as a pioneer of field historical operations, and he did not hesitate to proselytize the technique he had conceived."[24] Marshall was nothing if not self-assured; even one of his oldest friends and colleagues, John Westover, described him as "a cocky bastard; he never expressed any self-doubts."[25] The U.S. Army certainly never gave him any reason to doubt himself, as that institution became deeply invested in his work. Marshall was subsequently promoted to the rank of general (in the reserves) by the army, which apparently made alterations to its training programs on the basis of his recommendations. In 1950 Marshall wrote to British military theorist B.H. Liddell Hart claiming that *Men Against Fire* had "been accepted by the [United States] Army as doctrine, more or less, and [was] being put to increasingly greater use."[26] By the time American soldiers saw combat again in the Korean War, Marshall was claiming that the ratio of American fire had increased significantly, as a direct result of his own work and influence. He carried out more mass interviews with infantry rifle companies during the Korean War under the auspices of the U.S. Army's Operations Research Office, and claimed that, owing to his own previous discoveries, the ratio of fire had risen to over 50 percent among combat infantrymen.[27] Marshall proposed further improvements in training, and when the U.S. Army commissioned SLAM to carry out similar studies in Vietnam, he claimed that the ratio had risen again to the point where practically every American soldier was making use of his weapon in combat.[28] John Keegan has observed that Marshall had the experience, unusual for a historian, of seeing his message not merely accepted in his lifetime but translated into practice.[29]

Marshall's work on combat infantry and his ratio-of-fire findings have become the established knowledge referred to at the beginning of this chapter and hold a distinguished place in the pantheon of military history among the few empirically documented, rigorously researched examinations of the actual behaviour of soldiers in battle. *Men Against Fire* is a mainstay in bibliographies on infantry combat and human behaviour in warfare, and the book has attracted many supporters in the years following its publication.[30] Keegan acknowledged Marshall in the opening chapter of his own pivotal work, *The Face of Battle*, saying of Marshall's writing: "It is a flavour we can begin to call distinctively American, for his influence on military historians in his own country ... is becoming marked." Keegan referred to him as a "genius," and dubbed *Men Against Fire* a "masterpiece."[31] Indeed, Marshall and his observations on combat have helped to shape academic discourse on the Second World War since their first publication. Several major historical works have cited Marshall's ratio of fire as an authoritative statistic and based their analyses in part upon the assumption that his evidence was solidly entrenched.[32] As Spiller remarked in a 1989 article, "On occasion, the [ratio-of-fire] claim has been elevated to the status of a general principle of combat."[33] The idea that not even a quarter of American infantrymen would fire their weapons in battle also found some purchase among scholars who were inclined to characterize Allied combat performance in the Second World War as being extremely ineffective despite their eventual triumph.[34] All in all, Marshall's work, and in particular his ratio-of-fire data, has had a considerable influence in shaping the writing of military history in the past sixty years.

While Marshall typically confronted criticism of his work in a belligerent manner, he never had to face a serious critical discussion of his techniques or the potentially controversial ratio-of-fire findings before he passed away in 1977. Such discussion waited for over a decade afterward, when scholarly articles published in the late 1980s began to bring the question of "SLAM's" trustworthiness and the veracity of his research findings into the academic limelight. First among these studies were separate articles by Spiller and by historian Fredric Smoler in the *Royal United Services Institute Journal* and *American Heritage* magazine respectively, both of which critically examined Marshall's findings and the man himself. Both of these articles encountered the difficulty of disproving his argument without having any real means to do so. Marshall's assertions about the ratio of fire and soldiers not using their weapons therefore present an interesting case. The fact that little corroborating evidence has emerged in support of his study in any substantive way, explains in part why Marshall himself continues to be so widely cited. But at the same time, the question of soldiers firing their weapons was not one that participants in the Second World War were regularly asked, so there has been very little to disprove Marshall's ratio-of-fire numbers either. Most military men took it for granted that trained soldiers would be able and willing to pull the trigger if properly trained in how best to do so, and it was not a question that, outside Marshall's circle, was discussed at the time. The question "Did soldiers fire their weapons?" or any variation thereof does not appear, for example, in the excellent multi-volume social statistical surveys of American soldiers carried out by Samuel Stouffer and his team of psychologists during the Second World War; it was one of the very few questions that they did not think to ask.[35] Marshall's ratio-of-fire numbers were regarded as groundbreaking and revolutionary precisely because they represented a phenomenon that had not been systematically documented before; nor has it since.[36] Although the arguments of *Men Against Fire* have had to stand alone, many historians and military professionals opted to take Marshall at his word even in the absence of corroborating evidence.

During the 1980s, however, serious academic criticism of Marshall's ratio-of-fire numbers was advanced to suggest that his evidence was not as unimpeachably sound as had been believed. A number of historians and former soldiers attacked Marshall's conclusions, research methods, and personal credibility. Spiller's 1988 article in the *RUSI Journal* was among the first to deconstruct Marshall's arguments and to study the archived remains of the notebooks Marshall had taken with him in the field. Spiller's conclusion was that while Marshall had certainly carried out interviews, he could not have carried out anywhere near as many as he had claimed and, more important, that there was no sign that he was at any point or in any way collecting statistical data from those interviews. "The 'systematic collection of data' that made Marshall's ratio of fire so authoritative," Spiller concluded, "appears to have been an invention."[37] Smoler made similar claims in his *American Heritage* article the next year, and followed up his analysis with direct attacks on Marshall's personal life and credibility, providing evidence that Marshall had lied about his personal military service in the First World War, the number of mass interviews he conducted in the Second World War, and even about whether he had queried soldiers regarding their weapons use during those interviews. Smoler's conclusion was just as blunt as Spiller's: "It may just be that Samuel Lyman Marshall made the whole thing up."[38]

Both Spiller and – some time later – historian John Whiteclay Chambers II carried out interviews of their own with Marshall's former aides, who had assisted him in the field in northwest Europe and Korea, and who "could not recall Marshall *ever* asking this question [who fired their weapons?]" during the group interviews.[39] Another former aide, David H. Hackworth, who accompanied then-Brigadier-General Marshall on his tour of Vietnam, wrote a venomously critical account of his time with SLAM in his extremely popular 1989 autobiography, *About Face: The Odyssey of an American Warrior*. Hackworth portrayed Marshall as being more interested in selling new books and catering to the military establishment than in communicating the ugly truths behind the American problems in Vietnam. "Veterans of many of the actions [Marshall] 'documented' in his books," Hackworth remarked, "have complained bitterly over the years of his inaccuracy or blatant bias. It was a conscious effort on his part to give the audience the impression he was there ... he didn't seem to care that what he wrote was totally inaccurate and easily disproved. He seemed to have relied (and successfully so) on the notion that no one would ever dare to correct him."[40] Hackworth's *About Face*, which became a national bestseller in the United States, reached a much wider popular audience than any other critical examination of Marshall, though it was undoubtedly the most problematic of critical accounts and has not itself gone unchallenged.[41]

Although some of these accusations were subsequently addressed by Marshall's supporters, most remain unanswered. However, it is now a matter of record that SLAM exaggerated or at least partially fabricated his much-vaunted combat record in the First World War. Research done by his own grandson, John Douglas Marshall, revealed that Marshall never held the battlefield commission of which he had been so vocally proud, often claiming to have been the youngest commissioned officer in the American Expeditionary Force during the fighting.[42] John Douglas also ascertained that at least some of the events his grandfather claimed to have taken part in during the war could not have happened.[43] Although many of Marshall's critics have strayed too far into the realm of criticizing the man instead of his work, many of the points they have raised are quite valid: as a scholarly source Marshall has been found wanting in credibility, and his ratio-of-fire numbers are particularly suspect. There is a conspicuous lack of evidence that Marshall came upon his 15 to 20 percent non-firer statistic through the rigorous empirical procedures he claimed to have followed. There are no traces of any quest to document and compile statistics in the records of the theatre historian, European Theatre of Operations in the U.S. National Archives; nor have any been found thus far in the S.L.A. Marshall History Collection at the University of Texas at

El Paso.[44] Marshall is now known to have exaggerated and perhaps even fabricated the truth about a range of topics, from his First World War service record to the number and scope of interviews carried out, to the fact that his ratio-of-fire numbers were supported by hard data. Even the definitive defence of Marshall's work, F.D.G. Williams's biography of Marshall written for the U.S. Army Training and Doctrine Command, concedes: "Most people who knew or worked with Marshall admit that he was not a stranger to oversimplification, exaggeration, or manipulation."[45] At least one of his fellow analysts at the Operations Research Office in Korea, Colonel E.M. Parker, wrote that Marshall conducted his interviews and research in such a way as to support his preconceived ideas.[46] And Marshall's old friend and comrade Westover is on record prior to the controversy of the late 1980s as saying: "Marshall was an intuitive thinker. He did not gather evidence, weigh it ponderously, draw tentative hypotheses, then test them. If he did, it was not in an organized manner. Usually, from 'out of the blue' he stated a principle. Then he marshaled his evidence and statistics to back his concepts. Some of his statistics are subject to grave question as to source."[47] Marshall did little to aid his own credibility. In his memoirs he freely admitted that in his first historical assignment during the Second World War, the 1943 invasion of Makin Island in the Pacific, he saw clear and ample evidence of nervous, trigger-happy firing patterns among the American troops who landed there, characterizing them as firing their weapons too much rather than, as *Men Against Fire* attests, hardly at all. However, Marshall chose not to focus on this phenomenon and largely to ignore that particular evidence because it did not coincide with his conception of the "most serious problem," that of soldiers not firing their weapons at all.[48] There seems to be substance to Parker's and Westover's observations on Marshall. On his very first deployment as a combat observer, Marshall's preconceived ideas about the nature of battle were already sufficiently entrenched that he felt completely comfortable marginalizing important data in favour of his own presuppositions.

In terms of ramifications for historians and analysts, this observation alone should strongly imply that one of the most frequently cited studies on human behaviour in warfare since 1945, Marshall's *Men Against Fire*, cannot be taken at face value as a source on the sharp end of combat. It is interesting to note, however, that scepticism has not, by and large, been the response of the scholarly community to the criticisms. While Marshall's scholarly work has been treated with a somewhat greater caution since his critics began to speak up, his ratio-of-fire evidence is still cited as authoritative in recent works by historians and military professionals. Most often these citations come across as casual references in the text, such as in historian Niall Ferguson's *War of the World*, in which Marshall's ratio of fire is cited as supporting evidence for an argument about the combat performance of American troops in the Second World War.[49] Gender historian Joanna Bourke's *An Intimate History of Killing* uses Marshall's ratio of fire in a similar way, as it receives several pages of treatment in a chapter on training men to kill and allows only the barest mention that the numbers may not be fully reliable.[50] The new edition of journalist-historian Gwynne Dyer's *War* likewise employs S.L.A. Marshall's ratio-of-fire numbers and analysis to add credibility to arguments about how men are not natural killers, but fails to discuss Marshall's reliability.[51] The ratio-of-fire numbers continue to find their way into official military publications as well, even in Canada: in a 2006 collection on military disobedience Colonel Bernd Horn employs them in passing to support a discussion on fear in combat, again with no mention of their credibility.[52] Despite the largely unanswered allegations ranging from inaccuracy to outright fraud, Marshall's ratio of fire has evidently returned to academic vogue. A recent symposium on combat soldiers in the *Journal of Contemporary History* highlighted Marshall's ratio of fire and invoked it as evidence in almost every article. Simon Wessely, one of the contributors, demonstrates the general lack of awareness about the questioning of Marshall's credibility in the footnotes of his article, by recalling a recent gathering of peers: "None of my dinner companions was aware of the later doubts cast on [Marshall's] methods, and in particular on his famous 'ratio of fire' finding."[53] Such responses may well be typical, as the "famous ratio of fire" continues to make the rounds as key evidence in journals and books, largely unabated by published criticisms of Marshall, either because scholars are unaware of them or because they remain unconvinced.

References to Marshall's ratio-of-fire numbers are not limited to casual observations by academics, but are also presently being used as the explicit conceptual basis for more ambitious new studies on war and human behaviour. The grandmaster of this particular movement is Dave Grossman, a former lieutenant-colonel and U.S. Army Ranger, military psychologist, and professor of military science. His two major books, *On Killing* and *On Combat*, not only draw extensively upon Marshall's analyses but predicate many of their arguments on the twin assumptions that Marshall's observations on the ratio of fire were completely accurate, and that they remain largely unassailable as evidence.[54] *On Killing* was nominated for a Pulitzer Prize, and Grossman has toured extensively, giving presentations to military and police forces on the subject of his theories of human killing – which are founded in large part upon Marshall's work. His work is even cited by the Canadian Forces, listed in their *Guide to Reading on Professionalism and Leadership*, and has reportedly been prescribed by some members of the Canadian Forces' senior leadership as required reading for officers deploying overseas to Afghanistan.[55]

Grossman's fundamental point is really an elaboration of Marshall's speculation about an innate resistance to killing within human beings. He discusses at length "the simple and demonstrable fact that there is within most men an intense resistance to killing their fellow man. A resistance so strong that, in many circumstances, soldiers on the battlefield will die before they can overcome it."[56] In *On Killing* Grossman attributes this resistance to killing to vague conceptions of a Freudian "Eros" life-force, though in a thematically identical article written for *Christianity Today* magazine he prefers to name this resistance as "God-given."[57] Grossman's work is strangely Homeric in its conceptions of warfare, in that it puts the onus for fighting and killing back in the hands of the very few "elite" fighting men. It is an argument that is inextricably connected both ideologically and empirically to Marshall's, a fact that Grossman acknowledges with a defence of Marshall in *On Combat*:

> [Marshall's] work was widely accepted at the end of World War II when our Army consisted of a high ratio of veteran leaders who had led us through one of the greatest wars in history ... Were all of these military leaders wrong? Did Marshall fool all of them, and then, somehow, a few people discovered the "truth"? ... Let us hope that our life's work gets better treatment after we are dead and gone, than to have people question our work, and everyone thereafter simply assume that we had intentionally lied.[58]

While Grossman may be right that too much disrespect has been shown to Marshall personally, his beliefs – that one should not question the work of dead men and that a consensus of opinion among authorities is sufficient to determine truth on a matter – are fundamentally anti-historical.

However, this is evidently not a concern for him, as Grossman has made clear his belief that what we know of military history – and the work of military historians – is composed entirely of lies. He claims: "There are two things men will often lie about. They will lie about what happened on that date last night, and they will lie about what happened to them in combat. And therefore that means that what we think is happening in combat is actually based on 5,000 years of ... lies."[59] That Grossman has achieved such popularity and found enthusiastic reception within the military establishment should be worrying to historians. As we have seen, Marshall makes for a questionable source, and numbers derived from his disputed statistics are presently being touted by Grossman in partial answer to all the previously unknown elements of human combat. The popularization of Grossman's work has brought Marshall's questionable data back into the public eye, where they are being used to actively formulate military policy.[60] It would seem that John Keegan was more right than he knew in his comments about Marshall, as the man's work has come full circle to find practical application not once, but twice.

S.L.A. Marshall fundamentally believed in the importance of the human element of combat, and he wanted his readers to know, particularly in the early years of the atomic age when he was writing, that men, and not machines, had ensured Allied success in the Second World War. His discussion of small-group cohesion forms an indispensable part of the *Men Against Fire* thesis and, both as a military thinker and as a journalist, Marshall made valuable contributions. It is rather unfortunate that subsequent generations of army officers and historians have attached themselves particularly to the contention that most American infantrymen did not fire their weapons. However, whether we like it or not, Marshall's ratio-of-fire numbers have become the most enduring aspect of his legacy and they continue to have a direct, guiding influence upon the historical interpretation of human warfare. A number of Marshall's ideas – that human beings are not aggressive, that most will not fight in battle – continue, unproven, to find purchase in today's academic literature. The ratio of fire remains as pervasive an influence in military history as it has ever been, despite serious misgivings concerning its validity.

Given how problematic the ratio-of-fire numbers are, the question must be raised as to whether Marshall's assumptions, that soldiers in the Second

World War were not firing their weapons, form a credible historical theory, despite his faulty methods. If our understanding of what has gone on below the company level in combat has been so coloured by Marshall's work and the ratio-of-fire data still find strong support despite criticism of their accuracy, what can account for the longevity of Marshall's influence? It no doubt stems from the fact that, while the argument's credibility has been attacked (as has its author's), it has been difficult to produce historical evidence that speaks directly to the ratio-of-fire concept. Anecdotal evidence can be found either in support or in contradiction, but meaningful data on the subject have been lacking. Beyond Marshall's *Men Against Fire*, historical documentation on the subject of Allied weapons' usage at the small-unit level has not been forthcoming. Apart from individual accounts, unit diaries and reports are the sources closest to the actual infantry combat that have been accessible, and these tend to be mum on the subject.

New historical evidence for the actions and behaviour of soldiers in combat now allows us to examine many issues of combat – the experiences of soldiers, weapons usage, and the overall effectiveness of infantry combat – through a fresh lens, and from a Canadian perspective. The core evidence for this study comes from a series of questionnaires filled out by three hundred Canadian Army officers during the Second World War shortly after they were withdrawn from the front lines. These surveys contain a wealth of information on tactical questions and problems from 1944 and 1945. While collectively they offer new insights on the ratio-of-fire controversy, they are at the same time valuable pieces of evidence in terms of ascertaining the day-to-day fighting patterns of Canadian soldiers at the company level and below. When analysed, data from these questionnaires present a challenge to Marshall's conclusions in *Men Against Fire* – or at least to the universalist pretensions of those conclusions – and offer a revealing portrait of how junior officers led men into battle. This new material invites tentative new answers to some old questions: Were infantrymen truly such ineffective combatants as Marshall and others since have suggested? Was the Second World War truly won by technology and the weight of industrial machinery? What was the experience of "everyday" infantry fighting really like on the ground? The surveys grant personal access to infantry combat and the Canadian soldier in a way that might not be possible through individual memoirs, diaries, or unit reports. These sources delve into considerable tactical detail and, taken collectively, can yield vital information that may allow historians to permanently move beyond the ratio-of-fire paradigm created by S.L.A. Marshall's work.

## CHAPTER TWO

THE BATTLE EXPERIENCE
QUESTIONNAIRES

Junior and senior infantry officers who had seen active combat in the Canadian Army in 1944 and 1945, both in Italy and in Northwest Europe, were invited soon after their withdrawal from the front to fill out "battle experience questionnaires."[1] These surveys were drafted and printed by the British War Office's Directorate of Tactical Investigation (DTI), and were distributed to Canadian officers who had been personally involved in the fighting and were returning to England from overseas theatres. The questionnaires sought information from the returned officers on many tactical details of combat at the company, platoon, and section levels. Their distribution during the war was meant to provide the DTI with feedback on how congruent the realities of combat were with what was taught in soldiers' training programs. The cover letters attached to the Canadian battle experience questionnaires encouraged full responses: "It is important for all of us to make available as much information as possible concerning recent experience in order that we may keep all concerned fully informed as to the necessities of training in the light of operational requirements."[2] Prominent questions included inquiries about weapons use and effectiveness, night operations, mental and physical fatigue, co-operation among combat service arms, morale issues, and field communications. In addition to answering the formal survey questions themselves, the officer respondents were asked to attach loose-leaf memorandum paper as an addendum, for any additional comments, personal notes, clarifications, or elaborations they might wish to include. Many respondents were articulate and enthusiastic about the task, in some cases attaching a dozen pages or more of addendum notes that would include commentary, stories, and even hand-drawn maps and sketches to illustrate key points.

These battle experience questionnaires provide an uncommon entry into the details of combat as perceived by members of the officer corps of the Canadian Army. As they deal exclusively with tactical issues, these surveys are thematically similar to S.L.A. Marshall's post-combat mass interviews, although they deal with the sum of officers' tactical experiences rather than attempting to reconstruct any single battle or engagement, as Marshall's interviews did. While the battle experience questionnaires are therefore of less use for historians seeking details on specific actions during the war, they are an invaluable resource for gathering officers' overall impressions about the nature of close combat, based upon the totality of their personal experiences up to the point of writing. This sort of data, outlining overall impressions of tactical combat rather than isolated incidents and anecdotes, can be helpful in assessing the validity of Marshall's ratio of fire and other important elements of infantry effectiveness.

THE CANADIAN BATTLE EXPERIENCE QUESTIONNAIRES

The surveys were an official project of the British Directorate of Tactical Investigation (Questionnaire & War Diary Section), which had originally been a research branch independent of other directorates under the Imperial General Staff, but was renamed and made into its own directorate in December of 1943. The DTI's purpose was "to study and analyse the lessons of war and from them draw conclusions to assist in the formulation of tactical and organizational doctrine for the future roles of the Army and for its co-operation with the other Services; to keep in touch with new weapons and equipment and assess their tactical value; and to study developments in tactics and organization in relation to the present and future commitments of the Army."[3] Battle experience questionnaires were a significant part of the directorate's overall responsibility, as they constituted one of the most direct methods of eliciting potentially useful information from serving officers.

Because it was technically a semi-autonomous entity within the British command structure, the Canadian Army was included in the survey project. The DTI approached Canadian Military Headquarters (CMHQ) in London early in 1944 with the idea of expanding the Battle Experience Questionnaire program to include Canadian officers as well as British ones: the earliest archived correspondence between CMHQ and DTI on the subject dates to March 1944.[4] Members of CMHQ General Staff were in "complete agreement that we should participate in this scheme" in co-operation with the British War Office.[5] CMHQ would take responsibility for the initial distribution and collection, but would forward all questionnaires containing data of special interest to the DTI. The program was to include Canadian Army officers returning from active service overseas in the Mediterranean and, later, the Northwest Europe campaigns, and was distributed to respondents between July 1944 and May 1945, at which time it was discontinued with the winding-down of the war effort in Europe.[6] It included both officers who returned wounded as casualties of the fighting, and those returning uninjured to England for leave, training, reassignment, or repatriation to Canada.

The procedure for survey distribution was, according to the archived correspondence, as follows. British Movement Control staff were responsible for organizing the transportation and movement of armed forces personnel behind the lines, and they were therefore tasked with distributing an initial questionnaire, form "CFA-276," to Canadian officers, either on ships crossing the Channel to Britain or in British airports. Form CFA-276 was meant to provide the directorate with contact information for each of the officers while they were in Britain, but was also designed to find out which of them had seen actual combat while overseas; two questions, "Have you had actual Battle Experience," and "In what capacity have you served?" were the critical ones.[7] Officers who answered the former question in the affirmative were promptly sent a full battle experience questionnaire and a semi-personal letter either through the Canadian Reception Depot in England (for healthy respondents) or through the Canadian General Hospital (for casualty respondents).[8] If and when the officers returned the questionnaires via posted mail, the responses were first assessed by officers at CMHQ, who would forward the most "useful" of the surveys back to the British Directorate of Tactical Investigation.[9] Most of the questionnaires would be returned to CMHQ after processing, though a handful were permanently retained by the British War Office.[10]

The battle experience questionnaires actually encompassed all the combat arms of the Canadian Army, including infantry, armour, artillery, and engineers. In all, CMHQ reported that between July 1944 and April 1945 some 616 battle experience questionnaires were sent to returned Canadian officers from all arms, and that some 344 were sent back, 98 of which were forwarded to the British War Office.[11] As thirty questionnaires were permanently retained by the British, just over three hundred completed surveys remain, and can today be consulted in Library and Archives Canada (LAC) in Ottawa. Of these, 161 were filled out by officers of the infantry corps from about twenty different regiments in both the Mediterranean and Northwest European theatres in 1944 and 1945. This present study focuses exclusively upon the 161 battle experience questionnaires stored at LAC that were filled out by infantry officers, although a wealth of untapped information is contained in the surveys of the other arms as well.[12] Every officer was asked to complete a general survey as well as a survey specific to their fighting arm. For the infantry officers, this consisted of "Battle Experience Questionnaire 'A' – General" and "Battle Experience Questionnaire 'H' – Infantry."[13]

The battle experience questionnaires were limited in scope not only to the officer corps but to certain ranks of officer. Questionnaires were sent out to junior and senior officers who held the ranks of captain, major, and lieutenant-colonel, though many officers indicated that their combat experience had begun at the rank of lieutenant.[14] In theory, this list would limit the questionnaire circulation to officers with experience commanding units of at least company size, though in practice such was usually not the case. Many reported that they had commanded units ranging from platoons (for lieutenants and many captains) to companies and, in a few cases, to battalions, though they had often held second-in-command positions or positions other than commander in these units. Captains were often found to be commanding special-weapons platoons, such as anti-tank, mortar, or carrier platoons. Most had spent time commanding groups of around thirty to a hundred soldiers. While there is no indication in the correspondence between CMHQ and the DTI as to why they elected to limit the survey sample by rank, in all likelihood one reason would have been to keep the sample size manageable. In addition, they may have chosen to solicit the opinions of officers who they believed had the most experience with observing and commanding larger groups of soldiers at the tactical level.

The present study marks the first comprehensive examination of these battle experience questionnaires as historical documents. Historians Terry Copp and Bill McAndrew refer to them in passing in their excellent work, *Battle Exhaustion*.[15] No other major works – including later books on the Second World War by both McAndrew and Copp – seem to make any further substantial use of these documents. In some ways this is not surprising: the battle experience questionnaires give only scattered, incidental reports on specific actions that officers were involved in, and thus do not contribute to the temporal focus that narrative military histories would find most useful. The questionnaires are perhaps better likened to the Operational Research reports that form such a substantial part of Copp's work, although they have a less scientific objective, in that the data therein pertain to an accumulated totality of experiences rather than to specific instances. It might be more relevant to compare them directly, and favourably, to Marshall's group interviews.

Colonel C.P. Stacey, Canada's official historian of the Second World War, correctly suggested that in the matter of weighing evidence, "the vital element is that of time."[16] The validity and trustworthiness of battlefield testimonials and memories tends to decline sharply with the passage of years; interviews with soldiers carried out years or decades after the fact are of questionable value.[17] It is one of the tragedies of oral history that memories erode with time and cannot always be relied upon for accurate accounts of events that occurred long in the past – a point raised by one of Marshall's supporters to deflect the criticisms of ratio of fire brought up by Harold Leinbaugh, author of *The Men of Company K*.[18] The phenomenon of memory degradation has hampered many studies attempting to deduce the behaviour of combat soldiers in the Second World War, and has limited their potential usefulness.[19] One of the undeniable strengths of Marshall's interview techniques was that the interviews were carried out hours, days, or at most weeks after the event in question, so that memories were still fresh and the details of what actually happened could be captured with an expectation of some accuracy. These Canadian surveys share the immediacy of Marshall's work, having been filled out days or weeks after the respondent officers had last seen battle. While they might not have quite the same degree of immediacy that Marshall claimed to have had with his post-combat interviews, the survey accounts remain in close temporal proximity to the combat actions that they discuss. Furthermore, they lack the element of peer pressure that would have been present in Marshall's mass interviews. The LAC archives contain hundreds of catalogued CFA-276 forms filled out by officers and dated progressively from July 1944 through to May of 1945, as a steady stream of completed questionnaires was being returned to CMHQ during that time period.[20] This suggests that officers were receiving their questionnaires soon after returning to England from the front, rather than filling them out months afterward. In terms of historical veracity, the battle experience questionnaires are likely as reliable a source as any of Marshall's interviews, perhaps even more so, given that they represent the primary documentary evidence that is strangely missing from Marshall's testimony.

There are, however, inherent dangers in simply accepting the battle experience questionnaires without further question. In his major work on the analysis of the Canadian national censuses of the nineteenth century, *The Politics of Population*, sociologist Bruce Curtis critically examines the accumulation of statistical data for populations, and his comments on the creation of survey knowledge bear some attention. Curtis derides the idea of such statistical surveys being "scientific" and "factual," and scorns the very concession that "populations" are real entities that can be empirically measured. "Because no large-scale census of population can be based on direct physical observations of equivalent bodies in time and space," Curtis claims, "it is practically necessary to generate and assemble opinions of such things. Typically, only some opinions are solicited, and relations of authoritative opinion-making thus tend to intervene between the state agency and the individual."[21] Although the Canadian censuses that Curtis is concerned with are treated by contemporaries as objective, verifiable facts "taken" of the population body, they are more usefully construed as being "made" by the authorities, largely on the basis of opinions, rather than as collections of "facts" gathered from respondents. Similar comments could be directed toward these questionnaires from the Second World War. While much of the information from the battle experience questionnaires has been tabulated in statistical form for this study, the "data" are still derived from the opinions and memories of its respondents, rather than from "objective facts." Curtis goes on to say: "While others are skeptical of the pseudo-scientific pretension that privileges census returns as 'hard data' because of their numerical form, I share the delicious irony that such returns ... were typically worked-over oral history and third-hand hearsay."[22] Rather than being statements of definitive, quantitative fact, returned questionnaire data, perhaps even more so than Curtis's censuses, reflect a multiplicity of subjective experiences.

We need, then, to approach this historical evidence both with great care and with a full acknowledgment of the potential difficulties and limitations associated with such a project. To address some of these limitations, a brief review of some of the themes of questionnaire theory and design will be useful. Elements of this theory can then be applied to the specific case of the battle experience questionnaires in the following section.

QUESTIONNAIRE THEORY AND DESIGN

What constitutes a questionnaire and what functions can a questionnaire serve? Patricia J. Labaw, in the Introduction to her book *Advanced Questionnaire Design*, gives a fundamental caveat: "What people do not understand is that writing questions does not give you a questionnaire. A questionnaire is *not* simply a series of questions, nor is a question merely a series of words."[23] A.N. Oppenheim, another survey analyst, continues in the same vein: "A questionnaire is not some official sort of form, nor is it a set of questions which have been casually jotted down without much thought. We should think of the questionnaire as an important instrument of research, a tool for data collection. The questionnaire has a job to do: its function is measurement."[24] This is a good way to conceptualize questionnaires, with the reservation that questionnaires are measuring something ephemeral rather than concrete: the opinions of the respondents. Few professional surveys are haphazard amalgamations of questions; they exist to serve a very specific function and are structured accordingly. According to Labaw, the questionnaire must be viewed holistically; as a totality that is more meaningful than the sum of its questions.[25] The key to both designing and interpreting a questionnaire, therefore, will be in finding out the original intent behind it.

Labaw and Oppenheim agree – though Labaw's book emphasizes it to a greater extent – that rather than just being instruments to gather facts, questionnaires in their totality exist to test the hypotheses of the researchers designing them. When a small group or sample of a population is being surveyed, it is because a researcher wants to be able to generalize from the results and predict what might happen in a corresponding larger group in the future. The hypothesis, or research design, outlines the basic plan or strategy of the research and the logic behind it, thereby supposedly making it possible and valid to draw more widely applicable general conclusions from it.[26] "Although it is not obvious," Labaw tells us, "when a survey researcher writes a questionnaire, he constructs it on the basis of certain hypotheses he holds, whether he is aware of them or not … You cannot begin to formulate questions and worry about wording *unless you know what you want to accomplish* with your questions and words."[27] What needs to be accomplished will be determined by who the "client," the original commissioner of the questionnaire, happens to be, and what that client's perspective and goals are in mandating the research. The questionnaire as research tool therefore works as a problem-solving instrument and as an advocate, its ultimate goal being to inform policy decisions. It is more useful to think of a survey as an actively probing instrument rather than a fishing expedition or a blank slate upon which to inscribe results.[28]

Practical concerns over *research techniques*, that is the actual methods used in the collection of the survey data, also need to be assessed. Labaw and Oppenheim outline three main kinds of questionnaire distribution techniques: postal surveys, telephone interviews, and face-to-face interviews (in a contemporary context one would also include electronic surveys). Questionnaires distributed to respondents via post, as the battle experience questionnaires were, pose unique research challenges. As Oppenheim indicates, surveys done by post have advantages: the low cost of data collection and processing, the avoidance of interviewer bias, and the ability of the questionnaire to reach respondents at widely dispersed addresses.[29] Postal-return questionnaires also have serious disadvantages, however. They tend, for example, to have the lowest response rates, and samples are therefore skewed toward those who do respond. They may also be unsuitable for respondents with low or limited literacy, for the visually handicapped, or for those who have other language problems. Postal questionnaires allow no opportunity to correct misunderstandings or to probe more deeply, and the researcher cannot control the order in which questions are answered, check for incomplete responses, or monitor the passing on of the questionnaire to others.[30] As the battle experience questionnaires can be considered postal questionnaires – they were filled out without an interviewer present and returned by mail to CMHQ – these are potentially valid points that should be raised concerning the questionnaires' integrity.[31]

One must also ask if the data obtained from a questionnaire are *meaningful*. In *Advanced Questionnaire Design*, Labaw discusses several ways in which data can be rendered *meaningless* on questionnaires. Respondents can simply lie about their answers, either to protect their true feelings or so as not to appear stupid to the researcher. Questions can be phrased in a manner that does not allow respondents to truly tell what they thought. Respondents may genuinely not know how they feel about the particular issue being addressed by a given question. Or, finally, respondents may give meaningful answers that the *researcher* may misunderstand.[32] Even fully completed postal questionnaires may fall victim to some of these shortcomings.

Labaw continues, however, by pointing out that one of the best methods of safeguarding the reliability and meaningfulness of questionnaire results is for the researcher to be aware of how *conscious* respondents are of their answers.[33] "As a rule," Labaw writes, "people have not thought about and do not know their feelings about most issues that have not directly affected them."[34] This can be potentially endemic in data from questionnaires, particularly in public opinion polling, since in such cases people are typically surveyed on a breadth of subjects that may not all relate to their lives. An effective method in questionnaire design for weighing the potential consciousness of respondents on issues, Labaw proposes, is to determine how close to a respondent's personal experience a particular question falls. In this light one can identify three kinds of knowledge: first-hand personal knowledge, factual knowledge derived from a second-hand source (reading, indirect exposure, etc.), and computational knowledge derived from the ability to compute an answer. "Feelings based on [personal] experience," Labaw explains, "are much more stable than either feelings based on salience as a result of media exposure or feelings based simply on habit not related to any direct personal experience."[35] The "closer" respondents are to the subject of a survey question, the more likely they are to have both strong feelings and a general consciousness of those questions. Labaw uses the example of the Vietnam War, and the observation that a veteran soldier returning from a tour of duty there would be much more likely to hold a personal opinion on the war than someone who had not participated.[36] The greater a respondent's personal interest in or experience with a subject, the more conscious he or she will be in answering a question about it. Conversely, those who are less conscious of their feelings on a subject will be correspondingly apathetic toward it. The relation between personal experience and consciousness of feelings can subsequently be reflected in the extent to which respondents' opinions and answers will be developed and meaningful.

There is a considerable body of literature on the theory and practice of designing, distributing, and tabulating results from questionnaires, and many of the elements that underlie survey construction can be usefully applied to the battle experience questionnaires of this study.[37] They are particularly helpful when bearing in mind Curtis's thesis that censuses and other "official" collections of potentially subjective data are *made* rather than *taken.*

BATTLE EXPERIENCE QUESTIONNAIRE ANALYSIS

Elements of Labaw's and Oppenheim's theories of questionnaire construction allow the historian to analyse the form, function, and data derived from the battle experience questionnaires in a substantive manner, rather than accepting them at face value. Examining the surveys through the lens of questionnaire design provides some good starting points: the hypotheses, research techniques, meaningfulness, and degree of consciousness reflected in the questionnaires. From these beginnings one can assess the validity of placing our historical trust in these documents, and point out some potential pitfalls that await their use.

What were the hypotheses and underlying assumptions of the researchers in the British War Office and the Directorate of Tactical Investigation? What can be said about their intentions and beliefs in creating the surveys? We have already mentioned their stated intent: to obtain combat officer feedback to help "make our training fit with operational requirements."[38] There is some good evidence that officer feedback was indeed being implemented for this purpose on at least some level. In September of 1944 the Deputy Director of Tactical Investigation sent a memo to CMHQ that mentioned how, in the questionnaire of one Captain D. Dawson of the 3rd Canadian Infantry Division, "remarks on Aircraft Recognition were of particular interest as confirming other reports on the same subject. The necessary action to improve the training in this subject has been taken."[39] However, the case of Captain Dawson was the only readily apparent instance that could be found in the archives of the DTI specifically noting how training had been modified during the war in response to data collected from the battle experience questionnaires. If the DTI implemented other alterations to the training programs while the Second World War was still being fought, they don't appear to have told CMHQ about it. Almost a year after the end of the war the DTI began to circulate a series of reports, evidently from data gleaned at least in part from the battle experience questionnaires. Two of them, "Illumination of the Battlefield" and "Wireless Communications within the Infantry Battalion," were sent to the CMHQ in March of 1946, but there is little archival evidence that information gathered from the questionnaires was circulated before this date.[40]

Nevertheless, in terms of hypotheses and research goals, some of the administrative documentation surrounding the battle experience questionnaires can be helpful in identifying less explicit underlying motives. Despite the breadth of the tactical questions presented, the DTI believed that a few areas of combat were of particular importance at the beginning of the survey program in summer 1944. They outlined their criteria in some detail for the personnel of CMHQ in order to give them a better idea of which questionnaires would be of most interest to the DTI and worthy of forwarding. While the DTI laid out numerous "important subjects" for the artillery, anti-aircraft, and armour branches, all that was initially noted for infantry was "(i) Co-operation with armour; (ii) Generally, problems of communication, etc."[41] Several months later, the DTI would expand its view of what was considered to be the "most important" information to be gathered from the battle experience questionnaires, particularly for the infantry, and listed information on flame throwers, tactical handling of machine guns, German minefield-laying methods, tank-killing, and "points of general interest including new or unusual use of weapons" as being of special interest.[42] These became the criteria by which Canadian staff officers were to determine which surveys the DTI would want to see; questionnaires that contained particularly "useful" data on any of the above were to be flagged.

Of course, every battle experience questionnaire included, for the infantry, a wide range of survey questions as well as explicit directions for respondents on what subjects additional notes were "particularly required."[43] But while the DTI was casting a wide net in searching for tactical information, its private correspondence with CMHQ shows that there were topics within the questionnaire that they had pre-selected as the most pressing ones. The fact that they specifically requested that *only* questionnaires providing "useful" data on particular subjects be forwarded to them implies that the other data was ancillary to the original DTI researchers. Since over two-thirds of the Canadian questionnaires were never seen by anyone at DTI at all, their selection criteria for the "most valuable" surveys had a profound impact on what data the DTI researchers who commissioned the project were going to see. The selection criteria clearly changed between July 1944 and May 1945, but it remained true that the DTI hypotheses for what data would be most important from the questionnaires were central to determining which questionnaires they viewed.

It is also noteworthy that the British War Office had a strong inclination to keep the data from the questionnaires to themselves, rather than circulating the results freely. It was made clear from the beginning of the battle experience questionnaire program that Canadians were to be left out of the loop on the conclusions that the DTI drew from the surveys they had been sent. In a memo dated 16 August 1944, the Deputy Director of Tactical Investigation explicitly spelled out its expectations for the benefit of CMHQ officers: "It is not proposed to send you any consolidated or collated statement based on the information gained from Canadian officers and indeed it would not be possible to do so. The general conclusions based on such information will however reach you through the usual channels, such as ... Liaison Letters, Current Reports from Overseas and the Like."[44] There is evidence that the British were not even as forthcoming through "the usual channels" with this information as they had indicated. Just after the aforementioned two DTI reports on battlefield illumination and wireless communication were received in March 1946, a strongly worded letter was written to the British Under-Secretary of State by Lieutenant-General J.C. Murchie, the CMHQ Chief of Staff. The letter asked for "any drafts or completed notes on this subject [of lessons learned during the war] in order that relevant points can be extracted and incorporated into training programmes in Canada."[45] Murchie's letter indicates that such had not previously been done, even nine months after the end of the fighting in Europe. Whatever the reason, Canadians were not kept informed of the final conclusions that the DTI had drawn from the questionnaire responses; nor did they ever conduct any serious analysis of the questionnaires on their own. Proposals to tabulate statistics from the questionnaires with the "Hollerith System" card-punching computer of the National Defence Headquarters back in Ottawa were rejected, as the project was deemed to "not warrant additional staff."[46]

The research techniques employed in the distribution and collection of the battle experience questionnaires are also worth examining briefly, as they make a further point about some of the project's goals. First, Oppenheim's consideration of the weaknesses of post-based questionnaires gives us an interesting perspective. Literacy rates were likely not a serious obstacle to the survey, since the great majority of officers in the Canadian Army during the Second World War had at least completed high school.[47] Of the 616 Canadian officers who had reportedly been sent battle experience questionnaires to complete, about half of them sent their surveys back to CMHQ.[48] While this may seem a low number, it is actually a very favourable return rate compared to average post-based survey returns, indicating a much higher-than-normal willingness among the officers to participate in the questionnaires.[49] Furthermore, while officers were given the opportunity to go outside the formal structure of the questionnaire with their attached notes, there was still a fairly significant chance of misunderstanding between the respondents' comments and the researchers. We should also note that the structure of the DTI's survey analysis was fundamentally different from that of modern public-opinion polling. While recent surveys attempt to generalize findings through the compiling of data and the creation of statistics, the DTI apparently designed their questionnaire apparatus to do the exact opposite. Given that less than a third of the Canadian Army questionnaires were sent to the DTI, and that less than a third of *those* were permanently retained, there was clearly no attempt on the part of the British to gather or compile statistics from the battle experience questionnaires, as a much larger sample of questionnaires was available than they took advantage of. The evidence indicates, in fact, that they were more interested in combing through the data to locate intriguing or unusual individual reports and comments within the surveys than they were in examining the questionnaire project holistically or as a totality of information.[50] If the DTI's treatment of the Canadian surveys was indicative, there could never have been a serious effort to formulate representative statistics from the battle experience questionnaires. Their research techniques were structured around searching through hundreds of respondents for individual questionnaires of merit.

We can also take some steps toward assessing how *meaningful* the responses to the battle experience questionnaires were. As we have seen, this assessment relates explicitly to the extent to which respondents were *conscious* of the subject matter. As Labaw proposes, questionnaire responses can be rendered largely meaningless and worse than useless in many ways, including respondents lying about their answers, misunderstanding what was being asked, or not having any real feelings about an issue but answering anyway.[51] These are all potential concerns, particularly in regard to mailed-in questionnaires, for which there is no face-to-face contact between respondent and researcher, and no personal observations on the behaviour of the respondent can be collected and weighted.

We do, however, have indications that the battle experience questionnaire responses can be treated as reliable historical documents. Issues of respondents misunderstanding the intent behind questions or not having a chance to fully elaborate upon their answers are largely dealt with through the questionnaire structure. Officers were given complete latitude, and indeed were encouraged, to fully develop their ideas not only in the formal survey but in the addendum notes as well. Every battle experience questionnaire advised the officer: "If you have opinions and/or experiences of value which are not covered by the questionnaire, please attach them to the questionnaire on separate sheets. It will be helpful if you give as much factual evidence as possible."[52] In addition, while the surveys included considerable military "jargon" that can be nonsensical to the non-specialist, they were still relatively straightforward in their wording, and were written in military language that would have been familiar to serving officers. All the questionnaires were penned by British officers in the DTI. While it could be argued that a cultural gap might therefore have existed between the British researchers and the Canadian respondents, many Canadian officers had been living in England for up to six years by 1945, serving under British command and becoming acquainted with British military culture. The questionnaires would have been entirely comprehensible to the great majority of officers.

In the battle experience questionnaires, when the respondents did not in fact understand a question, or when they did not know the answer, they were not hesitant to indicate this on their surveys. Officers were clearly instructed: "Please answer every question. If you have no information on any particular question insert the letters N.K. (Not Known)."[53]

Although Labaw's view is that one cannot assume that a "don't know" category on a questionnaire will accurately represent people who do not know an answer, many officers followed the printed instructions and wrote in "N.K." when they did not know an answer.[54] Most officers did not in fact answer every question, and many left at least one blank instead of writing "N.K.", but the prevalence of "N.K." answers in the battle experience questionnaires suggests that there was, generally speaking, little hesitation on the part of the officers to admit when a subject was outside their realm of knowledge.

According to the questionnaire design theory outlined by Labaw and Oppenheim, evaluating how conscious of their own feelings respondents are is also critical to analysing the value of a questionnaire. Respondents are allegedly most conscious of their own feelings on subjects with which they have direct, personal experience. This was an aspect of questionnaire design that the DTI was clearly familiar with, as it was built into the architecture of the battle experience questionnaires. The initial CFA-276 forms, which were distributed to every Canadian officer returning from overseas, contained one important vetting question: "Have you had actual Battle Experience?"[55] Anyone answering "no" was eliminated from further consideration; anyone answering "yes" was sent a cover letter and two surveys – a general questionnaire and one specific to their combat arm. Although "Battle Experience" could be interpreted broadly, the initial selection of the officers provided by the CFA-276 virtually eliminated all staff and support officers from the survey body: all but a bare handful of final questionnaire respondents confirmed that they had led combat units in battle in either the Mediterranean or northwest Europe. Those who remained, and who took part in the questionnaire program, had all claimed to be combat veterans. Given that the questionnaires, and particularly the "H" Infantry questionnaire, dealt exclusively with details from tactical combat, one can safely assume that the respondents were writing about a subject with which they had some personal experience. And even if that personal experience did not allow the officers to give comprehensive answers to every question on the battle experience questionnaire, it would have represented a sufficient personal connection to the topic to allow for them to fit Labaw's definition of the conscious respondent.

It must be admitted that there is no way to be absolutely certain of the integrity of the answers given on these questionnaires; there is no method by which the historian can know beyond a doubt that all answers were given truthfully, that all opinions were informed, and that officers did not pass the questionnaires to others to complete for them. However, as soldiers and particularly as officers, the respondents were operating within the context of a professional military ethos that by 1944 was becoming very strong. A good working definition for "ethos" is the characteristic spirit and beliefs of a community, organization, or person. There is no doubt that we should view the Canadian officers of the Second World War as members of a "profession of arms" and therefore personally subject to a range of professional, personal, and ethical responsibilities.[56] Historian J.L. Granatstein affirms this in his book *Canada's Army*: "In effect, during a half-dozen years of active service, [Canadian officers] became professional soldiers, whatever their pre-war occupation."[57] Particularly in democracies, military officers have a special responsibility to conduct themselves according to the rules, values, and customs of the democratic nation that they serve and, even more important, to ensure that the soldiers they lead are trained and led according to those same values.[58] Naturally this cannot be taken as proof that all Canadian officers responded with complete honesty at all times, but every officer who participated in the battle experience questionnaire program was explicitly told in the semi-personalized cover letters that his comments and personal experiences would be put to use in improving the training of soldiers "in light of operational requirements."[59] For those who took the time to reply, providing false information on the questionnaires would have constituted not only dishonesty but a breach of professional trust and responsibility as well. Unlike ordinary civilians responding to a public opinion survey, who risk no personal consequences for answering falsely, the military officers filling out the battle experience questionnaires would have been under additional pressure to provide truthful feedback, given the expectation that this information would be used in the training of future soldiers. Non-response to the questionnaire indicated that not every officer wanted to invest the time or effort, but there is a significant difference between not responding to a questionnaire and knowingly responding with false information. Under such circumstances, lying on the questionnaire would have been tantamount to a serious breach of professional ethics and responsibility. The weight of such responsibility, if nothing else, would in all probability have kept respondent answers truthful. There is a possibility that some respondents lied regardless; this analysis, however, would suggest that the officers' responses can be considered to be, if not representative of objective truth, then at least representative of their own truthful opinions and observations.

A final note should be made about the extent to which the historian can generalize conclusions on the basis of these questionnaires. It terms of representation, the battle experience questionnaires are fairly broad, though they have some limits. Given that every Canadian officer (between the ranks of captain and lieutenant-colonel) returning to England in 1944 and 1945 had to pass through British Movement Control[60] – either by air or by sea – it is fair to say that almost all Canadian officers who returned to Britain from theatres of operations during this time period would have been handed a CFA-276 form. It is impossible to say how many sent in the CFA-276 forms and how many did not, but 616 officers with stated combat experience were sent the actual battle experience questionnaires; over half, 344, responded. Of those, almost exactly half were infantry officers, and are the focus of this present study. It is doubtful that the overall number of "combat-experienced" officers holding the required ranks in the Canadian Army during the required period of time could be tabulated, given the fluidity of battlefield commissions and the possible subjective interpretation of "combat experience." Most Canadian officers held administrative and staff positions and never saw combat personally. A precise calculation of what "proportion" of the overall Canadian officer corps the responses to battle experience questionnaires represent is therefore not possible. However, while the surveyed officers cannot necessarily be said to mathematically represent the entire officer corps, the project was still of considerable and useful scope. The officers who responded were obviously self-selected rather than randomly sampled, so the questionnaires are also clearly biased in favour of those with sufficient motivation to take the time to fill out the survey. The historian has to be cautious in generalizing when, mathematically, the numbers cannot be guaranteed to be representative. But as Curtis has demonstrated, the idea of an objective scientific "representation" being based upon personal opinions and hearsay itself lacks credibility. What can be said with certainty is that it was the stated intention of the DTI to reach *all* the officers of these ranks who had combat experience, insofar as it was possible. Within those boundaries there were no intended exclusion criteria. For the purpose of this study I will therefore propose that we accept that such a goodwill effort to include as many officers' opinions as possible in the collection of surveys would have yielded a significant, well-rounded sampling of the combat-experienced officers in the Canadian Army.

RESEARCH METHODS

We know, then, what information the Directorate of Tactical Investigation wanted to get out of the questionnaires and how they intended to do so through the survey structure, we have an idea of their representativeness, and we possess reasonable criteria by which to weigh the veracity of the officer respondents. The framework is now in place for engaging with the contents of the battle experience questionnaires in more depth. Even Bruce Curtis, for all his criticism of the processes underlying the taking of censuses and surveys, concedes that social science depends heavily upon systematic social observation, and that "the construction of social statistics, including statistics of population, offer[s] the potential for practical purchase on otherwise unknowable dimensions of social relations."[61] The formulation of statistics and the gathering of data, even opinions, from a population body provides valuable insights unavailable elsewhere. But at the same time, the problematic elements of employing such data "must be addressed directly, and the tactics employed to manage the essential uncertainty of social observations should not be concealed."[62]

From the perspective of questionnaire design theory, there clearly are potential difficulties with employing a source such as the battle experience questionnaires. Great reliance is placed upon what the officers wrote down in their questionnaires, and the accuracy, conscientiousness, and honesty of the respondents, although trusted, can never be guaranteed. Since much of what the officers wrote was generalized and not specific to any one time or place, it is difficult to corroborate the evidence by turning to the historical record.

We do know, however, many details of how the questionnaires were constructed by the DTI, including some of its underlying assumptions and hypotheses in carrying out the study. We also have strong indications that the officers, using Labaw's definition, were personally connected to subject matter of the questionnaires through their combat experience, and were thus fully *conscious* of their answers. While there can be no foolproof guarantee that the officers reported truthfully on their experiences, we can take some assurance from the fact that to do otherwise would have been a serious breach of their own professional responsibilities. The fact that many officers failed to turn in their questionnaires at all gives the survey sample an inherent self-selection bias, but those who were sufficiently able and motivated to go through the questionnaires would have been unlikely to deliberately return false information. Given the high response rates, a picture of willing compliance begins to emerge. Accidental misunderstanding or misinterpretation of survey questions are somewhat more likely to have happened, but again, the corps-specific questionnaires were being sent only to officers of that combat arm, so that every officer who received one would be, essentially, a specialist in the tactical material being covered. Not every officer had an answer for every survey question, but it is doubtful that any question on questionnaire "H" for infantry, for example, would have been beyond the average infantry officer's understanding.

The battle experience questionnaires thus offer a unique look into the combat experience of the officers of the Canadian Army during the Second World War. As historical artifacts they also hold considerable value for the historian in engaging the details of the sharp end of war, particularly since they have seemingly never been used to significant effect before.[63] In sum, the battle experience questionnaires seem able to stand up to analytical scrutiny.

Some mention should be made at this juncture of the precise methods used in collecting and compiling the data for this study. As previously mentioned, from the approximately 300 questionnaires that were on file in the LAC, 161 had been filled out by infantry officers and the remainder filled out by armoured, engineer, and artillery personnel. Every individual survey, with its addendum notes, was assigned a sequential reference number by CMHQ personnel during the Second World War, though the reference numbers were shared between the infantry and the other arms. On the cover of each survey is a "YES" or a "NO," handwritten in red pencil; those marked "YES" represent the questionnaires sent on to the DTI (and subsequently returned to Canada, except for the thirty permanently held by the DTI), and those marked "NO" were retained by CMHQ.[64] In September and October 2007 I took several thousand digital images of the surveys in the archives, documenting each infantry officer's survey answers as well as any other attached notes and comments that respondents had provided on loose-leaf. Subsequent trips to Ottawa in early 2008 resulted in additional digital imaging of many administrative documents and pieces of correspondence from CMHQ concerning the battle experience questionnaires in 1944 and 1945. These images were taken as carefully as possible so as to retrieve and record all available information from each survey.

Once the surveys were recorded in their entirety, two things were done. First, the roughly "quantitative" answers from the questionnaires themselves were entered in computer spreadsheet format. These survey questions typically allowed for "yes," "no," or "not known" answers, and included inquiries about weapons effectiveness, tactical fire-and-movement, German counter-attacks, artillery and air support, troop morale, average section strength, and the prevalence of close-quarters fighting, among others.[65] The officers' answers to these questions were tabulated through the spreadsheet, so that results could be viewed as a whole or broken down according to theatre of operations, regiment, dates spent in combat, or even rank. While this study makes no claim to be statistically representative of the entire Canadian Army in the Second World War, officers from over twenty different regiments were surveyed; given the relatively small size of the Canadian armed forces that saw combat in the war, they amount to a modest, but important, statistical sample of the combat officers in the army.[66] These answers have been compiled to allow readers to perceive commonalities among in the experiences of these combat veterans and view the patterns that emerge.

These figures and responses should not be taken as precise statistics or measurements of "hard data," despite any urge to assign "scientific" status to any numerical data. In one section of the survey officers were asked to estimate the number of times specific enemy weapons (rifles, mortars, artillery, tanks, and so on) had been used against their unit.[67] Some gave specific numbers of times, but most responded with "often" to denote many instances of the weapon being used against them, or "never" to indicate that they had never seen it used in battle. My point here is not to compile precise statistics or to try to determine that the average officer witnessed x weapon being used y number of times against his unit. Rather, the purpose for including this material is to indicate broad trends of what officers experienced in combat. It is not relevant whether the average officer remembered being engaged by German armoured cars three or four separate times, though one could indeed choose to tabulate such data. What is more helpful to this study is knowing that almost every officer surveyed encountered German rifle, mortar, and machine-gun fire, and that German mortars were overwhelmingly marked down as the weapon most devastating to the morale of Canadian soldiers. The statistics presented in this study are therefore useful for indicating broad trends that can be interpreted and analysed. They are also, fundamentally, measurements based on *stated opinions*, not measures of some objective reality. As Curtis said, the truth of the matter should not be concealed.

My second procedure, after digitally recording all the surveys, was to transcribe and record any personal comments, elaborations, and suggestions by the officers that were attached on loose-leaf paper as addenda to the survey. Although a very small minority were unreadable owing to illegible handwriting, faded pencil marks, or, in a handful of instances, faulty digital imaging discovered after the fact (*mea culpa*), the great majority were successfully transcribed. Many officers had a great deal to say, attaching up to a dozen pages of additional commentary, tactical map sketches for visual aid, and a few illustrative examples. Of the 161 infantry officers, 98 attached legible addendum notes to their surveys. These comments provide the vital qualitative corollary to the more quantitative statistical data garnered from the answers to the survey questions themselves. They provide personal commentary on the same tactical issues, with examples that go beyond the survey questions and offer the historian a more rounded view of officers' combat experiences.

Wherever possible, I have tried to combine the two major aspects of the questionnaires – the more quantitative formal survey questions, and the personal commentary of the addendum notes – so that whatever statistical evidence can be gleaned from the breadth of the survey is supported by the specific comments and critiques of the officers. Commonalities that appear between the stated experiences of the officers can therefore be assessed and supported with more explicit commentary. While these surveys cannot tell us everything about the experience of the Second World War on the ground, they can bring fresh information to historical debate about the war. They are also available to be used in the future to support broader studies, but for now it is sufficient that these surveys can address, as contemporary documentary evidence, the question of infantry effectiveness as it relates to the Canadian Army during the Second World War.

## CHAPTER THREE

THE OFFICER RESPONDENTS

On the night of 30 July 1943, the West Nova Scotia Regiment, fighting in Sicily with the rest of the 1st Canadian Division, spearheaded an attack upon the German-held town of Catenanuova.[1] Captain A.H. Maclean, a company commander, would later write in his battle experience questionnaire that to him this action was one of the most important and instructive of the war. In his addendum notes Maclean said that in the course of the night attack his battalion called down heavy artillery fire upon the town itself, irrespective of civilian casualties; he bluntly stated that German prisoners of war captured were shot on the spot, since "it was impossible to take prisoners under the circumstances"; and finally he ordered a bayonet charge in routing the Germans from Catenanuova, noting the efficacy of "cold steel" in cutting down the enemy.[2]

At least two of the three major elements of Captain Maclean's above account could be construed as atrocities or potential war crimes, but in his battle experience questionnaire the captain expressed no regrets, admitted no culpability, and indeed would probably have been surprised to have heard any accusations of wrongdoing levelled against him. Maclean was merely recounting his experiences, and while his questionnaire responses may be particularly chilling to today's reader, they underscore an important historical fact: the Canadian officers who put ink to paper on the battle experience questionnaires lived in a different time from our own and in a different moral climate and context, and held beliefs and values different from those of today. Maclean may be an extreme example, but his words highlight the need to understand the context in which historical actors and events have existed. To remain blind to these factors is to risk projecting the historian's values onto historical actors.

Having assessed the validity of the battle experience questionnaires themselves as historical documentary evidence, we need to devote some attention to examining and historically situating the subjects of the questionnaires, the Canadian Army's combat infantry officers. While much has been written about Canada's other ranks (OR) during the Second World War and even more about the commanders and generals of the Canadian Army, less attention has been paid to the officers who personally led the soldiers into the fight. Although not an invisible class of warriors, these officers are frequently neglected both by the grassroots social histories that focus on the experience of the beleaguered OR or the toil of the home front, and by the "great man" histories and biographies of high-profile leaders and personalities. Since the junior and senior officers who held ranks between captain and lieutenant-colonel constitute the voices of the battle experience questionnaires, it is worth exploring who they were and what their cultural context was. A broad "portrait" of these Canadian combat officers of the Second World War can emerge from the framework established by some excellent secondary literature on the subject, and the supporting evidence from the battle experience questionnaires themselves. This portrait will help acquaint the reader with the circumstances in which the Canadian infantry officers developed, how they were selected for commissioning, and what their duties were in combat.

CULTURAL BACKGROUND

A popular perception has existed from at least as far back as the Second World War which conflates "Western culture" or "Western civilization" with values of peacefulness and humanitarianism. Although typically vague on what "Western culture" might actually consist of, this perception has infiltrated military history in an important way. It is often understood that Western liberal society is blessed by an inherently peaceful, humanistic culture that cherishes human life and abhors unnecessary violence – and only accepts the use of "necessary" violence with the greatest reluctance.3 These assumptions have been put to work in supporting claims that Western culture therefore produces poor soldiers who are inclined to shrink from killing in close combat. Such loose reasoning makes infantry combat ineffectiveness a function of the supposed peacefulness of Western civilization. This idea is particularly linked with the generation raised between 1919 and 1939, who would go on to fight the Second World War. The accuracy of this particular portrait needs to be assessed.

The historiography identifying "Western civilisation" during the interwar years – and perhaps even before that – as inherently peaceful and inclined to promote non-violence and co-operation can be traced at least as far back as S.L.A. Marshall. Writing in 1947 to buttress, and in part to explain, his extraordinary ratio-of-fire findings, Marshall argued: ["The Army] must reckon with the fact that [the soldier] comes from a civilization in which aggression, connected with the taking of life, is prohibited and unacceptable. The teaching and the ideals of that civilization are against killing and against taking advantage ... this is his greatest handicap when he enters combat. It stays his trigger finger even though he is hardly conscious that it is a restraint upon him."4 Repeating Marshall almost word for word but referring specifically to the Canadian experience, Captain W.R. Chamberlain, in the *Canadian Army Journal* in 1951, likewise claimed: "Western civilization has set as its highest ideal the prolongation, amelioration and preservation of human life. From his mother's knee the citizen is taught 'safety first' and respect for the welfare of his fellow-man. Our culture is a constructive one, in which destruction is frowned upon as anti-social. As a consequence a mental block ... has been established in the normal law-abiding citizen's mind against the taking of human life."5 Other, more recent works have reinforced this perception that the interwar period specifically – and Western "civilization" more generally – produced individuals who were psychologically disposed to be ineffective soldiers due to their upbringing.6

Marshall and Chamberlain did not elaborate upon the specific cultural values that they deemed responsible for making most "Western" soldiers so combat-ineffective, and were content to fall back upon the rather simplistic notion that Western culture was inherently "civilized" during their time period.7 This is a point worth examining, particularly in the context of the Canadian officers being discussed, since it is their own cultural landscape and upbringing that are subject to such assumptions. Furthermore, these assumptions – about general Western peacefulness and shyness in the face of aggression – sound rather disingenuous when an actual examination of interwar society and culture is undertaken. Particularly in the case of Canada, but in most of Western Europe as well, it has recently been amply demonstrated that society did not set an abhorrence of violence and the necessity of killing as its "highest ideal." Some of the dominant cultural trends of the day involved the celebration and memorializing of war and sacrifice, with an undercurrent that accepted the necessity of mass violence.[8] The Second World War itself stands as a mockery of any attempt to paint "Western" culture as inherently "good" or pacifist. Although it would be an exaggeration to suggest that Canadian society was a war-mongering society, Canadians were no strangers to violence. The context in which the officers who filled out the battle experience questionnaires were raised needs at least to be tacitly understood to appreciate their actions in war.

A key distinction to make here is the difference between *espoused* values and values *in use*: what a group or organization claims its values to be as opposed to those that are most frequently put into practice. Edgar Schein, an expert on organizational culture, noted that *espoused* values could be considered the conscious, articulated values, the primarily normative statements that reflect a series of attitudes, hopes, and beliefs about how people would *like* things to be, as opposed to how they really are.[9] Values *in use* (which Schein refers to as basic assumptions) represent, on the other hand, a group's deepest core assumptions, normally taken for granted, which represent the implicit, underlying premises that deal with fundamental aspects of life.[10] When the two are in concert greater cohesion within a group can be developed. All societies, however, are rife with contradictory and antagonistic cultural tendencies, and are rarely so harmonious. The values a society claims as its own are frequently incongruent with what it puts into practice.

The values that Marshall, Chamberlain, and others have attributed to interwar "Western" civilization as a whole certainly bear the marks of espoused values. We would all like to think we are peaceful, co-operative, and generally benevolent toward our fellow human beings, understanding human life to be both important and sacred. The attributes of meekness and non-violence are not such clearcut ideals but they are still well in accord with the higher values underwriting the "Western" experience, particularly the strong influence of Christian morality. While Christian moral theories have articulated ethically acceptable applications of violence they have only condoned defense of self or others, and never promoted aggression, or "unjust war."[11] "Western" civilization has popularly portrayed itself as beneficent and humanitarian, though at times more convincingly than others.[12] Owing much to the Christian tenets of "turning the other cheek" and placing other's needs before the needs of the self, such values certainly represent the way the Christian West would like to be able to see itself, and, indeed, how it frequently succeeds in seeing itself.

But can these ideals also be portrayed as the actual values *in use* for Western society? Setting aside for the moment the blanket "Western" label and focusing specifically on Canada during the interwar years (1919–39), it becomes rather obvious that the espoused values of non-violence, peacefulness, and the sanctity of life were not always in harmony with the social practices in use. Although a "fear of aggression" may have been inculcated through the upbringing of some Canadians, such fears do not appear to have been central features of Canadian cultural at the time. The reality was far more complex.

None of the officers surveyed in the Canadian battle experience questionnaires would have had living memories of the First World War; they belonged to the generation born either during or immediately following that conflict. Although many Canadian officers at the outbreak of the Second World War had fought in the Great War, most were by then either the army's senior commanders or had been quietly removed from combat positions prior to the Canadian forces' seeing sustained action in 1943. No platoon, company, or battalion commanders – the officers of the battle experience questionnaires – were old enough in 1943–45 to have served in the Great War.[13] However, as they were growing up in the wake of the war, when its impact was still immediate and personal, the First World War would have been one of the central cultural events that shaped their early lives. It could hardly have been otherwise: almost 60,000 Canadians died in the trenches, from a 1914 population of just under 8 million; another 150,000 survived wounds, the scars of which they brought back across the Atlantic.[14] Such numbers are beyond the capacity of the human mind to fully grasp, but the tangible result was certainly a great rent in the social and demographic fabric of the country in the interwar years. Canadian society was inundated with veterans, memorials, and mourning, and the future officers of the Second World War were born and raised in the shadow of this colossal event, the human legacy of which would have been inescapable at the time. As historian Jonathan Vance has emphasized in his acclaimed work on interwar social memory, for the modern reader to simply assume that Canadian society was inclined toward pacifism because of the "psychic scars" of the trenches "is to misconstrue the past. It is to assume that simply because we judge the First World War to have been an appalling slaughter, people who lived through it must also have judged it in this way. This is clearly an assumption that the historian cannot make."[15] In his book, *Death So Noble*, Vance explores the creation and maintenance of a particular "mythology" of how the First World War was remembered in Canada during the interwar years: a "mythology" that, whether fully congruent with reality or not, was vigorously defended as a social memory that communicated an interpretation of the past. Contrary to what our present-day "popular memory" of the First World War might be, Canadians in the interwar period were "determined to see 1914–18 as the progenitor of good [and] refused to countenance a preoccupation with the horrors of battle or the grief of loss." Instead, the vision of the war that was promoted before the start of the Second World War was that the Great War had marked an unequivocal triumph, not just for Canada, but for all of "civilization":

> The Hun had been vanquished, and civilization had been saved
> from the threat of barbarism. Still, there was no guarantee that the
> salvation was permanent, and the memory of the war accepted that
> such a struggle might well have to be waged again. In this way, it
> acted as a powerful antidote to pacifism, for it assumed that the
> truest lovers of peace were those people who were willing to fight for
> it. Because the country had gone to war to preserve peace, Canada
> could look back with pride at its first world war.[16]

Far from perceiving the "War to End All Wars" as the literal end of world conflict, or perceiving it as a nightmarish butchery, the Canadian generation born into the interwar years heard the message that the war had been glorious, just, and waged for noble purposes. In the dominant social discourse war was constructed as triumph rather than tragedy, iconized by monuments to Winged Victory rather than the somber grave of the Unknown Soldier.[17]

In practical terms, the Canadian officers who would go on to fight the Second World War grew up in a cultural environment that had chosen to sanctify the sacrifices of the Great War rather than recoil from them. There were dissenting voices, of course, but the predominant social remembrance being negotiated at the time, in Canada as in many European countries, was one that emphasized the war's purposefulness rather than its tragedy. The aim was to make a highly unpalatable past acceptable to those who survived it, and to find both meaning and justification in what the war had been fought for.[18] There was a widespread acceptance of the fact that the application of deadly violence, though a necessary evil, had indeed been necessary and might well be required again in the near future.[19] Far from inculcating a fear of aggression and violence toward one's fellow man, the collective social remembrance of the interwar period in Canada commemorated the brutal violence with the message that the staggering loss had been worthwhile, socially sanctioned, and even *holy* in a profoundly religious way.[20] Undoubtedly some of the officers referred to here had heard different tales about the horrors of war when they were growing up; dissenting voices did exist, but they were normally ignored or drowned out. The established paradigm and pattern of collective remembrance of the Great War was of the glorious dead and an earthly triumph that underwrote the social acceptance of mass violence as legitimate and praiseworthy, however implicitly or indirectly. This generation was not raised to think of war as a grand adventure, as the scars of war would have been too real to sustain such an illusion for long; young men growing up in interwar Canada would have listened as veterans related their own personal truths about the terrors of modern warfare.[21] But they were nonetheless raised in the context of a Canadian culture that, as a basic assumption, portrayed its Great War experience in a positive commemorative light. Growing up in a culture inundated with the images and remembrance of the trench battles and heavy casualties of the First World War may well have been psychologically fortifying for soldiers in 1939–45. As British historian G.D. Sheffield has pointed out, no matter how bad things got, soldiers could always reassure themselves that their fathers had once been through worse, regardless of whether this was objectively true. While the physical conditions of the Mediterranean and Northwest Europe battlefields of the Second World War were frequently just as gruelling as those their predecessors had faced in the Great War, many soldiers were partially sustained by the belief that the Western Front of the previous war had been a much worse experience.[22]

The subject of the viciousness of war leads to another dimension of interwar culture that bears further meditation: the idea that Western cultures had, as a direct result of the First World War, undergone a continuing process of brutalization. The term was coined in relation to interwar culture by historian George Mosse. Brutalization, as Mosse outlines it, was "an attitude of mind derived from the war and the acceptance of war itself. The outcome of the process of brutalization in the interwar years was to energize man, to propel him into action against the political enemy, or to numb men and women in the face of human cruelty and the loss of life."[23] Although it is difficult to pinpoint the moment empirically, the First World War seems to have been a turning point in cultural attitudes toward mass violence, as the peoples of war-wearied countries became increasingly apathetic or numbed toward large-scale killing. For instance, in a 1903 pogrom in Kishinev, in modern-day Moldavia, the killing of forty-nine Jews provoked international outrage; but in 1919, when 60,000 Jews were killed in Russian pograms, nobody seemed to care. The Armenian Genocide was treated with similar apathy at the time.[24] Every society that had sent soldiers to fight in the Great War was overwhelmed by personal loss, scarred by the unfathomable number of soldiers killed in the war, and found itself increasingly unable to view mass violence as exceptional or even unusual. Sustained violence had, from 1914 to 1918, become widely approved, accepted, and engaged in by millions in Europe, from every social group. As historians Stéphane Audoin-Rouzeau and Annette Becker have written on the subject of brutalization: "Unprecedented violence became integrated with disconcerting ease into the daily life of every civilian and every soldier [during the First World War] to the point where it became commonplace."[25] For many years afterward it would have been difficult to re-establish the previous ethical lines; in some countries, and in some circumstances, the lines had become distorted. "The First World War," writes Jay Winter, "changed what was thinkable, what was imaginable, about human brutality and violence. It opened a door through which others passed a brief two decades later."[26] One is drawn, as Mosse was in his original brutalization thesis, toward the conclusion that "an obvious relationship exists between the confrontation with mass death and the holding of individual life as cheap."[27]

This process of the brutalization of everyday life was obviously most pronounced among the defeated powers, particularly in interwar Germany and Russia, where the political landscape was made "enduringly brutal" by the practices and representations of war,[28] but there are signs that it had taken a hold in even the victorious Allied powers like Britain and Canada.[29] Vance's research, for example, has done a superb job of un-covering some of the darker sentiments underwriting Canadian society during this time. The end of the war was marked not just as a return to peace, but as a victory over an evil foe, and many Canadians demonstrated a long and unforgiving memory for the losses sustained and the atrocities committed by the Germans, both real and propagandized: civilian mas-sacres, attacks on hospitals, and the destruction of cities.[30] Writing in 1939, popular Canadian journalist Pierre van Paassen complained that, even twenty years after the Great War, "hundreds of thousands of easy-going citizens of the Dominion [were] firmly persuaded that ... Belgian babies were ... carried on the point of German bayonets, that Bavarian yodelers took a particular delight in cutting off the breasts of Flemish nurses, and that the Huns boiled enemy corpses in order to extract grease for the soap in the Kaiser's bath."[31] Even in its defeat the enemy was demonized, per-haps understandably; the 60,000 of their soldiers who had died at German hands had not disposed Canadians toward forgiveness or reconciliation.

It is also worth recalling that interwar Canada was far from idyllic and peace-loving on the domestic front. The country was ravaged by labour unrest, political turbulence, economic depression, and more than a small amount of violence. "Industrial warfare still simmered," historian John Herd Thompson writes of Canada between 1921 and 1929, citing an aver-age of ninety-four strikes or lockouts every year during that time; in Au-gust of 1922 there were 22,000 coal workers on strike across the country. Violence accompanied many of these actions. The militia was deployed domestically several times during the interwar period to preserve "peace, order, and good government" and, more often than not, corporate prop-erty.[32] The working-class movement's struggles were not a new phenom-enon during the interwar years either. As labour historian Craig Heron describes it:

> The prosecution of the [First World War] and the (mis)management of the wartime economy, which gave the national state such promi-nence, had unified many previously fragmented struggles around the country and given them some common focus. Wartime ideals, espe-cially the fight for democracy, had also injected into public debate in Canada and abroad a moral fervor that piqued workers' imagination and heightened their expectations about the future. Old ways of viewing (and justifying) social relationships in capitalist society were

dissolving. The wartime convergence of material and ideological forces thus facilitated the creation of the most broad-based, anti-capitalist workers' movements that had ever appeared in Canada.[33]

The interwar years in Canada were wracked by widespread and violent labour unrest even before the Great Depression set in. After 1929 social upheaval and dislocation became epidemic throughout the country, cul-minating in even more violence, including "The Bloodiest Day of the Depression," the Regina Riots of 1935.[34] To claim that interwar Canada bred peace-loving and non-violent men in these years is to disregard much of the conflict inherent within their society and hide behind the Western-centric myths of the "modern" and "civilized" nation.

The strongest evidence of a cultural undercurrent of acceptance of everyday violence, however, is the fact that another half-million Canadi-ans voluntarily enlisted in the army in the course of the Second World War. There was no lack of prospective soldiers ready to take up the colours upon the outbreak of war, just as there were sufficient men to sustain and continually expand the Canadian Army throughout most of the war. The volunteers of 1939 enlisted, as Copp puts it, "aware that war might turn out to be hell [and] those who volunteered after June 1940 also knew that the war would last for a very long time. Few doubted the need for action."[35] Audoin-Rouzeau and Becker also comments on the apparent willingness to go to war: "Even more troubling, the about-turn – from a social state where violence had become very controlled, repressed, and unreal to a state of war where extreme violence had free rein – occurred in an extremely brief span of time. In a matter of days and with hardly any transition between the two, Europeans who had bene-fited from the 'civilising process' left their work, their families and their often sophisticated, cultivated social life to accept extreme violence."[36] Although they were speaking of the First World War, their comments are just as pertinent to the Canadian experience in the Second World War. Despite the language of valiance, determination, and sacrifice that serv-ice in wartime frequently evokes, the underlying truth was that half a million Canadians left behind their jobs and families so that they could fight, or help fight, a distant enemy. There was no overwhelming "rush to the colours" as there had been in 1914, no spontaneous mass demon-stration of support for the war, but enlistment quotas were consistently filled through the first five years of military expansion during the war. Regardless of the perceived horrors of 1914–18, come the outbreak of hostilities in 1939, war could still be justified, even if its day of popular glorification had passed into history.[37]

This discussion is not intended as a slur, or an implication that the officers of the Second World War were born and raised in a morally bankrupt or war-mongering society. Undoubtedly that was not the case; nor is it my intention to present interwar Canada as such. But in examining the officers' backgrounds, the historian should be aware of the complexities, tensions, and ambiguities prevalent during the post-1918 decades in which these soldiers developed as individuals, particularly as they might affect the way society then viewed violence and death. Canadians of the interwar years were kind, loving, helpful, co-operative, greedy, spiteful, and everything else within the full gamut of human emotion and experience, often unpredictably so. But they were also products of a culture that had accepted, encouraged, and celebrated the massive application of violence from 1914 to 1918; whatever their espoused values may have been, the societal core assumptions accepted the legitimacy and the necessity of war.[38] To discuss in vague generalizations the "civilizing" influences of Western culture that purportedly erode the ability of soldiers to fight is to misunderstand the complexities of the society the soldiers were drawn from. It is to presume that Western culture instinctively rejects – and has always instinctively rejected – violence, and has conditioned its members to do so from an early age. It is to assume, anachronistically, that survivors of the Great War must have remembered the conflict as the senseless butchery it is typified as today. As an examination of the historical literature can demonstrate, however, such assumptions are difficult to sustain.

The officers surveyed in the questionnaires came of age in a Canadian culture still fixated upon its Great War experience and determined to commemorate the loss and sacrifice, even though by the late 1930s cracks in this cultural paradigm were showing.[39] Nonetheless, far from being raised from mother's milk with the imbibed values of pacifism, non-violence, and a fear of killing, Canadian soldiers were often taught that their parents' war had been glorious, justified, and completely sanctioned by society. Although an over-generalization, it would probably also be accurate to surmise that they had been raised with the knowledge that their fathers had fought, died, and killed in battle, that those actions were socially acceptable and commendable, and that they too might someday be required to do the same thing. The Second World War proved this. The onset of "total war" in the twentieth century simultaneously made civilians an integral part of the war effort and, in the eyes of all major combatants, made them legitimate targets for the application of mass violence.[40] The list of the barbarities and horrors inflicted upon both civilians and combatants is well known, but all sides of the war, Allied and Axis alike, visited mass violence upon one another with virtually no restraint or restriction, destroying entire cities and populations alongside armies and soldiers.[41] Given the unfathomable scope of the violence unleashed in the Second World War, it seems curiously naïve, to the point of denial, to argue that Western culture abhors violence.

This discussion has perhaps provided an outline for demonstrating that the assumptions that Marshall, Chamberlain, and other writers held toward the "civilizing values" of Western culture are inadequate to explain infantry ineffectiveness, particularly as pertains to Canada. The cultural values and attitudes of the interwar period were simply not the same values and attitudes as are accepted today or even following the war. Today's values, especially concerning war, are largely informed by the brutality of the Second World War, which, according to Mosse, "brought about a decisive change in the memory of war in Western and Central Europe, seeming to put an end to the way in which wars had been perceived by most peoples and nations ever since the wars of the French Revolution."[42] It was a new kind of war, one that was perhaps the final embodiment of the brutalization of attitudes following the First World War, and central to its conduct was the wholesale destruction of towns, cities, and civilian populations. "The Second World War helped to put an end to the rich set of traditional languages of commemoration and mourning which flourished after the Great War," wrote Jay Winter in *Sites of Memory, Sites of Mourning*. "Before 1939, before the Death Camps, and the thermonuclear cloud, most men and women were still able to reach back into their 'traditional' cultural heritage to express amazement and anger, bewilderment and compassion, in the face of war."[43] Afterward, this was no longer possible. Perhaps the post-1945 theories of commentators such as Marshall and Chamberlain reflect this break in attitudes, and an appeal to sentiments of how Western society would prefer to view itself, rather than the grim reality of the values that it actually held.

BACKGROUND AND SELECTION

Although the battle experience questionnaires themselves give almost no personal information for the officers who filled them out beyond name, rank, position, and regiment, a few general comments can still be made on the constitution of both the Canadian Army Overseas and the officer corps during the six years of war. Canada in 1939 had a population of around 11 million, of whom just under half still lived on farms or in small towns and villages. Some 5.7 million Canadians considered themselves to be British in origin; 3.5 million identified themselves as French-Canadian. The other 20 percent were predominantly of European or American origin. By that point, most Canadians – around 9.4 million – had been born in Canada, a marked change from the time of the First World War, when a much larger proportion of the population had been born in the British Isles.44 The officer corps for the Canadian military, however, did not reflect these demographic realities during the war. A disproportionately high number of army officers were of British heritage, despite there being four French-speaking infantry battalions in the Canadian Army Overseas, as a much smaller proportion of the potential military manpower – males aged 18 to 45 – enlisted in Quebec than in the Western or Atlantic provinces of Canada.45 Most of the other ranks were aged between 18 and 25, and the younger officers who would rise to become the platoon, company, and battalion commanders that the questionnaires are concerned with were only a few years older than the men they led. The officers tended to have a markedly higher level of education than the ORs, however; almost all of them had completed high school, whereas only one in eight ORs could claim that distinction.46 At the outbreak of the Second World War the militia and Permanent Force officer corps were still weighed down with veterans of the First World War, men who were judged too old to hold field commissions. Most of these, however, had been weeded out over the four or five years spent waiting in England, so that by the time the Canadians went into action, almost all their commanders except those at the highest ranks – were younger officers who had not fought in the Great War.47

Until 1945, when the first soldiers conscripted by Canada's National Resources Mobilization Act (NRMA) began to arrive in Europe to alleviate the manpower shortage, the Canadian Army consisted of the largest all-volunteer active force in the world. By the spring of 1944, Canada had mustered some 405,834 men and women volunteers for general service overseas in the army alone, to say nothing of the air force and the navy.[48] Additionally, some 12,908 conscripted NRMA soldiers were sent overseas in early 1945 to help reinforce the battered Canadian infantry divisions in Europe, and arrived just prior to the end of the war. According to the official history, this group of conscripts suffered only 315 casualties, of which sixty-nine were fatal.[49] Therefore, the most decisive part of Canada's contribution to the Second World War, the soldiers fighting on the ground, consisted almost entirely of men who had enlisted voluntarily, with the full expectation – if an incomplete knowledge – of what lay ahead of them. In total, some 1.2 million Canadians volunteered for service in the Second World War.[50]

The fact that Canada's overseas army was an explicitly voluntary institution until the very last months of the war is worth some reflection, because it constitutes one of the most distinctive and under-appreciated elements of the military culture of the day. Some analysts have elected to see no difference between volunteers and conscripted soldiers, treating both methods of obtaining servicemen as qualitatively similar techniques for acquiring sufficient "human material" for the armed forces.[51] There are, however, some fundamental differences between the two types of soldier in terms of potential effectiveness. American military analyst and war-gaming simulation designer James Dunnigan has commented that an all-volunteer force produces an overall level of excellence that approaches that of traditional elite units.[52] While this might be overstating the point, there are likely to be notable differences in the combat motivation of the average volunteer soldier and the average conscripted soldier who may be serving under various compulsions. It has been suggested, for example, that one of the reasons that the Canadian divisions waiting in England in 1941 took more zealously to the "battle drill" training fad than their British counterparts was because it conformed more readily to the purpose they thought they had crossed the Atlantic for: to fight, rather than to carry on with the mundane but safe routine of garrison life.[53]

All the Canadian officers, of course, were volunteers, but this is not unusual for a Western military; even in conscript armies the officers are typically all volunteers. While one can compel soldiers to serve, follow, and obey with some expectation of success, forcing them to adopt the leadership qualities necessary to command others is far more problematic. What was more unusual about the Canadian officers was that they had the responsibility of leading a force of soldiers composed entirely of other volunteers as well.[54] Apart from the other Dominion armies such as those of South Africa and Australia, few officers among the Allied forces in the Second World War could make similar claims.[55] In Great Britain, for example, less than a quarter of the army's 3 million wartime inductees were volunteers, meaning that the British Army, within which the Canadian Army had to operate institutionally, took the conscripted soldier as its basic unit.[56]

The Canadian Army expanded exponentially during the war, increasing to about 125 times its prewar strength.[57] The officer corps needed to expand at a similar rate. While at the beginning of the war expansion was accomplished by commissioning officers from the Active and Reserve lists, after the fall of France in 1940 Canada began to implement a policy whereby all officers would be commissioned from the ranks, meaning that every officer candidate had to have spent a minimum amount of time – initially four months, but later fixed upon five – in the ranks.[58] While a system of direct battlefield promotion was never implemented, non-commissioned officers in the ranks were screened for "good officer material" and subsequently sent to Officer Training Centres, where the large-scale development of reinforcement officers took place.[59] It was acknowledged by the Canadian General Staff that commissioning from the ranks was both more legitimate and more likely to produce competent officers, since candidates would have already had a background in soldiering. All told, 42,613 officer commissions were granted between September 1939 and June 1946; and between April 1941, when the policy of commissioning from the ranks took effect, to the end of the war, 19,322 officers were appointed from the ranks.[60] By the time Canadian soldiers saw battle in the Second World War, their officer corps, particularly the group studied here, was at least theoretically structured as a meritocracy, aimed at cultivating the best officer material within its ranks.

The selection process for officers drawn from the ranks is also of interest in this context, since the way a military organizes and allocates its personnel within its infrastructure is at least as important in understanding war as any technological factors.[61] In this process, Canada was influenced by the British experience, although a step behind. After the initial mobilization requirements of 1939 had been fulfilled, it became official policy in the British Army that all potential officers had first to spend six months in the enlisted ranks.[62] Much as in Britain, the initial machinery for "screening" candidates and finding quality officer material involved interview panels of senior officers, which would meet with officer candidates and then forward a recommendation to the battalion commander, who made the final decision.[63] By early 1943, Canadian Officer Selection and Appraisal Boards had been established with the intention of bringing "scientific" authority to the selection of officers. Described as "impartial Boards," these new selection panels were composed of senior officers, psychiatrists, psychologists, and educational officers, and were presided over by brigadiers with long personal experience in selection and training.[64] At Officer Selection and Appraisal Centres, candidates were put through a series of rigorous tests lasting a week, in order to demonstrate their fitness for commissioning, and then they were given a final interview with the Board before the decision was made. This process mimicked in most details the concept of the British War Office Selection Boards, which had been created in January 1942. These selection boards adhered to a supposedly "German model" of officer selection in which psychologists, psychiatrists, and military experts shared in the vetting of the potential officers, although psychological testing on a smaller scale than the Selection Boards had been implemented in Britain in 1941.[65] It was actually General Harry Crerar, later the commander of the First Canadian Army but in 1941 serving as Chief of the General Staff, who laid the groundwork to establish a partially civilianized personnel selection apparatus for the Canadian Army, "to develop a systematic program of personnel selection, ultimately classifying all men in the army, and seeking to identify potential officers."[66] The goal was to utilize civilian specialists in the realm of human behaviour in order more efficiently to allocate personnel on a supposedly scientific basis, although, as C.P. Stacey points out, Canada adopted this approach for army officer selection rather late in the war, at a time when the Canadian army was actually about to experience an officer surplus rather than a shortage.[67]

It should be emphasized, however, that the "scientific" authority surrounding selection was something of a mirage. When it came to personnel selection, "military experts based their approaches to these problems on science as they knew it ... but science is not an entirely objective undertaking."[68] In both the British War Office Selection Boards and the Canadian Officer Selection and Appraisal Boards, a great deal of subjectivity was inherent to the process, as senior officers were willing to entertain input from civilian specialists but were generally unwilling to cede their ultimate authority in appointing or recommending future officers. Regardless of "scientific" input, the president of the board – a brigadier in Canada – normally had the final say.[69] As historian Jeremy Crang notes in his study of British officer selection techniques, owing to the nature of the interview and the rather mutable standards for what qualities collectively constituted good officer material, "a candidate still stood or fell by the first impression he created."[70] Even in the course of a week at one of the Officer Selection and Appraisal Centres, it would have been very difficult, if indeed possible at all, to identify the subjective leadership qualities that would have been necessary for combat officers. Moreover, until at least 1943 the selection process remained almost completely theoretical, as the implemented procedures had never been tested in battle for validity.[71] So, despite the scientific veneer, most of the officers who filled out the battle experience questionnaires would have been chosen as successful candidates because they appeared to fulfill the traditional criteria of "intelligence, personality, and powers of leadership" that remained difficult to quantify.[72] This process did, however, help at least to establish the perception of rigorous analysis of officer candidates, and their subsequent eligibility for ranking on the basis of ostensibly scientific criteria. It was also a superior system to earlier selection processes, which had been entirely subjective in their operation. The fact that officer selection could be defended on scientific grounds, helped to reduce the perception that membership in certain social groups or personal educational distinctions would constitute the final prerequisites for commissioned ranks. Candidates saw the process as being more fair to them as individuals, allowing them to compete on merit rather than background. Given the reputation of politicization that the Canadian officer corps had possessed prior to the Second World War, any system that could work to decrease this perception was sure to reduce resentments.[73]

THE ROLE OF THE OFFICERS

Finally, to aid our understanding of the battle experience questionnaires, and especially to establsih their credibility as evidence of combat performance, it will be helpful to look at the roles that officers fulfilled within their infantry units and how these related to combat operations. This issue is particularly important to address, because it touches upon a potential criticism that might be levelled against officers' observations of infantry effectiveness: S.L.A. Marshall's claim in *Men Against Fire* that officers – even junior ones – were never aware of what their troops were doing in combat. In crafting his ratio-of-fire argument, Marshall stated: "In the course of holding post-combat mass interviews with approximately four hundred infantry companies ... I did not find one battalion, company, or platoon commander who had made the slightest effort to determine how many of his men had actually engaged the enemy with a weapon. But there were many who, on being asked the preliminary question, made the automatic reply: 'I believe that every man used a weapon at one time or another.'"[74] According to Marshall's interpretation, the subsequent group interviews "proved" the officers to be incorrect, though he goes on to say that after the mass interviews had been completed, "there was no case of a commander remaining unconvinced that the men had made a true report" of what had taken place in combat.[75] In Marshall's judgment, then, combat officers would make an untrustworthy source, and the Canadian battle experience questionnaires would therefore be useless as historical evidence. As with much of Marshall's work, however, the basis of his claims regarding the haplessness of officers is highly questionable and needs to be subjected to scrutiny.

As previously mentioned, three ranks were asked to complete the battle experience questionnaires: captains, majors, and lieutenant-colonels, although many officers indicated that they had first received their combat experience as lieutenants. Their leadership responsibilities extended from commanding platoons, companies, and, in a few cases, battalions, or serving as second-in-command or in other positions in those formations. Among those surveyed, "rifle company commander" was the most frequent position listed; these officers had command of about a hundred riflemen, although many also indicated that they had held positions as the officer commanding for support companies, which provided a battalion's supporting elements, particularly the carrier, scout, pioneer, anti-tank, and mortar platoons. Rifle companies provided the main fighting strength, and there were normally four to a battalion; the support company provided specialized weaponry, transportation, and other services in support of the rifles.[76] Only seven of the respondents were lieutenant-colonels, the commanding officers of battalions, and the overwhelming majority of voices in the questionnaires came from officers operating at the company level or lower.[77] Seventy-eight officers held the rank of captain at the time when they filled out their questionnaire, and seventy-six held the rank of major. For all intents and purposes, therefore, the questionnaire reveals the tactical combat experience of officers at the platoon and company organizational levels; although company commanders predominate, most of them had combat experience first at the platoon level, and could speak with authority from several positions within the army organization. A few battalion commanders are included, but since they can be seen as outliers, this discussion will focus on company and platoon commanders.

While tactical doctrine is frequently discussed in the historiography of the Second World War, what that doctrine says about the roles of officers is not often articulated.[78] The *Infantry Training* manuals and *Field Service Regulations* in effect during the Second World War give an idea of what the intended role of the company and platoon commanders on the battlefield was.[79] The *Infantry Training 1937 (Training & War)* manual indicates in its chapter on "Attack" that the company commander position involved considerable administrative work and training duties. When in action the company commander was also responsible for interpreting the battalion commander's intentions, performing reconnaissance of the situation, formulating a plan of attack for his company, co-ordinating with supporting arms, and keeping abreast of the tactical situation once the attack commenced.[80] No small task, especially with approximately a hundred men to command (or two hundred for support companies). The manual also lays out the following: "Commanders should not be tied to their headquarters during operations and depend on others entirely for information. There are occasions when a commander's presence at his headquarters is essential; on the other hand there are many occasions when it is of much greater importance that he should go forward to see the ground and the situation for himself, to get in touch with his forward sub-units and thus control the situation personally."[81] While company commanders were not frequently in the front lines and had a small staff to manage, it was still laid out in doctrine that they should take every opportunity to personally observe, ascertain, and control the situation on the ground.[82] This policy contrasted with British doctrine, which typically erred on the side of centralized, autocratic control.[83] Rifle platoon commanders, on the other hand, only had approximately thirty men to deal with (the number could vary considerably for the more specialized platoons in the support company) and was expected to take a much more active hand in the actual tactical conduct of the battle. "The platoon commander," declared *Infantry Training 1937*, "will move where he can best control the action of his platoon; before deployment, at the head of his platoon; after deployment usually with or near his reserve sections; during the assault, once more at the head of his platoon."[84] The platoon commander's central obligation, as historian Allan English put it, was the "conspicuous sharing of risk with subordinates" that forms an integral part of Western leadership style.[85]

Such was the tactical doctrine as written. However, examining some of the evidence on the actual role and place of the officers, directly from the primary sources, can also be extremely helpful. According to research done by the 21st Army Group's No. 2 Operational Research Section in 1944 and 1945 (recently compiled by Terry Copp), officers tended to suffer a much higher proportion of casualties than the soldiers they led. While much of Copp's data is for British divisions, the findings likely apply to the Canadian Army as well, since it was part of the same 21st Army Group and engaged under similar conditions and circumstances. A survey of seven infantry divisions gave results on officer-to-other ranks casualty ratios everywhere from 1.28:1 to 1.70:1, so that in one division (the British 51st) the proportion of officer casualties was almost double that of other ranks.[86] A further analysis of those casualties showed that rifle platoon commanders and rifle company commanders suffered almost identical casualty rates between 6 June and 6 November 1944: every month 31.2 percent of rifle platoon commanders and 30.0 percent of rifle company commanders became casualties.[87] Most officer casualties tended to take place in the attack phase (69 %) as opposed to defence (23 %) and patrolling (8 %). Furthermore, most casualties took place either when troops were engaged in "close fighting (within 500 yards of the enemy)" (40 %), "moving from one position to another, visiting troops, etc. (18 %), or in "[forming-up points] or concentration areas" (13 %). Becoming a casualty "in command post" was uncommon (8 %).[88] Generalizing from these figures, the job of a rifle platoon or company commander was an exceptionally dangerous one in the infantry, the branch of the armed forces that was itself the most hazardous occupation. The Operational Research data would suggest that officers were killed or wounded when leading either from the front or very close behind it, amid their troops. The heavy casualties and the near-parity of casualties between platoon and company commanders further suggest that company commanders were following the suggestions laid out in the doctrinal manuals and were indeed operating very close to their soldiers, rather than staying back at the company headquarters. Proceedings from meetings of the Canadian Small Arms Users Committee from around the same time showed that junior and senior infantry officers, who were frequently in a position where they needed to directly defend themselves against the enemy, would much rather have been equipped with automatic carbines than with the near-useless .38 pistol that was the standard-issue weapon of officers.[89] Officers in the supporting arms preferred to keep their pistol sidearms, but infantry officers were among their troops so frequently that they needed the added measure of protection – and ability to engage the enemy – offered by an automatic weapon.[90]

Interestingly, the above evidence that junior and senior officers were in the thick of the fighting is congruent with the information collected from commentaries within the battle experience questionnaires. Many officers, from their reports on their own actions and the actions of those around them, were regularly directed and led from the front and were in a position to observe directly or participate in a combat action. Officers frequently wrote about the need for their presence (or at least the presence of "an officer") on active patrolling missions during periods when the front was static. Captain G.C. Watt of the Royal Winnipeg Rifles, commander of a carrier platoon, insisted that for infantry reconnaissance patrols, "it was found imperative to have an officer in charge."[91] Two French-Canadian officers, Captain Charles Lévesque of Le Royal 22e Régiment and Major G.P. Boucher of Le Régiment de la Chaudière, both noted that junior officers always accompanied patrols, even for minimal-strength scouting missions of only two or three men.[92] Captain Mark Tennant of the Calgary Highlanders differed in opinion somewhat, and emphasized that while everyday scout patrols – meant to ascertain the enemy's position and report back – could be carried out by NCOs, "Fighting Patrols" sent out to engage the enemy's static positions were always led by a commissioned officer.[93] Captain A.J. Willick, a Canadian assigned to the British 5th Wiltshire regiment, similarly noted that junior officers were physically and mentally exhausting themselves leading regular patrols due to a consistent shortage of platoon commanders, and had started using benzedrine tablets (an amphetamine) excessively to compensate for their exhaustion.[94] While there is some disagreement on whether officers always led patrols, this disagreement merely reflects the differing experiences and practices of the various battalions, and of the companies and platoons within the battalions. The impression given by the surveys is that junior or even senior officers personally led most of the significant patrolling actions.[95] Major Harrison, also a rifle company commander with the Calgary Highlanders, came to a more general conclusion on the lessons learned from his experience in battle: "Men will follow their commanders if well led."[96] This seems to have been true in the Canadian Army during most of its battles in Europe, as the available evidence indicates that platoon and company commanders did, in most cases, lead their troops from the front, and personally engaged in combat enough to demand more effective weapons and to sustain a conspicuously high casualty rate. In fact, Copp's Operational Research Reports provided figures for how officers had been killed or wounded: 57 percent from high explosives (shells and mortars), and 35 percent from small-arms action. Curiously, the casualties sustained by British and Canadian ORs were thought to be above 70 percent from German mortar and *Nebelwerfer* (multi-barrelled mortar) fire alone. Officers were less likely to be killed by high explosives, but significantly more likely than their troops to be killed at relatively close range by enemy small arms.[97]

There can be little doubt that Canadian junior and senior officers were frequently forward with their troops, either controlling movements or else conspicuously leading patrols and other actions. Contrary to Marshall's belief, the officers would frequently have been in positions allowing them to observe what was going on in combat, and certainly close enough to notice if, for example, only 15 percent of their rifleman had been making any use of their weapons at all. In *Men Against Fire*, and in more recent works that use Marshall's data as their basis, such as Grossman's *On Killing*, the response to such reasoning is that soldiers will generally fire when an officer or NCO is standing over their shoulder yelling orders or trying to "move up and down a fire line booting his men until they use their weapons," but will cease as soon as he leaves.[98] Grossman refers to this as the proximate power of leadership and authority in enabling battlefield killing: as the proximity to a leader increases, the soldier's desire or ability to fire his weapon increases.[99] Both of these points, however, seem to stem from a faulty assumption about combat. First, they assume that a soldier would always know when he was being observed by an officer, which is possible, though if any officer who made himself conspicuously known to all of his subordinates in the middle of combat would have been making himself similarly conspicuous to the enemy. Second, they also assume that not only would officers not observe this non-firing behaviour themselves, but that they would not hear reports of it from NCOs (who, according to Marshall, *were* typically aware of the low firing ratio among their men).[100] Such a position is predicated upon there being no effective communication between officers and NCOs within a unit. The argument is made even less convincing in the Canadian case by what was established earlier in this chapter: that virtually all Canadian combat infantry officers in 1943 and 1944 had in fact been commissioned from the ranks, meaning that most had been NCOs themselves not long before.[101] By 1945, owing to the heavy officer casualties, it is probable that most new officer replacements had been NCOs who had actually had combat experience as NCOs as well. Given this information, Marshall's theories regarding the obliviousness of junior officers cannot be viewed as credible in the Canadian situation.

I do not mean to suggest here that every Canadian officer in the Second World War was a sterling leader, as the rapidly expanding army experienced many growing pains, including occasional shortfalls in leadership. The policy of commissioning from the ranks is itself a somewhat dubious military practice, since, as John English has pointed out, it skims the cream from the NCO corps and leaves units in desperate need of good non-commissioned leadership.[102] However, the evidence strongly indicates that, at the very least, Canadian platoon and company officers were frequently exercising personal leadership from the front, were in a position to observe their troops' actions, and generally had the personal connections to the other ranks to keep abreast of what was happening within their unit. Despite the numerous administrative duties that they also had to perform, there is every indication that the officers of the battle experience questionnaires would have been in a position when the fighting commenced to observe the combat effectiveness of their own units. And indeed, as subsequent chapters show, the officers did observe and offer commentary in their questionnaires on many different facets of the effectiveness of their troops. What the evidence from doctrinal manuals, Operational Research, and battle experience questionnaires indicates is that these observations were valid, and reflected first-hand experience from the front lines of the Second World War. They are as legitimate a historical source on the nature of Canadian tactical combat as presently exists, and they illuminate a great deal about infantry effectiveness that has previously been unknown.

## CHAPTER FOUR

THE COMBINED-ARMS TEAM

A persistent theme in the military historiography of the Second World War is that the German armed forces consistently out-performed and out-fought the armies of the Allies, falling short of victory only because of extreme material and manpower inferiority, or because of inexpert high-level command decisions.[1] Particularly in the domain of infantry tactics and combat German forces have been venerated as the model of combat effectiveness and, in the words of one historian, "deserve to be studied more thoroughly for application in future conventional war."[2] Trevor Dupuy's computational models have calculated German "fighting effectiveness" to be on average 20 percent higher than that of the Allies, as a result of their practice of "institutionalizing military excellence," which led to stunning early *Wehrmacht* victories and, later, to its resilience when being driven back toward Germany.[3]

A judgment of German effectiveness implies a corresponding Allied combat mediocrity or outright ineffectiveness. It is sometimes argued that after 1942, when both the Soviet Union and the United States had joined the war, the Allies' economic and industrial superiority was so overwhelming that they succeeded in grinding the Axis powers down through material attrition rather than through tactical or operational skill.[4] Little tactical skill was necessary, in fact; the extent of Allied production advantage meant that they could liberally afford to expend tanks, airplanes, bombs, and shells on the battlefield, using fire-power as a "crutch" and an equalizer, so that their qualitatively inferior forces could wear down the tactically adept *Wehrmacht*.[5] The post-war accounts of high-ranking German officers are partly responsible for this perception, as they reached a wide audience in the West and emphasized that the Allies had won because of their material advantages.[6] As one critic has recalled: "From some [German accounts] one would believe that the [Allied] logistical situation was so extravagant that U.S. Army Air Force Thunderbolts routinely buried German positions under refrigerators and cartons of razor blades."[7] But the idea of Allied tactical ineffectiveness owes just as much to S.L.A. Marshall and his ratio-of-fire argument, which was popularly regarded as an authoritative measurement of effectiveness for decades. If only 15 to 20 percent of American or Allied soldiers were participating in combat, then they would have been no match for the Germans, the narrative sometimes unfolds, and thus material factors would be the only reasonable way to explain the outcome of the war.[8] The argument has developed that the Allies could only have relied upon their excellent artillery, virtually unlimited supply of armoured vehicles, and complete dominion over the air to grind down the German military machine, since their tactical unfitness prevented them from pursuing more finessed strategies.

Although there are elements of truth to this account, such as the fact that Allied material superiority influenced doctrine, the thesis of German tactical supremacy and relative Allied tactical ineffectiveness has been poorly researched and heavily weighted toward idolizing the *Wehrmacht*. This argument is a restatement of the theories espoused by German officers after the war to explain their own defeat, theories that became widely adopted because of Western military authorities' acceptance of the former Nazis themselves after 1945.[9] Some of the long-standing theories on the *Wehrmacht*'s superiority have more recently been seriously challenged, and scholarship is moving toward a more balanced view: that the Allies were generally a match for the Germans, with obvious fluctuations owing to inexperience, technology, and circumstance.[10] As new evidence is gathered and new studies are written on the topic, it is becoming apparent that the Allied victory owed much to the combat capabilities of the soldiers on the ground.

Before entertaining a discussion of infantry effectiveness in combat, one should understand the central place of infantry fighting within the combined-arms systems of the Allied, and specifically Canadian, armed forces. The primary documentation concerning infantry co-operation with artillery and armour underscores the degree to which arguments claiming Allied victory through simple material preponderance are, as military historian Richard Overy has affirmed, overly simplistic and bordering upon inaccurate.[11] The Allies out-produced the Axis by a substantial margin, but the way they put that equipment to use was infinitely more important than the quantity they could stockpile. In addition, and more to the point, original sources are now making evident that serious shortcomings in the Allied application of both armour and artillery during the Second World War have frequently been understated in the historiography.[12] Such shortcomings meant that infantry riflemen remained the Canadian Army's main arm of decision; while infantry could be supported by tanks, artillery, and air power, their ability to fight and win battles was determined foremost by their own tactical skill. None of the other arms supplanted the need for strong infantry forces to engage the enemy and seize ground; nor were any of the other arms, in the Canadian experience, potent enough to reduce the need for skilled infantry fighting, on the offense or defensively.

Also worth noting is the contention that the Allies' tactical doctrine and operational art were both imperfect tools for the tasks that needed to be accomplished. Historian Bill McAndrew, for example, has written that Canadian tactical doctrine was derived from the attrition-based warfare of the First World War, and that it sacrificed the potential for operational manoeuvre on the altar of centralized control and overwhelming firepower.[13] This is not an unreasonable argument, and is valid in some ways. Canadian doctrine was imperfect: it invested too much authority in higher-formation commanders at the expense of unit leaders – though the battle experience questionnaires do not indicate that this was as serious a problem as McAndrew claims – and targeted German strengths rather than German weaknesses.[14] The emphasis was indeed upon expending firepower rather than lives. However, given the difficult terrain and the nature of the offensive battles they were fighting, it seems doubtful that Canadians could have done much better than they did. The doctrine and methods they used were highly rational and derived from the successes of the First World War, and were put into use for a reason. Despite charges that the doctrine relied too extensively upon artillery, a strong, skilled infantry arm was absolutely essential for the type of warfare that the Canadians undertook in the Second World War.

This chapter examines the roots of Canadian doctrine, as well as the effectiveness of armour and artillery on the battlefields of the Second World War, using data from the battle experience questionnaires and, where appropriate, evidence gleaned from Operational Research reports originally compiled by historian Terry Copp. While the Canadian Army derived strength from its well-developed artillery doctrine and the power of its armoured formations, both had severe battlefield limitations that put the onus of fighting and dying upon the infantry; over 70 percent of casualties in the Canadian Army were from infantry rifle companies, who made up less than 15 percent of the army.[15] Canadian infantry effectiveness has been as severely underrated as the German Army's effectiveness has been overrated, and a critical examination of the arms that normally receive credit for the Allied victory is of central importance to determining the fighting skill of Canadian infantry.

TACTICAL DOCTRINE AND THE LEGACY
OF THE GREAT WAR

The actual ground combat of the Second World War would not have been an unfamiliar environment for soldiers who had fought in the First World War; indeed, the tactical similarities between the two wars are greater than is normally understood. The increased mechanization, seemingly decisive operations, and global scope of the Second World War sometimes conceal the fact that, at least in Western Europe, the wars were more alike than not. In 1939 the tempo of operations was faster and the weapons were somewhat more modernized and destructive. But the tank changed land warfare less than is assumed. Even in 1945, armoured vehicles were still extremely vulnerable, to the point where it was rarely clear whether tanks were protecting the infantry or vice versa. Motorization and the much-touted restoration of mobility to the battlefield were never as significant during the war as is sometimes believed; motorized transportation helped revolutionize logistics and the movement of troops behind the lines, but it had less impact at the sharp end once the shooting began.[16] Artillery, although more mobile, was still the workhorse of battlefield firepower; and air support, although more technologically advanced and comprehensive, still played a fundamentally similar role as the planes that had taken to the skies in 1918.[17] Infantry remained decisive, particularly where technology for anti-tank weaponry kept pace with the technology for the tanks themselves. The battlefields of the Second World War were surprisingly little removed from the trenches of the Great War – temporally, geographically, or doctrinally.[18] This investigation into the effectiveness of the Canadian Army in the Second World War must therefore trace its roots back to the precursor conflict, and to its precursor organization, the Canadian Corps.

The First World War coloured all the military thought that developed in the twenty years after 1918, but it did not colour them evenly, and the belligerent nations who studied the war's lessons came to radically different conclusions about how future war should be fought. In significant ways, the First World War was actually a series of smaller self-contained wars on geographically disparate fronts, none of which resembled the others. The deadlocked Western Front, with its archetypal trench warfare, bore little resemblance to the conflicts along the Italian-Austrian border, or at Gallipoli and Salonika, where natural geography was far more pressing an issue than any man-made defences. None of those fronts bore any likeness at all to the smaller colonial-style wars that erupted in German East Africa, the Middle East, and the Pacific. None of the above bore any similarity to the Eastern Front, where the war of movement had not disappeared in 1914, but had resulted in a much more fluid, decisive form of warfare than in the west.

All these "fronts" produced unique styles of war-fighting suited to their specific conditions; consequently, each one presented a different set of lessons to be absorbed and digested by the combatants during the conflict and in the two decades afterward. Military analyst James Corum has theorized that the German learning experience of the First World War emphasized the Eastern Front, where the kaiser's Imperial Army had achieved stunning victory. Most of the German generals who would lead the *Wehrmacht* in the 1940s, including Rommel, Kesselring, von Kleist, von Manstein, and von Rundstedt, had acquired much of their Great War combat experience on the Eastern Front against Russia, Serbia, and Romania.[19] By contrast, almost all the Allied generals of the Second World War, including Montgomery, de Gaulle, Patton, and Canada's Harry Crerar, had their baptism by fire on the Western Front, and had virtually no experience with the fluid war of movement characterized by the east, save for the semi-mobile conditions that developed in 1918.[20] The fronts upon which their soldiers fought, died, and achieved success shaped the lessons that the respective powers would take from the war. For Germany, fluidity of movement and mobility, embodied in the General Staff's development of the "storm-troop" tactics of 1917 and 1918 on the Eastern Front, was the main doctrinal legacy from the war.[21]

The Canadian experience was framed entirely by the Western Front, and the Canadian military learned its lessons on modern warfare from the trenches. This experience was less characterized by maneuvre than by operationally static deadlock. During the First World War, however, the Canadian Corps developed a doctrine based upon combined-arms warfare and firepower that was consistently able to crack, though not rupture, the trench deadlock. The Germans never found an adequate response to this doctrine. Ian Brown has pointed out that the German "infiltration" and "storm-troop" tactics of the 1918 offensives have won a great deal of misguided praise from historians who view the "glamour" of maneuvre warfare as the height of innovation; however, these were not tactics that won the war.[22] Indeed, it was the Allied armies – with the Canadian Corps acting as a spearhead unit in the final hundred days – that ultimately tore apart the German Army and forced the armistice.

It was during the Western Front deadlock that the facts of infantry vulnerability to modern firepower were first internalized by armies. All the combatant nations developed new techniques to allow infantry a chance to safely close with the enemy. Most of these techniques included massive artillery support on timed programs, using mathematically predicted fire against targets that were over the horizon or otherwise unseen. The Canadian Corps relied heavily on the creeping barrage attack: "[Artillery] gunners, by firing on German positions until the last possible instant while simultaneously putting up a moving curtain of destruction a few hundred yards in front of the infantry, would ensure that German defenders would remain in their dugouts until attackers were close enough to use their own weapons."[23] The infantry had to "lean" into the barrage, getting as close to their own falling shells as they dared, in the hope of making it to the opposing trenches before the Germans – theoretically driven to ground by the intense bombardment – could get back up out of their dugouts. It did not always work, sometimes with disastrous consequences, but detailed planning, careful co-ordination, and rigorous training helped to increase the chances of success.[24] Although the employment of infantry weapons and (to a lesser degree) tanks played significant roles as well, the unprecedented application of indirect artillery fire in support of infantry was the hallmark of the Canadian tactics First World War.

Especially in 1917 and 1918, the Canadian Corps became particularly adept at applying elaborate artillery programs in support of their offensive actions, which were highly orchestrated and rehearsed, and were termed the "set-piece attack."[25] Brown defines the set-piece attack as "a deliberate, closely timed attack under the cover of an intense rolling artillery barrage" employing all arms to attain a limited objective rather than attempting a general breakthrough of the enemy front.[26] German defensive doctrine called for an elastic, thinly held forward defensive line, and an aggressive, immediate counter-attack, the *Eingreif*, using strong reserves against any gains that the Allies made during an offensive, hoping to catch the attacking infantry when they were exhausted and disorganized from their own advance.[27] The Canadian set-piece attack was designed to turn German defensive doctrine against itself. The Canadian Corps employed overwhelming force to secure limited gains along its front, rapidly consolidate them, and then inflict massive casualties upon the inevitable German counter-attack from the newly formed defensive line.[28] Also known as "bite-and-hold," these tactics demanded close infantry-artillery co-operation. Objectives were limited so that friendly forces did not outrun their fire support, and every effort was made to bring firepower forward as quickly as possible to the new front. These tactics were ideal for repelling German counter-attacks, as they deliberately created a killing ground in front of the new Canadian positions.[29] All of this was founded upon exceptionally well-orchestrated artillery support, which helped troops move forward, broke up counter-attacks, and silenced enemy artillery through counter-battery fire. As historian John English puts it: "In a highly positional war that left little room for strategic maneuver, tactical innovation effected through meticulous staff work was critical."[30] These Canadian Corps tactics, although extremely costly in blood and casualties, were the most consistently successful of the First World War on the Western Front; and from Vimy Ridge in 1917 to the final Hundred Days' offensive of the war, Canadian troops were extremely effective when assaulting static German positions, and in cutting their counter-attacks to pieces. This earned them their place at the spearhead of the Allied armies in 1918.[31] It is true that such tactics were concise, and tended to target German strength rather than exploit German weakness.

What is sometimes misunderstood is that this was the objective. In the First World War fighting on the defensive was always easier and less costly than attacking.[32] Forcing the enemy to abandon his defensive stance to engage in local counter-attacks against units undertaking bite-and-hold tactics was a highly rational, if grinding and attrition-based, method of fighting a war in static circumstances.

The Canadian Army, along with the British military, of which it served as a subset, took extensive planning, organization, control, and careful orchestration of operations as their most important lessons from the war. The legacy of their successes could be felt through the interwar period and into the Second World War.[33] The British and Canadian armies had triumphed in the First World War through the meticulous planning, preparation, and execution of highly orchestrated offensives predicated upon the skillful co-operation of infantry and artillery. The prewar and wartime doctrine employed by the Commonwealth armies was heir to this Great War experience, and the War Office's 1935 *Field Service Regulations* (*FSR*), re-issued in Canada in November 1939, stated the theoretical foundation upon which the British and Canadians built their land forces for the Second World War.

The 1939 regulations portrayed a British General Staff that was grappling with the lessons learned in the previous conflict.[34] Historian David French has explored how the *FSR* promised security and predictability to the individual, and "persisted in attempting to bring the same regularity and order to the battlefield, through the application of the principles of war, as industrialists had brought to the modern factory."[35] Unwilling to countenance a chaotic view of the battlefield, British and Canadian doctrine remained grounded during the interwar years in the notion that proper combined-arms co-operation could only be achieved through unity of control and careful co-ordination of artillery, supporting weapons, and troop movement. The 1935 *FSR* placed more emphasis on the consolidation of a position than on the ruthless exploitation of success.[36] Doctrine therefore favoured tactics that were designed to achieve limited objectives but annihilate enemy counter-attacks, rather than push for breaking through their lines in a war of manoeuvre.[37] These tactics were clearly products of the lessons derived from the Western Front battles of the First World War. Given how the Allied ground war between 1943 and 1945 consisted almost exclusively of offensives against static German positions, it should come as no surprise that the successful experiences of the Western

Front in the Great War influenced the way the Allies, and particularly the Canadians, fought during the next conflict. The Canadians normally engaged in well-planned and finely coordinated battles against dug-in enemy units that remained devoted to the defensive counter-attack doctrine.[38] Well before June 1944 it had become clear that even a best-case victory over the German *Wehrmacht* in Western Europe was much more likely to resemble the hundred days of 1918 than the *Blitzkrieg* tank assaults of 1940.[39]

This Anglo-Canadian doctrine for the Second World War has, with some justice, been criticized by military historians for being too autocratic, and for centralizing too much decision-making power in authority figures too distant from the battlefield to be able to adapt to the pandemonium of battle.[40] However, set-piece manoeuvres such as the Canadian attack that seized Vimy Ridge in 1917 were successful in large part thanks to the rigorous planning, training, and orchestration of all arms; it is with reason that military writer Shane Schreiber uses the metaphor of a musical symphony so successfully in his book on the Canadian Corps, *Shock Army of the British Empire*.[41] A tremendous amount of staff work and calculation underwrote most attacks, and in the First World War this investment paid dividends both in terms of objectives seized and successive victories over the German Army; one side-effect was the entrenchment of a more autocratic, controlling command style.[42] During the Second World War this doctrine was successfully revived by the Canadian Army. As Lieutenant-General Guy Simonds wrote in his operational policy notes for 2 Canadian Corps prior to Normandy: "The success of the offensive battle hinges on the defeat of the German counter-attacks ... The defeat of these counter-attacks must form part of the original plan of attack which must include arrangements for artillery support and the forward moves of infantry supporting weapons – including tanks – on the objective. Further, in selecting the objectives, the suitability from the point of view of fighting this 'battle of counter-attacks' must receive important consideration."[43] Certainly there were local variations and instances where the Canadians fought for a breakthrough battle rather than an attritional one, such as at Falaise. But Canadian tactical doctrine emphasized a cautious, grinding style of fighting designed to wear down the key element of the German defensive arrangements: the counter-attack.

Of special note here is that the continuity between the Canadian doctrines of the First and Second World War meant that the importance of infantry remained high. Despite the coming-of-age of tanks, air power, and advanced artillery, infantry from 1943 to 1945 was still called upon to seize and hold ground, and to defeat German counter-attacks at close quarters. Historians have sometimes taken a negative view of this doctrine and its emphasis upon artillery supporting fire, claiming that the barrage became the "arbiter of tactical movement" and that infantry were chained to it too slavishly.[44] But a closer examination shows that this doctrine magnified the importance and need for skilled infantry fighting, given the inherent limitations of the supporting arms. While artillery, armour, and air power are regarded as having revolutionized warfare, the fighting that ultimately liberated Europe from German control was still as dominated by infantry action as it had been during the First World War.

THE POWER AND LIMITS OF ARTILLERY

The legacy of exceptionally heavy reliance upon artillery from the First World War, when the power available to gunners had been a deciding contributor to the static deadlock of the Western Front[45] became a hallmark of the Anglo-Canadian armies during the Mediterranean and Northwest Europe campaigns of the Second World War, both in doctrine and in practice. It made sense to afford artillery such a central place in battle; doing so was in part a reflection of the Allied willingness to wage what the Germans referred to as *Materialschlacht*, a "material battle" in which equipment was expended lavishly. Certainly the Allies could afford such an undertaking. Combined Allied Gross Domestic Product was, by 1943, three times that of the combined Axis nations, and the gap increased steadily through 1945.[46] Just as important, of course, was the impressive Allied infrastructure that allowed industrial power to be harnessed for the war effort so that maximum advantage could be derived from this imbalance, something that Nazi Germany and its partners were never able to accomplish.[47] Producing, fielding, and keeping well supplied the thousands of artillery pieces used so expansively during the Second World War was a monumental expression of the Allied material advantage. As historian Niall Ferguson remarks, the Allies and the Americans in particular "were the masters of overkill, whose first principle was: 'always have on hand more of everything than you can ever conceivably need.'"[48]

The decision to employ heavy firepower also had its basis in manpower considerations. The British General Staff had been developing its doctrine through the interwar period on the assumption that Great Britain as a country would not or could not again sustain the mass casualties suffered during the First World War, and searched for a conservative approach to war-fighting that would minimize casualties.[49] During the Second World War, such fears were partly realized, as the three Allies with major contingents on the western front – Britain, Canada, and the United States – all suffered from manpower shortfalls. An emphasis on artillery firepower allowed the Allies, in theory, to expend equipment instead of lives, obliterating enemy positions from afar through concentrated barrages and reducing the opposition that the infantry would face.[50] Playing to their industrial strength was a strategic decision for the Allied powers, given their critical manpower crisis. Munitions and guns could swiftly and easily be replaced; the same could not be said for trained soldiers once the bottom of the manpower barrel had been reached, as it had been for the British and Canadian armies in 1944 and 1945.[51] For armies short on soldiers but with surplus material strength, such a doctrine was the pragmatic choice.[52]

However, the major precedent for the successful use of overwhelming firepower as part of a set-piece battle came from the Western Front experience of the First World War. During the Second World War, British and Canadian commanders fell back upon these ideas, hoping to expend shells instead of lives and, at the same time, to take full advantage of their established doctrinal and material strengths. The result was the extraordinary magnitude of Anglo-Canadian reliance upon artillery fire support. For the Germans in the Second World War, the ferocity of the British, American, and Canadian artillery fire was something altogether new, even for veterans of the Eastern Front. Soldiers of the 2nd Panzer Division fighting in Normandy, despite extensive service against the Red Army in the east, described the Allied barrages as being able to "trample the nerves" of seasoned veterans, and as "literally soul-destroying" to inexperienced men.[53] The punishing weight of Allied artillery was used everywhere along the front lines, particularly in Northwest Europe. As Canadian Brigadier Stanley Todd stated during Operation SWITCHBACK against the Leopold Canal in Belgium in October 1944, one of the goals was to give infantry "fire when they want it for as long as they want it."[54]

The Canadian officers who participated in the battle experience questionnaire surveys were familiar with the support that artillery lent them, and discussed it at length. Despite being a holdover from the First World War, the creeping barrage remained the best way to support advancing infantry forward through a fire-beaten zone during the Second World

War. Some 80 percent of the officers reported that they and their troops had carried out attacks under a creeping artillery barrage, although when the surveys are broken down by theatre of operations, officers fighting in Sicily and Italy were somewhat more likely to indicate that they had attacked under a barrage (86 %) than those fighting in Northwest Europe (78 %).[55] A number of officers commented on the application of the creeping barrage technique. Captain Donald Findlay, who served with both the Canadian Queen's York Rangers and the British 1/6 Queen's Royal Regiment, wrote about advances supported by a creeping barrage that could reliably advance over a mile per attack against opposition – not an inconsiderable amount.[56] Captain S.R. Lambert of the South Saskatchewan Regiment reported at least one instance, a night attack on the village of Rocquancourt during Operation GOODWOOD outside Caen, where his troops achieved "success due to accurate [artillery] support and confidence in same" with a timed creeping barrage.[57] Major J.G. Stothart of the Stormont, Dundas and Glengarry Highlanders was particularly satisfied with the old-fashioned artillery technique, and wrote: "It is my firm opinion that if the Army can register and even in some cases when they cannot the closer the inf[antry] can get to a … barrage the better the final result. The casualties they may suffer are not in proportion with those they may incur through hesitation or a lack of speed in reaching the objective. We have had several experiences which substantiate this opinion … and I know from discussing it with [the troops] that they do appreciate the advantage of being close to a barrage."[58]

Major John Irvin Mills, a company commander in the Queen's Own Rifles of Canada, on the other hand, mentioned in his notes that his infantry encountered the same problem as the soldiers of the First World War: if they failed to keep up with the pace of the barrage – roughly 100 yards every four minutes – they were held up in the open without fire support.[59] Indeed, keeping up with the creeping barrage's timed program was a significant problem for many units. One-third of officers serving in Italy and just over 20 percent in Northwest Europe reported experiencing difficulties with their troops keeping up with the creeping barrage.[60] Units that became bogged down in the terrain, were pinned down by pockets of enemy resistance, or otherwise failed to keep pace with the artillery barrage could be in danger, noted Captain G.C. Watt of the Royal Winnipeg Rifles: therefore, "the infantry must follow close in behind their artillery and not bog down and allow [the artillery] to do [the infantry's] job."[61]

On the flip side of these numbers, however, just under 80 percent of officers in Northwest Europe reported that their soldiers had never experienced difficulty keeping up with the barrage. This was undoubtedly due to improved wireless technologies, which allowed better direct communication between the advancing troops, artillery observers, and the guns themselves. So, while Canadian troops were sometimes left behind by their covering fire, the majority of the time, particularly in Northwest Europe, they seem to have been able to keep up.

Reliance upon the creeping barrage was indicative of the widely held Canadian preference for the set-piece attack, based upon detailed staff planning and preparation, and normally featuring an orchestrated offensive supported by timed artillery programs for creeping barrages and concentrations on enemy positions. Captain Warren Harvey, a mortar officer with the North Shore Regiment, stated that he believed success was due to thorough preparation. "Without these thorough preparations I feel that while the final result might have been the same, there would have been considerable confusion and higher casualties."[62] Despite the extent to which the artillery-dominated set-piece attack influenced Canadian tactical thought, however, there were still several significant problems to overcome. An evident disconnect existed between what was occurring in training and what was being put into practice on the battlefield. In spite of the large percentage of officers who indicated that their units had taken part in attacks supported by creeping barrages, barely half of them indicated that their troops had ever operated beneath a creeping barrage as part of a training exercise.[63] This number did not vary significantly, no matter which theatre of operations the officer was engaged in, though officers who had served longer in combat were more likely to report that their troops had not received any such preliminary training.[64] Given how dangerous training under a live creeping barrage would have been, and given Allied unwillingness to accept a high level of casualties in training, there may have been few opportunities to do so. This lack of training may also have reflected the fact that Canadian replacement soldiers were hastily trained before being dispatched to reinforce units in the field.

The other serious limitation of an artillery-heavy doctrine has only recently been appreciated by historians, who have found that artillery was not nearly as effective a weapon of destruction as has been popularly assumed, particularly in the context of infantry support. While the artillery was capable of producing massive, even "soul-shattering" amounts of fire, evidence suggests that predicted fire by indirect artillery was disappointing in terms of effectiveness. Terry Copp's examination of documents from the Operational Research Section of the 21st Army Group uncovered studies demonstrating that, between D-Day in June 1944 and Operation VERITABLE, the attack on the Rhineland in early 1945, indirect fire support was only marginally effective. Operational Research scientists discovered that the "50 percent zone" – the area in which half the shells fired could be expected to land – was far larger than had been projected, and that only 5 percent of rounds fired by prediction could be expected to fall in an area 100 yards square.[65] Using aerial photographs taken immediately after a counter-battery shoot, the Operational Research Section determined that, on average, only 4.8 per cent of the rounds fired fell within a hundred yards of a target, meaning that the artillery had to fire 2,000 rounds at a predicted target in order "to cause 100 rounds to fall in a field 100 yards square." Gunners had operated on the assumption that it would require only 170 rounds to accomplish this.[66] Their accuracy was stunningly poor, and even though measures were introduced to correct this, they had little effect. A follow-up Operational Research study of the accuracy of predicted fire in Operation VERITABLE suggests that after months of effort, "on average not more than 5.1 percent of the rounds aimed at a target fell in an area 100 yards x 100 yards at that target position."[67] Anything that could be seen could probably be destroyed, but observation was often spotty, as communications were sometimes poor.[68] Direct fire was not usually an option for artillery. While the artillery thus continued to serve an effective suppression role, and heavy concentrations could force an enemy to go to ground, its actual ability to concentrate a destructive barrage upon a designated target via predicted fire was highly doubtful.[69]

Many Canadian soldiers had known this all along, and comments on the ineffectiveness of the artillery recurred throughout the battle experience questionnaires. While it was not a subject dealt with by any of the survey questions, many officers brought it up independently in their attached notes. Captain T.H. Burdett, a rifle company commander in the Royal Canadian Regiment, noted that for keeping troops' nerves down "it might help if all new reinforcements were instructed in the little damage that is actually done by shelling, or mortar fire."[70] "Timed [artillery] barrages were not very effective," wrote Major J.W. Ostiguy, company commander in Le Régiment de Maisonneuve, "as the … German defensive emplacements in some sectors were so strong that they were not harmed by [artillery] and could not be bypassed."[71] Canadian troops would often approach a German position that had been targeted by a heavy barrage, only to be caught off-guard, and sustain heavy casualties when they found the position still fully manned and defended despite the barrage.[72] Lieutenant-Colonel T.P. Gilday, a battalion commander in Italy, perhaps summed this up best: "Artillery only keeps enemy heads down and does not kill. The heads are always up and guns firing when the infantry closes."[73] While one officer rightly observed that the Germans feared the Allied artillery, more prevalent were comments that, while artillery support was normally very good, any dug-in German position was going to be quite safe from the worst of its effects.[74] Captain D.A.J. Paré, also of Le Régiment de Châteauguay, wrote of one encounter: "Jerry was well dug-in on high ground, and he didn't bother much with [Canadian artillery]."[75] Finally, long-serving (July 1944 to March 1945) rifle company commander Major Froggett noted in his questionnaire that he regularly took advantage of the artillery's inability to destroy Canadian dug-in targets. If his company's defensive position was being overrun, he would not hesitate to call down artillery fire on his own position; relatively secure and dug-in, the defending company would probably be fine, but the effects upon the attacking enemy, who was still above ground and had less effective cover, could be devastating.[76] Simply put, plans for even the heaviest artillery fire could never be counted on to obliterate the enemy, independent of other action. The artillery undeniably inflicted heavy casualties, and was one of the war's greatest killers; but its high degree of inaccuracy meant that its killing power was dispersed almost to the point of being randomized, and that attempts to concentrate predicted fire upon key positions – where it was most needed – were futile. Given the heavy reliance of set-piece attacks upon timed, predicted artillery fire, this inefficiency could cast a distressing light upon their tactical procedures. At best, indirect artillery could exercise an effective suppressing or neutralizing power over the enemy; as a concentrated weapon of destruction its efficacy was far more questionable.

The 21st Army Group's Operational Research Section also discovered, when studying casualties, that at least 7 percent of identifiable shell fragments removed from British and Canadian casualties had come from Allied ordnance, and that the extent of total friendly casualties from Allied fire may have been as high as 19 percent.[77] This report, dated 20

April 1945, was not widely publicized, but as Copp points out in *Cinderella Army*, the evidence is compelling that "friendly fire" casualties from artillery were much higher than has previously been believed. The battle experience questionnaires support this contention as well. The Calgary Highlanders' Major John Campbell reported that, during an advance in Normandy against St. André-sur-Orne, Canadian artillery fell considerably short and managed to fall on the Calgaries not once, but twice.[78] Major J.G. Stothart, despite having indicated that the closer an infantry unit could stay to a creeping barrage, the better, conceded: "The confidence of the men in the [artillery] can be seriously disturbed by one bad show (and we have had those too)," and recounted friendly artillery fire being brought down on top of them.[79] The very idea of being caught by one's own artillery was profoundly disturbing both to the officers and to the soldiers that they led.[80] It ranked high on the questionnaires as a demoralizing factor for the troops.[81]

On the other hand, these shortcomings demonstrate the true role of artillery in the combined-arms team, and help us understand why so many Canadian officers wrote about artillery barrages and fire plans in favourable terms. The artillery was useful not for its outright destructive role – which is not mentioned once in any infantry officer questionnaire – but as a way of keeping enemy troops' heads down and their fire suppressed so that the Canadian infantrymen could advance to their objectives and avoid sustained exposure to enemy fire. Commanders of higher formations may not always have appreciated this dynamic, but officers leading infantry units on the ground were well aware of it. The fear that the guns inspired in the Germans, combined with the need to huddle in trenches or bunkers to avoid the worst of the barrage, made artillery the perfect weapon to "shepherd" infantry through a normally fire-swept area to come into close-quarters with the enemy. This was the reason that many officers favoured the creeping barrage; as in the First World War, "leaning into" the edge of a creeping artillery barrage minimized the time between when the barrage lifted and when the infantry were on top of their objectives. As Major Daniel Tremblay pointed out: "If you come in just after the barrage, it is much easier [to take an objective], but [this is] not always possible."[82]

Artillery was not a guaranteed method of moving forward by any means, and German troops who braved the barrage and kept their "heads up" throughout were able to catch Canadian troops rushing forward.

Casualties from the use of these techniques and tactics were very high. But with the Allied material advantage keeping the guns well supplied, artillery fire could prove effective in escorting infantry to close with the enemy, suppressing enemy fire if not destroying it outright, and providing cover for the movement of infantry behind the barrage. A great majority of officers, particularly in Northwest Europe, reported that their troops could keep up effectively with the barrage even when they had not received preliminary training – a testament to how well Canadians typically performed under this system.[83]

With predicted fire being largely ineffective at destroying anything (unless employed on a truly staggering magnitude to compensate), and inflicting a substantial number of friendly casualties when used, the old French doctrine of *l'artillerie conquiert, l'infanterie occupe* was untenable.[84] Artillery was not the senior partner of the combined-arms team; the massive barrages characteristic of Allied doctrine, particularly in Northwest Europe, frequently left the German defenders still alive and the core of their defence intact and fully operational.[85] The skillful application of infantry small-arms fire was still necessary to seize, consolidate, and hold an objective, no matter how powerful of the barrage that preceded it. When it came to the final advance on a position, infantry would have to employ their own personal weapons and initiative to engage and kill the enemy in a fight for the position. The artillery was a support, but against the prepared German defences that Canadians in all theatres were required to assault, it could not have been the decisive instrument. As Copp has said: "Historians who argue that the Allies won the war by 'shelling and bombing the enemy into submission' might wish to reconsider their view."[86]

THE LIMITS OF ARMOUR

The Canadian Army's experience with armour during the Second World War paralleled their experience of artillery in terms of importance to infantry riflemen. This was to be expected. The British Army, and its associated dominion formations, had gone to war in 1939 with the interwar debate on the correct application of tanks and mechanized warfare still largely unresolved.[87] The decision to mechanize the cavalry during the 1930s had resulted in a doctrinal schism in the British General Staff.

The heirs to the cavalry tradition were the "all-armour" school of tactical thought, which focused upon lighter "Cruiser" tanks to replace traditional horse cavalry as free-ranging reconnaissance and exploitation forces. The other school emphasized heavier, slower "Infantry" tanks that were exclusively responsible for infantry support.[88] The two arms had little to do with one another. The wrong lessons were taken from the supposed *Blitzkrieg* successes of 1939 and 1941, and in the first phase of the British campaign in the North African deserts the "all-armour" school seemed ascendant, emphasizing speed, maneuvre, deep penetration, and the dislocation of enemy command and control. By the time Canadians first saw sustained land combat in 1943, however, the "all-armour" school of thought had been proven largely bankrupt and the rest of the war was spent attempting to replace this misperception with a more balanced, combined-arms approach to battle.[89]

By the time Canadians joined the fight in Sicily and Italy, Allied tanks had largely resumed the long process of learning their role of supporting infantry in combat. The only operation in which the Canadian Army took part that relied upon the all-armoured attack was Operation GOODWOOD on 18–20 July 1944 near Caen, which purchased the British and Canadians some ground in Normandy at a heavy price in armoured vehicles, but failed in large part due to a lack of infantry support.[90] GOODWOOD demonstrated to the Canadian Army what the Germans had taught the British in North Africa: the vulnerability of armour, not just to other tanks and artillery but to dug-in infantry, minefields, and especially to the excellent German anti-tank weapons.[91] Tanks were extremely ineffective weapons, as British General Bernard Montgomery put it, when employed as though they were part of a fox hunt.[92] Armour could not replace or minimize the role of infantry; its primary role, in the Canadian experience, was to act as another tool for supporting infantry.

These remarks are not meant to downplay or deny the importance of tanks, of course; the introduction of armoured and otherwise motorized vehicles changed the face and pace of warfare. Tanks could provide valuable, highly accurate direct-fire support to a battle, and had a sometimes-overlooked role in carrying infantry sections into battle. They were also great morale boosters for the infantry: generally the presence of armoured vehicles on a battlefield was tremendously encouraging for the foot soldiers operating alongside them.[93] In the battle experience questionnaires, thirty officers specifically listed "tanks" or "tank support" as being among the greatest factors contributing to the raising of morale in their units.[94] But at the same time, tanks could also be a considerable source of frustration, nuisance, and even danger for soldiers, and in the Canadian experience were rarely instruments of decision on their own. Their primary role became to support what Canadian Lieutenant-General Simonds termed the infantry "sledgehammer," as tanks never had the staying power to overcome organized German defences independently.[95]

One of the main troubles with the tanks employed by the Canadian Army was their vulnerability, in themselves as well as in comparison with German tanks. Allied armour, plentiful thanks to American industry and mechanically very reliable, was tactically disadvantaged on the battlefield. The American-made M4 Sherman tank, the mainstay armoured vehicle for the Canadians, was "vulnerable and under-gunned," and is sometimes treated by historians as the embodiment of the qualitative disparity between Allied and German equipment.[96] The Sherman tank's armour plating was relatively light, and while this made it faster over open ground than German tanks, its speed was only infrequently a serious advantage, and it was an easy target for enemy tank and anti-tank fire. The 21st Army Group's Operational Research Section estimated that 95 percent of hits from armour-piercing ordnance fired from enemy anti-tank weapons successfully penetrated the Sherman's armour, and that the tank's vulnerable areas were so extensive that re-armouring was not practical.[97] Worse, the tank tended to catch fire easily and "brew-up" fiercely due to its petrol, rather than diesel, engine. These vulnerabilities were exacerbated by the fact that, as Canadian Major R.A. Cottrill of the Queen's Own Rifles reflected, the Sherman's silhouette was too high and its profile too large, making it easier to spot in the field than other vehicles.[98] At the same time, the standard Sherman 75mm gun tended to "bounce off" the frontal armour of a German Mk V "Panther" tank, and could only hope to damage a Mk VI "Tiger" tank from the rear or point-blank from enfilade positions, which Shermans had a difficult time reaching, given the tank's other weaknesses.[99] While a modified British version of the Sherman, called the Firefly, mounted a superior 17-pounder gun that could take on heavy German armour, the Firefly was only issued on a limited scale and tended to draw disproportionately heavy enemy fire. British and Canadian armoured regiments eventually managed to deploy two per tank troop; the Americans never received enough to make any difference to their operations.[100] Even Copp, a vociferous advocate of the Canadian Army's performance in the Second World War, admits in *Fields of Fire*: "Neither Shermans nor Cromwells and Churchills [the major British-built tanks] could lead an advance against even hastily constructed German defences without supplementary suppressive fire" from the artillery and infantry.[101]

The fundamental problem with tanks, and the reason the "all-armour" doctrine failed, was that despite visions of massive pitched tank battles, the guns on most models of tanks were inadequate. Infantry units had access to a variety of anti-tank and field artillery weapons that, while not as mobile as tanks, packed a heavier punch. Anti-tank weapons deployed along static defensive lines could shred a tank attack, and typically had to be dealt with by infantry assault before tanks could hope to break through the "anti-tank screen."[102] The Germans certainly preferred to engage Allied tanks with their anti-tank guns rather than their own tanks, particularly the 88mm anti-tank guns but also the infantry-carried *Panzerschrek* (literally "tank-terrorizer," a shoulder-mounted infantry anti-tank weapon).[103] British and Canadian infantrymen similarly preferred to use their own anti-tank weaponry to engage German tanks. While the original British anti-tank gun, the 2-pounder, was an inadequate weapon, its replacements, the 6-pounder and 17-pounder anti-tank guns, were exceptional pieces of equipment, and in 1944–45 both were highly effective against both the German Mk V Panther and the Mk VI Tiger, something the Sherman tank could never claim.[104]

The British-made Projector, Infantry, Anti-Tank (PIAT), a shoulder-mounted weapon firing hollow charge ordnance, was appreciated by Canadian troops in both the Mediterranean and Northwest Europe theatres as a highly effective weapon against German armour. The PIAT's hollow charge bomb, fired by means of a heavy spring that ignited the projectile's propellant charge, had many less-conventional applications, including demolitions in urban combat and use against enemy slit trenches and prepared fortifications.[105] Curiously, while both Operational Research reports and recent historians have tended to deprecate the PIAT's performance in combat, it was an exceptionally popular weapon among the officers filling out the battle experience questionnaires.[106] When surveyed as to which infantry weapons had been particularly effective for their units in combat, more officers chose the PIAT than any other weapon, with the Bren light machine gun coming up a distant second.[107] Generally speaking, the threat posed to armour by well-equipped infantry meant that the "all-armoured" concept of tank warfare became impracticable against strong infantry positions. Ironically, infantry assaults were often needed to clear out anti-tank weapons before tanks could safely move forward in the attack.

Evidence gathered from the battle experience questionnaires strongly corroborates historians' accounts of the weaknesses – actual and perceived – of Canadian armour during the Second World War. According to the surveys, most Canadian infantry co-operated with tanks regularly: 80 percent of the officers serving in Northwest Europe and 77 percent serving in Italy reported having carried out combined-arms operations alongside "Infantry" tanks.[108] But if tanks were ubiquitous in Canadian operations, so were the problems encountered in co-operating with them. In their personal notes, many officers expressed disappointment or frustration with the vulnerability of the Shermans they operated in conjunction with. Major John Clarke of the 48th Highlanders recounted that, during the assault on the Hitler Line in Italy, fifty-two out of fifty-four tanks were lost in less than half an hour owing to minefields and concealed German 88mm anti-tank guns.[109] Captain William Bennett of the First Special Service Force (FSSF) described a similar incident at Anzio Beach: "At one point I saw six of our [Sherman] tanks (American 1st Arm.) knocked out by what appeared to be one Tiger firing 6 consecutive shots."[110] Some officers, such as Major Daniel Tremblay, understood the root of the problem: "We had Sherman tanks, and they are very good as far as speed is concerned, but too high + not enough armour. I know if you want speed, you have to eliminate armour."[111] This contention, that Allied tanks were "frail" and could not match German tanks in battle, is repeated with some frequency by the officers filling out the surveys.[112] Lieutenant-Colonel T.P. Gilday's comment is perhaps most telling: in his opinion, if the infantry was well-trained and knew the ground, it was always better for them to attack by night *without* tanks than by day *with* tanks.[113]

Moreover, even the morale boost that the presence of tanks could bring to infantry was highly contingent upon the tanks' actions and role in combat. Lieutenant-Colonel E.T. Jacques of Le Régiment de Maisonneuve commented: "The infantry were always very enthusiastic and morale high when it was known that tanks were co-operating. However, after a couple of shows the men and officers were not so happy as they found that the tanks expected the infantry to lead [in the attack]."[114] It was an established element of combined-arms tactical doctrine by 1943 that tanks should support infantry from the rear, rather than leading the way themselves:

supposedly their high-explosive guns could best assist infantrymen by sitting in unexposed hull- or turret-down positions to help gnaw through an enemy defensive position from afar.[115] This was a much more ponderous role for tanks than the original disciples of mobility had intended, and it was doctrine with which Canadian officers expressed a great deal of dissatisfaction in the battle experience questionnaires. "Infantry [co-operation with] tanks," wrote Major Ostiguy, "often took the shape of cover by the tanks guns from an area, the tanks moving up after success. This was bad for the morale of foot troops who often got out of touch with the tanks due to the nature of the ground and were pinned down by enemy fire which could have been dealt with by the tanks had they been closer."[116] The vulnerability of the Sherman tanks to German anti-tank weapons was widely recognized by the infantrymen as the main reason for the timidity of the tank crews. As Major John Wesley Burgess of the Essex Scottish Regiment wrote: "My experiences with tanks cooperating with [infantry] were all unfortunate ... Canadian tanks attached to us always seemed singularly reluctant to engage enemy with fire or expose themselves to possible enemy fire, as a result they never rendered material help. This obtained ... 19–20 June [1944] at Verriers and in the night breakthrough near Rocquancourt, on which occasion the [Regiment] of tanks responsible for maintaining direction of embussed column moving at night in enemy territory, broke and disappeared when a single 88mm gun opened fire. Infantry was left short of objective without tank support."[117] Along similar lines, Major Tremblay noted: "We found out most of the time that [tanks] don't like to come ahead with us, and would prefer to shoot us in far behind when there are bunkers of 88mm [anti-tank guns], as they are very vulnerable to them."[118] Captain Paré likewise mentioned: "As far as tanks are concerned, they are as vulnerable by an 88[mm anti-tank gun] as a man is with a bullet, and did they know it! What they do is, take a turret-down or Hull-down posit[ion], and after firing and the infantry coming in they moved in too, but like infantry."[119] Other officers also expressed their frustration at the circumspect behaviour of their tank support. Major R.C. Graves of the North Nova Scotia Highlanders made a sour remark when discussing infantry weaponry: "I have never used a German 'Bazooka' but I know that our own tanks will NOT go forward until we can assure them that there are none in the area."[120] According to the data compiled from the officers' survey answers, the experience of these officers was not exceptional. In an assessment of all survey responses to a question regarding whether the infantry usually moved in front of, behind, or among the tanks in combined arms operations, 42 percent of officers reported operating exclusively in front of the tanks, and only 12 percent exclusively behind the tanks, although 25 percent reported having moved in "all" positions relative to their armoured support.[121] The differences between officers serving in the Italian and Northwest Europe campaigns were not noteworthy in this instance; the trend among respondent officers indicates that the tactical norm was that tanks followed the infantry. And, as Major R.G. Liddell of the Royal Canadian Regiment pointed out in his addendum notes, this rearward positioning of the tanks could be profoundly destructive to infantry morale. Few could see good reason for the armoured tanks to be more skittish than the "naked" infantry.[122]

Of course, some officers understood the tactical exigencies of tank use, and many found ways to make tank-infantry co-operation work, even when tanks were deployed following the infantry at a distance.[123] The problems presented by strong anti-tank defences were generally acknowledged, but there was a significant gap between understanding the fact and liking it. Infantry officers were reluctant to accept that armoured vehicles were somehow more vulnerable than unarmoured infantry in the field. Major Cottrill put it best: "Tank commanders rather slow in reacting to infantry's immediate needs. Appear to lose sight of fact that a good Rifle company commander won't risk losing [his men] any more than [the tank commander] will his own men."[124]

Another issue, and just as serious, was the problem of coordinating combined movements and fire due to breakdowns in communications between infantry and tanks; this was in fact one of the chief complaints of infantry officers. According to some surveys, wireless communication with tanks rarely functioned properly, and tank crews, owing to their restricted field of vision, could never see as much of the battlefield as the infantry could.[125] In order to communicate properly with supporting tanks while in battle – to point out an enemy strong point or coordinate plans – soldiers on foot typically had to leave themselves exposed. This often meant communicating via the wired telephone box fitted on the backs of some, but not all, tanks, although Major A.L. Saunders bitterly reported that even when they were equipped, these telephones were often "switched off; or out of order, or the tank crew [commander] being busy looking out for himself listening to his Signals ... would not take time to listen." Telephones were not reliable in facilitating tank-infantry communications.[126] As Major Cottrill pointed out, infantrymen were therefore often forced to "Climb turret [and] endeavour to point out hold up [to the advance] (Not very healthy!)."[127]

There were other creative, if decidedly inefficient, ways to communicate messages to tanks. Many officers claimed that they had used tracer fire, smoke, or flares to point out enemy positions to tanks.[128] Captain P.A.R. Blaker of the Argyll and Sutherland Highlanders Regiment noted, perhaps wryly, that his "most satisfactory method" of attracting the attention of a tank was to "throw a handful of earth at him."[129] Major John Clarke also recommended throwing "rocks and sand" at friendly tanks to attract their attention and avoid having infantry officers expose themselves, though less amusingly he also said that at Ortona they had to use bursts of Bren or sub-machine gun fire on the rear of the friendly tank turret for the same purpose.[130] Communication problems became most acute, and deadly, when friendly tanks were unable to distinguish friend from foe in the confusion of battle. Surveyed officers complained bitterly about "trigger-happy tanks" or "indiscriminate fire."[131] At best this halted infantry progress, and at worst inflicted friendly fire casualties, which were listed in the surveys as being among the most prominent causes of low morale among Canadians.[132] The restricted vision of the tanks meant that it was usually up to the infantry to "look out that tanks did not cause accidents either to personnel or vehicles."[133] This was another reason why some infantry officers preferred to work behind tanks, rather than in front of them. An inability to communicate could cripple attempts at co-operation between the two fighting arms, and it is understandable that infantry officers sometimes viewed tanks as a liability and could dislike working with them intensely.

Still, despite considerable problems, there is plentiful evidence that infantrymen generally appreciated having tanks present for their excellent fire-support. They were particularly helpful in blunting the tactically inevitable German counter-attacks, as they could bring accurate and powerful direct fire to supplement artillery barrages and infantry small-arms.[134] Tanks could move up to support a position quickly once the way was clear, much faster than anti-tank guns or artillery. Major L.P. Coderre of the South Saskatchewan Regiment made special note of their utility: "In an advance-to-contact role we have used tanks behind the leading company.

Their role there is to shoot-in the company. The method used in this case is that once the leading elements are fired on or brought to ground the tanks, from a position of about 500 yards to the rear of a company, and to either flank, will neutralize most any enemy strongpoint, thereby allowing the infantry to regain the fire initiative."[135]

It is unfortunate, then, that so many problems plagued this aspect of the combined-arms team. In the survey notes there are many more expressions of officer dissatisfaction with infantry-tank co-operation than there are mentions of successful co-operation between the two, although not every officer had anything to say on the subject. While this should not be taken as a statistical observation, the general impression from the battle experience questionnaires is that infantry co-operation with tanks was at its best quite effective, but in practice was often extremely problematic. Spotty field communications exacerbated the difficulties presented by the tanks' inherent tactical vulnerabilities and predilection for letting the infantry fight forward ahead of them. Whatever the case, the idea of *Blitzkrieg* warfare, with the armour leading the way toward a penetration and rupture of the enemy lines, was largely foreign to the Canadian battlefield experience. For all of its mechanized power, the Canadian army still required the infantry to act as its "sledgehammer" both in the attack and on the defensive.

AIR POWER

Mention needs to be made of another key component of combined-arms warfare, air power. Air supremacy was indisputably one of the great strengths of every Allied ground campaign after 1942. Particularly in Northwest Europe, the *Luftwaffe*, so dominant in the 1939 and 1940 campaigns, was almost completely absent from the skies above Allied infantrymen by 1944, having been driven away by the relentless application of Allied air power. More than 50 percent of the German day-fighter force was deployed for the defence of Germany in the spring of 1944, and not even 10 percent of the available fighters were sent to northern France. On 6 June, the *Luftwaffe* managed only three fighter sweeps along 50 miles of D-Day coast, perhaps wisely electing not to test their mettle against the umbrella of Allied fighter cover around the beachheads.[136] The Allies were the unquestioned masters of the sky over Western Europe, and this dominance is widely regarded by military historians as one of their most important advantages during the ground war.[137]

It is unfortunate, then, that the battle experience questionnaires are relatively quiet on the subject of the air support available to the Canadian Army. Only one short group of formal questions on the survey had anything to do with air support, and these mentioned it only in the vaguest of terms. From those answers, curiously, only 66 percent of all respondents claimed to have received "Direct Air Support," while 26 percent claimed never to have received any; of the officers serving in the Mediterranean 63 percent responded in the affirmative, and 29 percent answered negatively.[138] Of those who claimed to have received air support, over 80 percent indicated that this support had been "effective," and only a handful in either theatre of operations wrote that it had been "ineffective," although 16 officers wrote that the support had been only "partially effective."[139] In the addendum notes, the subject of air support was remarkably absent, with hardly any officers commenting upon it. A few indicated their disgust and their troops' fear of being bombed by their own planes; Major C.K. Crummer of the Lincoln and Welland Regiment was quite appalled after a pilot he met in hospital told him he had never before heard of yellow smoke being used to indicate friendly troops on the ground – the standard practice among ground troops in Northwest Europe at the time.[140]

On the other hand, air power was frequently mentioned by respondents in the area of the questionnaire detailing factors known to raise or lower morale in units. Over a quarter of all officers (47 in all) listed air support among the greatest factors in raising a unit's morale.[141] Most of these officers were specifically pleased by the role of the Royal Air Force's Hawker Typhoon, especially when armed with rockets and used for "direct support" in engaging enemy ground forces during a battle.[142] "Seeing Typhoons going after near targets," was what Captain A.C. MacCallum considered to be the best thing for raising his troops' morale.[143] Similarly, Major Cyril Wrightman commented that air support was vital to morale, and that "pounding by [Typhoons and bombers] always put the battalion in high spirits."[144] It was particularly appreciated by troops when nearby planes could be called down on short notice to concentrate bombing on enemy artillery that was giving the Canadians trouble.[145] As historian Paul Johnston has explored, the system (called a "cabrank"), by which RAF fighter-bombers would circle a specific point above the front, available to swiftly descend on enemy targets as soon as a forward controller called for support, was immensely popular with the army, a conclusion that the battle experience questionnaires bear out.[146]

Unfortunately, while air power was a huge morale boost for troops, it was not as available as would have been desired. Maintaining cabranks was expensive in terms of fuel and in terms of the drain on pilots and aircraft. Parcelling out of aircraft for tactical support to individual divisions or even corps was also contrary to the RAF doctrine of force concentration, so the presence of cabranks was the exception rather than the rule.[147] The RAF was also inclined toward using air power in ways that were less visible from the infantryman's "worm's-eye view" of the battlefield. By October 1944 the Royal Air Force's 2nd Tactical Air Force – partially tasked with supporting First Canadian Army's operations in Northwest Europe – was only flying one-third of its sorties in direct support of the armies; two-thirds were dedicated to other missions, such as cutting French and German rail communications and attacking other targets in Germany.[148] These interdiction bombing missions, meant to cripple German transportation, logistics, and communications ahead of the Allied ground advance, were arguably the most effective contribution of the air forces to the war in Western Europe. They would have been largely invisible to Allied troops on the ground, though highly visible to the Germans. Even when air support was tasked for direct support of army operations, it did not always make itself useful. Operational Research Section reports have shown, for example, that neither extensive heavy bomber sorties nor fighter-bomber direct support played any noticeable role in supporting the D-Day landings on 6 June, despite complete control of the skies.[149] As historian Allan Millett wrote concerning American tactical air support in the Second World War: "Close air support for ground operations improved during the war, but still proved less successful than ground officers hoped."[150] Johnston attributes this disappointment in part to the tendency of army officers to focus on the tactical level of fighting and lose sight of the operational dimensions of battle: "Unsurprisingly, therefore, the air support they called for was narrow in nature, tending toward a desire for on-call tactical help everywhere, with massive heavy bomber strikes to precede any advance."[151]

In reality this kind of support could not be counted on, even if it was a major morale booster for the infantry when it did appear. As mentioned, beyond the question on morale and one question on Direct Air Support in the questionnaire, there is a dearth of information in these surveys on the impact of air power, and the battle experience questionnaires can add little to the discussion of air power in the Second World War. The survey questions are not nuanced enough to provide anything but broad-stroke impressions, and few addendum comments add much texture to the topic. The officers may just have had little to say about air support – or just as likely, the questionnaire may have been structured in a way that, deliberately or not, downplayed the role that air support played. All that can be said on the basis of the battle experience questionnaires is that air support was greatly appreciated by infantrymen when it was present, was hated when it caused friendly fire incidents, and was not employed as often as it was demanded. While this should not imply that there similarly exists nothing further for the historian to say on the topic – quite the contrary – infantry officers evidently did not consider tactical air support to be a defining feature of their time in combat.

CONCLUSION

In the closing chapter of *The Face of Battle*, military historian John Keegan explores the idea that through the ages the common denominator in warfare has been the central role of the infantryman. Despite the march of science and technology, this was no less true for the Second World War. As Keegan explains: "A Second World War armoured division in action ... little resembled the fast-moving fleet of land ironclads, wheeling and shooting in unison, of which the visionaries of *Blitzkrieg* had dreamed ... their operations, losing the simplicity of ship-to-ship actions, became heavily intermingled with confused infantry combats of a kind little different from those which soldiers of the First World War had experienced in many of the great offensives."[152] The combat arms that embraced mechanization – the artillery, the tanks, the air force – have become the popular icons of the Second World War: and even the best histories can become bogged down in attempts to deduce which side had more tanks or fighters available at any given time, in their efforts to come up with a measurement of effectiveness. But while there is no denying the importance of these combat arms, their central role in the ground fighting of the war has perhaps been somewhat overstated. On virtually every front the Second World War was fundamentally just as savage an infantry "slugging contest" as the First World War. The infantry of all armies sustained by far the highest casualty rates, losses that were particularly disastrous for nations such as Canada, which concentrated such a small percentage of servicemen in the infantry. Casualty rates in several major engagements in Northwest Europe, and at any given time on the Eastern Front, were often higher than those of the First World War.[153] While armour and a general increase in available firepower contributed to the war's greater mobility, when compared with the Western Front of the Great War, at least, the evidence from both primary and secondary sources suggests that the importance of infantry in combat remained undiminished.

Artillery was neither as accurate nor as effective as it needed to be in order to act as a substitute for advancing foot soldiers. While it could prove devastating and demoralizing for the enemy, and served to neutralize positions temporarily, even the overwhelming advantage in munitions and manufacturing capacity enjoyed by the Allies was hardly ever sufficient to singularly obliterate German defenders. The role of the artillery – as it had been during the First World War – was to suppress enemy fire rather than to destroy it, and to escort infantry in close enough to make good use of their own fire. It was also used to excellent effect in blunting German counter-attacks against seized positions, when enemy troops were in the open and could be targeted through direct observation, but even then it was infantry that was needed to hold a position against the enemy.[154]

Likewise, while the tank remains the iconic weapon of the war, its decisive impact was limited, most notably by the power of the infantry arrayed against it. The anti-tank weaponry available to the infantry of all sides in the conflict, in the form of larger guns and man-portable shoulder-fired weapons, was simply too potent to allow tanks to habitually operate in a forward position. The German *Panzerschreck* anti-tank rocket launcher could penetrate over 200mm of tank armour, such as that found on the Soviet IS-2, which was far more heavily armoured than anything the British, Americans, or Canadians fielded. One shot from a *Panzerschreck* normally sufficed to destroy any Allied armoured vehicle.[155] Allied anti-tank weapons were of comparable, if somewhat inferior, potency. Not surprisingly, Canadian tanks were most often deployed in support of the infantry – usually from behind – rather than leading the attack themselves. In fact, even during the most decisive phases of the war, particularly in the German offensives between 1939 and 1941, success in battle did not come from massing tanks together, but from the intelligent application of combined-arms formations, typified by the excellent Panzer divisions of the *Wehrmacht*.[156] Armour in combination with infantry and artillery could be highly effective; armour operating by itself was easy prey for anti-tank platoons.

The battle experience questionnaires demonstrate that Canadian infantry soldiers were very aware of the limitations of their supporting arms. While one would expect the reports of infantry officers to reflect the experience and bias of riflemen, the surveys confirm what other historians have begun to recognize in recent years: that mechanized technology in the Second World War served to supplement the infantry, not to replace it or even seriously detract from its importance. Terry Copp has argued at length that Canadian infantry was the decisive arm. "Given a reasonable chance of success," Copp tells us, "the Canadian soldier proved capable of overcoming even the most elaborate defensive positions."[157] The armoured and artillery corps significantly increased this "reasonable chance of success," but it was upon the infantry that the greatest burden of the fighting, and almost all of the dying, fell.

In assessing the effectiveness of Canadian infantry during the war, this point is vital. The evidence supports the thesis that, in the case of Canadian ground combat during the Second World War, the infantry were the senior partners of the combined-arms team. However iconic mechanized firepower might have been, it was necessarily subordinate to the tactical reality that war was still being fought and won primarily by infantry action, the "sledgehammer" of the attack, when properly supported. If, for example, S.L.A. Marshall was correct, and only 15 to 20 percent of combat infantrymen would ever fire their weapons in combat, then that sledgehammer possessed only a fraction of its potential strength. Taking Marshall at his word would mean that infantry in battle would have to be subordinated to the firepower of supporting arms like the tanks, artillery, and tactical air power, given that infantry units would have been unable to generate sufficient organic firepower themselves. But as the historical evidence has testified, the supporting arms were simply that: in support of the infantry. Their inherent limitations and vulnerabilities meant that only in the closest co-operation with foot soldiers could decisive results be generated. Although this evidence is not conclusive in itself, it strongly implies that Marshall and others have sold the infantry short of its true importance in battle. It is difficult to believe that any infantry unit where scarcely one in five soldiers, on average, would do so much as fire their weapons in the air would be able to constitute the kind of sledgehammer that ultimately won the war against Germany.

An understanding of infantry effectiveness must be predicated on the knowledge that the so-called decisive arms beside which it operated were not decisive in themselves; if Canadian infantry truly was ineffective, then so was the entire army, because nothing except the infantry was going to win the battles for them. As the next chapter demonstrates, accounts of infantry ineffectiveness have been grossly exaggerated, and in evaluating the savage fighting carried out by Canadians during the Second World War, more credit needs to be given to the strength and skill of the infantrymen.

## CHAPTER FIVE

CANADIAN INFANTRY EFFECTIVENESS

The inability of armour and artillery to decisively alter the tactical balance underscores the extent to which Canada's Second World War was an infantryman's war. In virtually every engagement, it was the extent of the infantry's skill, resolve, and effectiveness that resulted in either victory or failure for the Canadian Army. Although the infantry was at its best operating as part of a combined-arms tactical machine, it typically shouldered the burden of decision.

One reason for this imbalance was the difficulty of the terrain that the Canadian Army was forced to fight upon, a difficulty sometimes forgotten or downplayed in operational or strategic overviews of the European campaigns. Particularly in Northwest Europe, the First Canadian Army, which suffered from a number of organizational defects and lack of experience prior to June 1944, was relegated by the Supreme Headquarters Allied Expeditionary Force (SHAEF) to inglorious positions in the line where their perceived weaknesses would, in theory, be less of a liability.[1] As a result, the Canadians bloodied themselves across unfavourable terrain: the sieges of the Channel ports, the flooded fields of the Berskens Pocket and northern Belgium, and the heavily forested areas of the Rhineland, all of which were fiercely defended by the Germans. The Canadians in the Mediterranean faced even unhappier prospects, having to contest with the mountainous Sicilian and Italian landscapes, the urban fighting in Ortona, and the heavily fortified defensive lines built by the Germans to check Allied progress. Even if the Canadian Army had been better prepared to engage in high-mobility maneuvre warfare, almost all the terrain in which Canadians fought between 1943 and 1945 precluded it.[2] Given the ground upon which they had to fight, and the normally extensive defensive preparations of the enemy, Canada's success was predicated almost entirely on the effectiveness of its infantry corps in battle.

Infantry effectiveness is the subject of this chapter, which assesses the tactical dimensions of Canadian infantry fighting during the war. Excellent narrative accounts of the Canadian Army in specific actions and theatres have already been written, and this discussion will not be adding to that literature. Instead, this chapter follows the thematic structure of the battle experience questionnaires upon which it is based to examine some of the most important tactical aspects of Canadian campaigns against Germany. The questionnaires asked officers to dissect their combat experiences and report on details and principles, and form generalizations from them. They are not after-action reports, and if they detail specific encounters it is in an incidental or illustrative fashion. As discussed in chapter 3, this method has acknowledged limitations, but every effort has been made to differentiate officers according to the theatre of operations that they served in and the specific engagements in which they fought, as ascertained from their time spent in combat and their assigned unit. More narrative histories, and particularly the recent work of Terry Copp and others, have helped to add texture and context to the questionnaire evidence.

A number of topics addressed in the questionnaires relate directly to the effectiveness of Canadian infantry in combat – topics such as bite-and-hold tactics, patrol actions, and night fighting. The evidence on infantry small-arms fire in combat is also of considerable importance in that it directly contradicts, with documentary historical evidence, the classic ratio-of-fire arguments advanced by S.L.A. Marshall. In presenting the survey data, I attempt to differentiate units and specific theatres of operations (complete lists of which can be found in the appendix), although it is worth remembering that Canadians faced almost uniformly hostile terrain and only slightly varying degrees of bitter enemy resistance no matter what front they were fighting on. While the geography of the Mediterranean and Northwest Europe campaigns was of course different, the kind of tactical fighting required on both fronts did not vary much: sustained infantry combat and assault, as part of a combined-arms attack with artillery and armour support, was always needed to overcome enemy defences.

The battle experience questionnaires paint an overall picture of varying effectiveness over time and place, as they highlight the successes, failures, and adaptations that accompanied the infantry war. As Copp has mentioned, the concept of an ascending learning curve is deeply entrenched in military historiography, as is the idea that the soldiers of the Canadian Army started out poorly but got better the longer they fought.[3] While it is difficult to monitor such trends through the questionnaires, the emerging picture seems rather to be that effectiveness tended to fluctuate. This was particularly true among infantry rifle companies, many of which, owing to high losses, had to be completely rebuilt with replacement soldiers several times in the course of Canadian operations. Nonetheless, while an ascending curve may not have been evident, the battle experience questionnaires suggest that Canadian infantry was generally operating at a much higher standard of proficiency than historians have previously acknowledged. Although their effectiveness depended upon local terrain and conditions, the soundness of planning, staff work, logistics, and the determination of the enemy, Canadian infantrymen were normally able to give good account of themselves in close combat.

"BITE-AND-HOLD" FIGHTING, AND FIRE-AND-MOVEMENT

The Canadian Army Overseas had the unusual experience of being on the operational offensive against the Axis throughout its time in combat. Aside from local counter-attacks, the only major German offensive against the Allies on the Western Front, the Battle of the Bulge in December 1944, missed the First Canadian Army entirely, as it was being held in reserve during that winter. In a war that is often characterized in historical writing by the slashing "lightning" warfare of 1939 and 1940, the Canadians faced the unenviable task of having to assault and crack open a series of prepared German defensive positions in every theatre they faced. Highly reminiscent of their role in the First World War, the task of the Canadian Army was to develop techniques that would succeed offensively across a variety of geographical climates and terrains, ranging from mountains to flooded polders to city streets and dense European forests, in the face of a skilled and resourceful opposition. The offensive techniques developed and employed by the Canadians warrant discussion in light of the battle experience questionnaires.

By 1944 experience in North Africa and Italy had reaffirmed for Allied commanders that the best way to exploit the German operational doctrine of the immediate counterattack was through old techniques. "The one certain way of defeating the Germans," writes Terry Copp, "was to find, fix, and then neutralize the enemy with overwhelming firepower. This would allow the infantry to assault and occupy vital ground, which the enemy would then counterattack."[4] These tactics, in an updated form that included tanks and gave the infantry greater organic firepower, were essentially the bite-and-hold techniques already used in the First World War. The infantry would follow a creeping barrage toward its objective rather than fighting forward entirely on its own, dealing with any neutralized German positions as they appeared; they would then seize their limited objectives with the help of tanks, consolidate, dig in, and bring up the heavier anti-tank guns to prepare for the inevitable counterattack.[5] Although often costly in terms of lives and resources, bite-and-hold tactics were likely to inflict serious damage on a defender who was doctrinally committed to counterattacking for every lost yard of ground. As discussed in chapter 4, the strength of bite-and-hold fighting lay in that it switched the combatants' places, so that the attacker, upon reaching the objective, could dig in and assume a defensive stance, with most of the advantages of the defence on their side if they could entrench themselves rapidly. It was in part a return to attrition warfare, with the twin objectives of seizing ground and wearing down an enemy. This manner of fighting was hardly elegant, and relied upon the artillery to cover the initial advance to the objective; but there were few better realistic options available to the Canadians at the time.[6]

The actual name "bite-and-hold" is not written anywhere in the battle experience questionnaires, but none of the officers were unfamiliar with the concept, especially since many aspects of it were built into pre-war doctrine.[7] In the surveys, just over 70 percent of respondents reported that their units had organized a "rapid defence against counterattack;" the number did not vary significantly between the Mediterranean and Northwest Europe theatres of operations.[8] Upon seizing a position, Canadian troops would be almost immediately counterattacked, normally with tanks as well as infantry, since German armoured divisions on the defensive were being primarily used as a floating operational reserve for local counterattacks.9 For rifle companies, assembling a rapid defence normally meant digging in as part of the "consolidation" phase, rapidly preparing slit trenches on positions that hopefully were not already sited by enemy artillery. According to the surveys, the Royal Canadian Engineers hardly ever did this digging for the infantry; as Major W.C. Allan wrote, the riflemen themselves had to dig with "pick and shovel and, if available, #75 [high explosive] grenades."10 And as the Cape Breton Highlanders' Major A.C. Ross mentioned: "Once the men are 'battle wise' – which comes very quickly – there is never any need to tell people to get slit trenches dug quickly. It becomes second nature to them."11 Once anti-tank guns, the mainstay defence against German armour, had been brought forward in the consolidation, they had to be dug in as well, or they would quickly be destroyed.12 However, infantry that had been properly dug-in and was adequately supported with both artillery and direct-fire weapons such as tanks and anti-tank guns, often had fewer reasons to fear German counterattacks, since these techniques were designed to blunt the enemy's reactionary counterattack system.13 Tanks could accompany infantry in the assault or "shoot them in" with supporting fire from behind, but they were particularly useful in consolidating the new defensive posture. Numerous rifle company commanders noted that tanks should accompany infantry onto the objective, but should not be "released" either forward or back toward friendly lines until after the anti-tank guns had arrived on the position; it was the effectiveness of anti-tank weapons like the 6-pounder that allowed forward units to stand against counterattacks.14 When the enemy counterattack came, though, it was up to the infantry, with the help of its supporting arms, to beat off the assault.15 With the combination of the powerful anti-tank guns and the shoulder-mounted PIATs, even German armoured counterattacks could normally be defeated. As Major Allan wrote: "Enemy tanks did not relish the PIAT and could be forced to turn tail moderately easily. As soon as the tanks turned the majority [of counterattacking infantry] broke except on very rare occasions."16 Mines would also be laid out in front of the new defensive position, and heavier crew-served weapons, such as medium machine-guns and mortars, would be brought forward as well to help consolidate.17 "Harassing fire" from artillery and indirect weapons in close communication with forward observers would be depended upon to try and break up enemy counterattacks and perform counter-battery firing to suppress enemy shelling.[18]

The essence of the bite-and-hold style of attacking was its ability to rapidly convert an objective into a defensive strong-point, in sufficient time to fight off the counterattack. Any serious delays in getting to the objective and digging in would allow the German defenders more time to launch their counter-stroke. During the initial attack behind the creeping barrage, officers encouraged their troops to bypass enemy strong-points *en route* to the objective, rather than risk getting bogged down in local fire-fights.[19] A lot could go wrong with this technique, however. Major Harrison of the Calgary Highlanders related a telling incident: once, when his company began moving forward to the assault line behind a creeping barrage, they were met by a blistering German counter-barrage sited to their position, which killed many soldiers and temporarily halted the advance. The delay, however, meant that the Calgaries were caught out in the open once their own creeping barrage had passed on, and the company was cut apart by the Germans' forward machine-gun outposts.[20] Major Thomas McCoy would have agreed that, generally speaking, the faster and harder troops advanced, the fewer of them would be killed.[21] Bite-and-hold tactics required a high degree of bloody-mindedness and determination, since their success risked a great deal of potential exposure to both friendly and enemy fire.

Bite-and-hold tactics did not require units to execute the "fire-and-movement" skills that had been a mainstay of Anglo-Canadian infantry training. Bite-and-hold was an artillery-based doctrine that "required the infantry to move forward at a steady pace, leaning into the barrage, so as to be on the objective before the enemy could engage the attackers," just as in the First World War.[22] The use of infantry weapons in the initial advance to the objective was actually discouraged, at least in the written doctrine. The 1935 *Field Service Regulations* stipulated: "Infantry should not open fire as long as it can get forward without it; a fire fight must be to the advantage of the defender, who knows the range and can more easily replenish his ammunition supply," not to mention that the enemy is dug-in and less exposed to fire.[23] Ideally, nothing was supposed to slow the infantry short of its objective ground; in reality any number of problems could develop.

It is tempting to generalize on this point and view Canadian infantrymen as suffering from tactical arthritis, yoked to the artillery that battered a way through the forward defences for them. But while bite-and-hold tactics were a mainstay in the Canadian art of war, they were not the only show in town. Fire-and-movement was still extensively employed throughout the Second World War by Canadian troops. In essence, fire-and-movement tactics called for the application of heavy small-arms fire to neutralize an enemy position for long enough to allow troops to move forward into another position, where they could then cover others in turn. The basic principles of this tactic had been drilled into Commonwealth riflemen in training as "battle drill."[24] As historian Timothy Harrison Place explains in his book *Military Training in the British Army*, although the barrage-based bite-and-hold tactics were central to operations, if something went wrong, the infantrymen would be expected to use fire-and-movement tactics to fight their own way forward. While the British, Place argues, had difficulty taking this kind of action,[25] the battle experience questionnaires suggest that Canadian soldiers had success with it. In their survey answers, 85 percent of officer respondents in both theatres indicated that they had put fire-and-movement tactics into practice in battle.[26] Of these, about two-thirds answered that they had put fire-and-movement into practice "Often" or "Fairly Often," with the remainder indicating that they had only employed it "Seldom."[27] Nonetheless, a significant majority of Canadian officers indicated that they regularly employed fire-and-movement tactics.

These numbers are given some nuance by the numerous questionnaire respondents who recounted instances when their units were forced to fight their way forward with their own small-arms using fire-and-movement techniques. Captain Robert Mainprize wrote about employing fire-and-movement against German machine-gun defence posts during aggressive fighting patrols in Normandy: "We split the patrol into three groups, 2 fire groups and an assault group ... The fire group led the patrol and one fire group was off to what the patrol [leader] thought was the dangerous flank. They moved in leaps and bounds ... If engaged before reaching their objective one of the fire groups engaged the enemy while the other fire group and assault group withdrew and tried an alternative route. In this way the patrol was maintaining its object."[28] Fire-and-movement was cleady an integral part of some patrol actions. In terms of major offensive actions, though, two separate officers – one from the Seaforth Highlanders and the other from Le Royal 22e Régiment – recounted that their assaults on the Hitler Line had taken place without appreciable tank or artillery support, and that the battle against the fixed German defences had to be carried out by infantry weapons almost exclusively.[29] The Calgary Highlanders' Major Harrison similarly wrote that while his unit never used the method of sending sections or platoons on long, exposed flanking movements, fire-and-movement of the "pepper-pot" method was employed frequently.[30] Major Crummer of the Lincoln and Welland Regiment wrote that fire-and-movement was employed "on almost every operation."[31] But it was Major R.D. Medland, a company commander with the Queen's Own Rifles, who articulated fire-and-movement most clearly:

> The principles of fire and movement is not battle drill. Rather, battle drill is only a form, a good one, of expressing and explaining fire and movement. To my knowledge battle drill, as such, has never been used. It is only the expedient by with the principle may be taught.
>
> The principle of fire and movement is as old as war itself, whereas battle drill, as we know it, is comparatively new. [Many] of the ideas embodied in the teaching of battle drill give a completely faulty impression of actual battle conditions. We can accept the principle of fire and movement, right – but the speed and inaccuracy with which battle drill movements are carried out would prove costly and unsuccessful. However, careful [reconnaissance], repetition, over and over, of plans and orders, then the employment of fire and movement, are a firm guarantee to success.[32]

The questionnaires indicate that many Canadian units had substantial experience fighting their own way forward on the attack, rather than re-lying exclusively on the steady creeping barrage advance as a "crutch."

There is no question that Canadian set-piece attacks depended more upon a creeping barrage to seize an objective than upon infantrymen having to fight their own way forward using their own organic firepower. However, the evidence demonstrates that fire-and-movement was still employed regularly by Canadian soldiers in battle: in lieu of a barrage, during patrol actions, and when things went awry during an advance. The advance to the objective was also only the first phase of the battle and, according to most sources, the easy part: it was much more difficult to rapidly consolidate a new position and secure it against enemy counter-attacks. While artillery could be pivotal in breaking up a counterattacking enemy force, such actions hinged upon the infantrymen being able to make effective, successful use of their own weapons and skills.

There were almost endless permutations and variations on how Canadian operations were structured and executed in the field: securing a bridgehead over the Leopold Canal was not fighting in Ortona or assaulting the Hitler Line. Given that Canadians were constantly on the strategic offensive and possessed the initiative of when, where, and how to attack, it is not surprising to find that their officers wrote that they employed a range of techniques in overcoming the enemy. Every situation presented new tactical challenges and demanded the application of more than just one tactic. While it appears to be true that Canadian sub-units did not enjoy the same degree of independence and decentralized control as German ones did, they were not chained to the creeping barrage and were typically capable of fighting forward without it, as local conditions and the German opposition allowed. Canadian success on the offensive varied, but it rested upon the effectiveness of its infantry rifle companies, and, generally speaking, they did not disappoint in this regard.

PATROLLING

Too much has been made of the supposition that this artillery-based tactical doctrine crippled infantry initiative and shackled all movement to the rain of shellfire that constituted the creeping barrage.[33] Such accounts suggest that Canadian soldiers only ever encountered their enemies during rigid set-piece assaults against German defensive lines. Although many major offensives of the Canadian Army were indeed characterized by firepower-intensive actions, these did not represent the entire scope of Canadian tactical experiences. Along relatively static fronts – which characterized most of the Canadian war experience – smaller actions were being undertaken constantly. A variety of different types of patrols, from simple reconnaissance and raiding to full-on fighting patrols, were mounted regularly by Canadian rifle companies in the line. These patrols, reminiscent of the trench raiding of the First World War, were highly fluid, often improvised affairs that demanded tremendous initiative from soldiers at the platoon and section levels. While the proclivity of Canadian soldiers for trench raiding in the First World War has been well established in the historiography, less attention has been paid to the patrols and raids carried out in the Second World War, where the lines could become almost as static as those of 1914 to 1918, if not as elaborately entrenched.[34] The evidence from the battle experience questionnaires shows that Canadians in all theatres participated actively in patrols, and that much of the time they succeeded in dominating the Germans at close quarters and controlling the ground between static positions.

Patrol activity was constant on all fronts and in every theatre. There were practical benefits: obtaining reconnaissance, gathering intelligence, and harassing the enemy. Commanders also believed that getting soldiers out of their defensive positions and patrolling no-man's land between major offensives would prevent stagnation and a deadlock mentality.[35] According to formal Commonwealth infantry doctrine, as laid out in the War Office's *Infantry Section Leading 1938*, active patrolling was to take three different forms: *reconnoitering* patrols, *fighting* patrols, and *standing* patrols. Reconnoitering patrols, which received the most attention, were broken down into patrols for the purpose of guarding against enemy surprise attacks, and patrols for scouting out enemy defences, learning the ground, and "maintaining touch with the enemy."[36] A fundamental flexibility in approach was deemed necessary, and particular stress was placed upon never taking obvious routes or otherwise making moves the enemy might expect. The manual recommended only two to three men per reconnoitering patrol to maximize stealth and silence.[37] Fighting patrols were an updated version of the trench raid, aimed at harassing the enemy, defeating hostile patrols, and capturing enemy prisoners. These were to be led, according to doctrine, by an officer or warrant officer, and would be two or more sections strong. Fighting patrols were also employed as a rear guard during withdrawals, to cover parties in defence, protect troops forming up at night for an attack, or to generally divert an enemy's attention.[38] Standing patrols, in contrast, were an active combination of sentry duty and a forward picket line, "sent out to watch approaches which the enemy is expected to use," and were also expected to "occupy prominent points which an enemy must capture as a preliminary to an attack." Standing patrols were expected to act as a flexible forward defensive line; unlike defensive posts, which were expected to hold their ground, standing patrols could shift position, manoeuvre, and fall back to more favourable ground when under attack.[39] All three forms of patrolling demanded a great deal of initiative and flexibility on the part of the patrol leader and the soldiers carrying out the patrol.

The Anglo-Canadian armies were not unique in their patrolling. The German operational and tactical doctrine for the Second World War, *Truppenführung 1933*, laid out a system of aggressive reconnaissance, with a greater emphasis upon *battle recon* for coming to grips with the enemy while active operations were being carried out, and always in sufficient strength to deal swiftly with enemy security patrol detachments.[40] The U.S. Army, in its 1941 field service regulations, placed a similar emphasis upon patrolling, but drew clearer lines between patrol activity for *reconnaissance* and activity for *security* purposes.[41] Most armies realized the necessity of being able to project flexible patrols beyond the main body of their force for a variety of purposes.

The Canadians were particularly disposed toward aggressive patrolling. They seem, in this instance, to have strongly adhered to established doctrine, and the questionnaire respondents wrote extensively on their patrolling habits. In practice, however, there was considerable variation according to the demands of the mission. While Canadian units frequently encountered problems, they seem to have been quite adept at engaging the enemy in a variety of ways during patrol actions.

Many officer respondents mentioned that patrolling was a dominant feature of life along the front lines, and patrols were mounted around the clock; soldiers were frequently sent out at a moment's notice on improvised patrols.[42] As Captain Gordon Crutcher mentioned from his tour in Italy, "the whole front must be kept under constant observation by trained personnel."[43] Sometimes several reconnoitering patrols would be sent out simultaneously, to keep the enemy confused and off balance, and to gather together more useful information at once.[44] Many officers complained that for their reconnoitering and fighting patrols they were not given adequate time to plan their patrol routes. Particularly at night, being able to move silently while following a predetermined route could mean the difference between making it home safely and being trapped behind enemy lines.[45] As enunciated by Captain Yuile, a platoon commander in Normandy, insufficient time to plan and study a patrol could lead to "many unnecessary casualties" or a patrol that "was not 100% successful."[46] But patrols were frequently sent out whether they were fully prepared or not.

The constitution of fighting patrols varied, as official doctrine made a point of giving officers latitude in this regard. Many preferred to carry out major patrolling actions in a fashion reminiscent of the large-scale trench raids from the First World War, which for all intents and purposes had been miniature pitched battles. Major G.P. Boucher of Le Régiment de la Chaudière wrote that fighting patrols were always of platoon strength, and supported by a full complement of artillery, mortar, and medium machine gun fire. Lieutenant-Colonel E.T. Jacques of Le Régiment de Maisonneuve wrote about a normal system of patrolling involving "several patrols of Company strength with [artillery] … [and] mortar support" for the purposes of grabbing German prisoners.[47] Similarly, Major D.S. Beatty wrote about patrols being "fired in" by at least two covering parties employing plenty of automatic fire to distract and harass the Germans so that "the actual [reconnoitering] party was only asked to show courage and determination for a few hundred yards, and NOT 1000 yards or more."[48] Major J.C. Allan of the Seaforth Highlanders likewise ordered patrols to go out armed to the teeth, with as many Bren machine-guns and sub-machine guns as possible, so as to be able to generate a hail of automatic weapons fire on a moment's notice.[49] And Major Thomas McCoy, in his questionnaire, angrily wrote that fighting patrols were never large enough (normally only ten all ranks) to take on even a small German defensive position, and that far too much stress was placed upon keeping a large proportion of bodies in the main position at all times.[50] On the other hand, some officers strongly advocated stealth, silence, and minimal numbers, even for fighting patrols. In contrast to Major McCoy, Major John Irvin Mills, operating in the same theatre, remarked that the size of some fighting patrols – such as entire companies being employed for the purpose – was grossly exaggerated and exceedingly difficult to control at night.[51] Company commander Major James Dandy advocated minimum-strength units for fighting patrols, and specialized tank-hunting patrols armed with PIATs.[52] Others suggested personal camouflage and specific training in stealthy movement, particularly at night, preferring to rely more on covertness than strength to accomplish an objective.[53] At least one officer integrated the two approaches, having soldiers from the scout platoon act as "guides" through hostile terrain for much larger fighting patrols.[54]

The various types and systems of patrolling being employed at any given time were strongly influenced by the peculiarities of the terrain, as well as the morale and strength of the enemy forces being probed or attacked. As the Royal Canadian Regiment's Major R.G. Liddell wrote, "No set rules [for patrolling] were found which would suit all situations," so the officers and NCOs leading the patrols had to be allowed maximum flexibility.[55] Most other officers who offered an opinion on the issue agreed: patrols that had been mandated at the battalion or brigade level seem to have sometimes been "too cut and dried," not allowing patrol leaders the opportunity to "use his own thoughts"; and much of the intelligence received from higher headquarters to plan patrols could be very inaccurate and far-removed from the actual operations.[56] It was preferred that patrol leaders and members be intelligent soldiers with plenty of initiative and ability to improvise should something go wrong.[57] There was a virtual consensus that more and continuous training was required, particularly for night patrols. The battle experience questionnaires also emphasized that, the soldiers would participate willingly in patrol activities, officers had to be explicit in laying out what their patrol objective was if they wanted to capitalize on that willingness.[58] As long as a definite task had been laid out for them, soldiers would usually patrol aggressively; if firm (and what would be considered "good") reasons could not be provided for why they should risk their lives even further by patrolling, then it became, as company commander Captain Thomas D. Murray wrote, extremely hard on men's nerves.[59] This was understandable, since casualties incurred on patrols could be heavy given that patrolling involved probing the enemy, often at night: dangers such as hidden mines and booby-traps were exacerbated, and the physical proximity to enemy positions was a mortal threat as well.[60] Canadian troops would stick their necks out if they believed there was a reason to do so, but were less inclined to put themselves at risk if they could not perceive the necessity. One can imagine that such orders had to be negotiated and renegotiated between officers and other ranks on a regular basis.

The patrol work done by Canadian units, though, seems to have been both effective and pervasive, particularly during the Italian campaign. As Major Harold Hudson Usher mentioned with some pride: "If we didn't patrol [then] the enemy did, but the Canadians did so much of it that enemy patrols were seldom out or encountered. Initiative can be maintained by dominating 'no man's land.'"[61] Other officers similarly reported that Canadians controlled all of the ground up to the German forward defensive line, and in doing so were able to keep the enemy in a constant state of confusion and indecision as to their movements and actions.[62] This was not universally regarded as a good thing: Major Liddell complained that "too much patrolling" by Canadians would drive the Germans to "hole up" in their defensive positions, and reduced the chance of capturing useful prisoners for interrogation.[63] Lieutenant-Colonel Gilday likewise wrote in his extensive notes that "Jerry did not patrol as much as we did" and was driven back to maintaining listening posts rather than actively patrolling in no-man's land.[64] The Canadians excelled at forcing German patrols out of disputed territory.

Since German doctrine called for aggressive patrolling to prevent the enemy from gaining the advantage of surprise, the Canadian ability to dominate the area in front of their lines reflects a policy of continuous reconnoitering and fighting patrols. In the Italian campaign in particular, the Canadians were able to impose their will upon the enemy during these skirmishes, frequently dominating no man's land and confining the Germans to their static defensive positions. In contrast, there is no mention in any of the infantry questionnaires of German patrol activity being particularly effective, despite the fact that the officer respondents were not shy about praising German tactical skill where they saw it. The Canadian ability to continuously mount and excel at smaller patrol actions implies tactical effectiveness on the part of the Canadian infantry, in a role where even large-scale raids demanded the soldiers' imagination and initiative. Canadian patrols were not always exceptionally proficient: they sustained heavy casualties, and patrols frequently went sour or failed to accomplish anything. When formations went into combat for the first time, they were less likely to mount effective patrols, particularly to guard themselves from enemy attack. But the overall impression from the questionnaire notes is that Canadian patrol work was competent and persistent in both theatres, and was normally more effective than German patrolling. This would seem to contradict some of the German sources, which sometimes disparaged the poor fighting qualities of Allied and Canadian soldiers at close quarters.[65] Regardless of the tactical flexibility exhibited by Canadian troops during formal set-piece attacks, their strength in undertaking difficult and dangerous patrol actions, reconnaissance, and raids suggests a reasonably high level of effectiveness at the platoon and section level.

NIGHT FIGHTING

Night fighting is another area that has received insufficient consideration in traditional accounts of the Canadian infantry's effectiveness in the Second World War. The battlefield vista was completely transformed at night; prior to the availability of useful night-vision technology, sunset left both sides blind, save for whatever moonlight or artificial lighting could be brought to bear. Tactics had to change; greater degrees of skill, initiative, and independence were required. The potential benefits of such operations, such as being able to move around the battlefield largely unobserved, were considerable. The battle experience questionnaires highlight the fact that Canadian soldiers undertook a great many operations using darkness as a cover, and that many companies achieved great tactical proficiency in night fighting. While a few set-piece offensives were mounted at night, the inherent difficulty of coordinating night actions involved patrolling, raiding, and infiltration attacks that could best take advantage of the darkness. Infantry units had to be quite tactically effective in order to execute successful operations after sunset.

Patrol and raid actions were frequently carried out at night to capitalize on the enemy's blindness. While some officers noted that patrols constituted their only night experience, many more wrote about larger engagements they had taken part in after sunset.[66] In reality, all sorts of Canadian operations were launched at night, or had an H-hour before sunrise, and a huge majority of officers took part in such actions. According to their battle experience questionnaire answers, about 88 percent of respondents indicated that their unit had taken part in night operations, and only 10 percent claimed that they had not.[67] Officers in Italy were notably more likely (92 %) to have engaged in night operations than those in Northwest Europe (85 %).[68] Of those who indicated having taken part in such actions, an even higher percentage counted them as having been "effective" (93.8 % in the Mediterranean, and 90.5 % in Northwest Europe).[69] Night actions were a major component of Canadian Army operations, and, by the officers' own reckoning, were normally highly successful.

Beyond the statistics, operating at night could take a number of different forms, depending upon the unit. Major William Ewing noted that while he had never taken part in a set-piece battle at night, he had nevertheless still commanded frequent major night operations on the

company-scale.[70] Platoons, companies, and battalions were also frequently re-positioned at night. The Calgary Highlanders' Captain R.D.
Bacon wrote of an experience toward the end of the war during Operation BLOCKBUSTER inside Germany: his unit, moving stealthily by night,
arrived at its objectives on the edge of the Hochwald Forest and surprised
the enemy by showing up right on top of them at first light.[71] Major
M.B. John mentioned a river-crossing in Italy at night, which featured
heavy support: the whole Corps artillery bombarded German positions
on the opposing bank while the Royal Canadian Regiment's crossing was
underway, ultimately driving the Germans back.[72] A number of other
units undertook major night operations that could be accurately described as "set-pieces," complete with timed artillery barrages and tanks
in support, though such actions required exceptionally meticulous planning and had a high probability of descending into chaos. Captain S.R.
Lambert of the South Saskatchewan Regiment remembered that in the
night attack on Rocquancourt, just south of Caen in Normandy, the
action was heavily scripted: "[a] well laid artillery barrage, timed to the
minute forward [companies] would enter town, and the quick positioning of anti-tank guns, mortars and carrier [platoon]" in consolidation
positions. Lambert attributed their success, and their low casualties, to
the artillery support and the soldiers' confidence in it, though other historical accounts of that action give total credit to the South Saskatchewan
troops themselves.[73] Lieutenant-Colonel Gilday reported having many
successful experiences with set-piece night attacks, and went so far as to
say: "In a set piece attack against known enemy defense, if your troops
are well trained in night work it is much better to attack at night without tanks than by day. This is particularly so in mountains where the
enemy is looking down on you ... At night the enemy is blind. You know
where he is, he does not know where you are. You suffer fewer casualties
and have more success in night fighting than in day against known enemy
positions."[74] However, John Campbell, also of the Calgary Highlanders,
wrote about another night attack in Normandy against May-sur-Orne
which was less successful, owing to the disorientation of the soldiers
milling about in the dark, and one company stumbling into a barrage of
friendly artillery fire.[75]

More likely to be attempted at night than full set-piece attacks, however, were infiltration attacks, where soldiers would move swiftly through

enemy lines and cut through along the lines of least resistance, bypassing strong-points in order to infiltrate vulnerable areas. The battle experience questionnaires indicate that Canadians deserve credit for frequent night infiltration actions, both for patrols and for major attacks on enemy lines.[76] Major John Clarke wrote that his unit, engaged in northwest Ortona in December 1943, used "stealth and good direction" at night to infiltrate "through enemy lines to hill overlooking enemy's only escape route from Ortona," effectively cutting the Germans off. He reported that they inflicted serious casualties on the Germans with mortars and small-arms fire once in position, and that on the way they managed such stealth and surprise that they captured twenty Germans enjoying Christmas parcels in their houses.[77] Similarly, Captain William Bennett's FSSF company, fighting in southern France in August of 1944, used the cover of darkness and the most rugged, heavily-wooded terrain they could find to slip around and through German defences, managing to occupy a small town "before Jerry was alerted." Although fierce fighting erupted during the day, "the Jerries were confused and hence disorganized" by the movement, and ended up taking "several hundred" casualties, including fifty-nine from snipers alone, for very few FSSF casualties.[78] Admittedly the FSSF was an elite unit and under American command, but even normal Canadian troops proved quite capable of conducting infiltration attacks. These techniques were reported to be quite good for quietly surrounding German tanks – which were normally deployed as portable pillboxes – and bringing infantry anti-tank weapons such as the PIAT to bear against their vulnerable areas, which Allied tanks had difficulty reaching by day.[79] Major Liddell likewise emphasized how the darkness, combined with an absolute silence of movement, could confuse and severely demoralize the enemy, as did strict fire discipline (discussed later) and infiltrating movements.[80] Of course, operating at night did not always mean avoiding close combat; sometimes it resulted in quite the opposite. Major Roy Styffe described a mad-dash night infiltration attack on enemy high ground in the Hochwald Forest which left his company engaged in a "horrific" twelve-hour firefight with the Germans until sunrise, when they finally seized the objective.[81]

Night operations of course had their drawbacks and underlying dangers. When employing infiltration at night, or at least exclusively at night, it could be extremely difficult for follow-up units to "clear" or "mop-up" an area with any certainty in the darkness; sometimes the bypassed enemy could cut off the lead formations if they were not dealt with.[82] Many officers noted severe, and very understandable, difficulties with the command and control of troops at night, which at its worst could result in a diffusion of effort and rampant confusion among the attackers. Mutual support between companies also became impossible to coordinate, placing a premium upon independent section and platoon actions.[83] A widespread "fear of the dark" among both officers and other ranks could also be a major stumbling block, as Captain Donald Smith noted.[84] To counter these difficulties, extensive and very specific training was needed, and the questionnaire respondents stressed that it was the key to success at night. As Captain Maclean put it: "Since much of our work in action was done at night, I would suggest that training in night operations and in movement at night is vitally important. Night patrols were quite frequent in Italy, and in these it is essential both to move silently and to be able to follow a predetermined route unerringly."[85] There were, however, serious problems with that training, and a surprising discrepancy existed between theatres on this matter. Asked in their questionnaires whether or not their units had received special training in night operations prior to engaging in them, less than 24 percent from Northwest Europe answered "yes," and 74 percent answered "no." In contrast, officers who had served in Sicily and Italy noted that they had received considerably more training: 53 percent of respondents from the Mediterranean theatre of operations answered "yes," and only 37 percent answered "no."[86] Many officers who mentioned the problems of night operations recommended increased training as a remedy, particularly for nighttime navigation with map and compass, and for obtaining an intimate knowledge of the ground prior to heading into it blindly. Captain Smith blamed "laziness" in training officers and NCOs tasked to teach night fighting, who normally had a fear of night training themselves.[87]

If there were systemic problems in securing relevant, quality training for soldiers engaged in night operations, however, they seem to have been largely overcome by experience in the field. In Northwest Europe, even though fewer than a quarter of the officers indicated that their units had received special training in nighttime actions, most units undertook night operations regularly and only a slim minority of officers believed that they had been ineffective. That Canadian soldiers worked well at night seems beyond question; while many, according to Captain Tennant, did not enjoy it, they nonetheless did it willingly, recognizing its efficiency. Tennant also noted that "the Germans as a rule did not like night work, and cracked easily" during night battles.[88] While such generalizations defy universal applicability, the evidence from the questionnaires suggests a measure of Canadian tactical proficiency in night operations, which by their very nature combined the need for careful planning and training with the need for initiative and quick-thinking when plans started to go astray in the darkness.

SMALL ARMS EFFECTIVENESS

A further major objective of the battle experience questionnaire project was to determine the battlefield use and usefulness of infantry small arms employed by the Commonwealth armies. The general survey and the specific infantry survey together contain five question groups dealing specifically with small arms and crew-served weapons use, as well as an explicit invitation for officers to attach additional notes on the best weapons for an infantry section and any novel applications that they had developed or observed.[89] The questions about weapon use were among the most prominent and asked which were used or not used, which were effective and had the most impact upon soldiers' morale, and even which weapons were being used *against* the Canadians by the enemy forces. Officer respondents offered commentary on the problems of small arms use in their attached notes, highlighting in particular the useful weapons and the ones that were found wanting or were simply not used at all. Given the emphasis upon these questions in the original survey, and their relevance to the issues of infantry effectiveness, the evidence from the questionnaires is worth consulting.

The statistics on weapons use, based upon the survey data, is of special interest, and is in line with the portrait of combat being developed in this chapter. Two questions on the battle experience questionnaires deal directly with these points: question #1 on infantry survey "H" asks which weapons were used by the officer's unit in battle, and question #1 on general survey "A" discusses weapons used by the Germans *against* the Canadians and their effects upon morale. Virtually every officer respondent answered at least these two questions; only five left them blank. In infantry survey "H," which asked about the weapons "actually used in action," almost every officer reported use of the Rifle (153 surveys), the sub-machine gun (149 surveys), and the Bren light machine-gun (152 surveys). The PIAT (141 surveys), 2-inch and 3-inch Mortars (139 and 140 surveys respectively), and the 6-Pounder anti-tank gun (125 surveys) were also extensively used.[90] Grenades, particularly the No. 36 fragmentation grenade, also known as the "Mills bomb," were also widely reported to have seen use (142 surveys), offering a stark contrast to S.L.A. Marshall's observations that grenades were almost never used by soldiers.[91]

Perhaps the most informative aspects of the questionnaires on the topic of weapon use are the questions relating to the effectiveness, or lack thereof, of small arms. Question #2 on survey "H"-Infantry asked officers whether any of the infantry weapons they had witnessed used in action had been "outstandingly effective," and question #3 asked the same thing about weapons being "ineffective." While the answers should not be interpreted as concrete statistics on small arms use in battle, they do offer some perspective on Canadian soldiers' use of their weapons in combat. These numbers should be taken for what they are: the general impressions of men in battle, not definitive, rigorous statistics on small arms and crew-served weapons. Nonetheless, given that the surveys were filled out by officers who had personally fought, and had commanded and observed other soldiers doing the same, the level of reliability of these impressions is likely quite high.

Not every officer wrote about a particular weapon being especially effective or ineffective in battle; those who did illustrate varying, some-times contradictory experiences with weapons' effectiveness. However, a few patterns stand out from a study of the surveys. The PIAT was listed in seventy-four surveys as being "outstandingly effective" far more than any other weapon.[92] Its effectiveness was due not only to its tank-killing role, but also to the fact that its high-explosive bomb could be put to uncon-ventional good use against "soft" infantry targets, either in direct or indi-rect roles, making it a good source of suppressing fire.[93] Furthermore, only three officers listed the PIAT as being an "ineffective" weapon. Weapons that could produce significant fire effects or high volumes of fire tended to be selected as "outstandingly effective" on this question. Next in line in order of effectiveness were the Bren light machine-gun (54 surveys), the 3-inch Mortar (44 surveys), the No. 36 "Mills bomb" grenade (33 surveys), and the standard-issue rifle (15 surveys). Officers indicated their confidence in the reliability, consistency, and volume of small arms fire being generated by their troops.

Perhaps more notable is the reaction of many officers to the perceived "ineffective" weapons. Officers typically listed weapons as "ineffective" for at least one of three reasons: mechanical difficulties inherent in the weapon, a perceived lack of "stopping power" on the weapon's part, or the troops' lack of confidence in the weapon leading to lack of use. The Sten sub-machine gun, for example, received over one-third of all complaints: forty-five officers listed the Sten as "ineffective," while sixty-seven officers complained about all other weapons combined.[94] Mechanically, the Sten was regarded as one of the least reliable weapons available to Canadian troops. Lieutenant-Colonel P.W. Bennett noted the Sten as ineffective: "due to liability to jam due to dirt, troops have no confidence in it"; and Major Cyril Wrightman reported that in his experience troops and officers threw their Stens away in favour of American-made automatic weapons. "Never very safe," Wrightman said of the Sten; "will let you down when most needed."[95] "Failure to fire when needed (frequent)," was Captain F.W. Grafton's comment on the Sten.[96] Many other Canadian officers noted the mechanical unreliability of the Sten, and a number also reported that the weapon did not have sufficient killing power, particularly when compared to the sub-machine guns available to the other Allied armies. "Not enough stopping power," reported Captain Orest Dutchak of the Algonquin Regiment, who went on to say that the American "Thompson Sub[-machine gun was] preferred."[97] Captain Tennant likewise claimed that, in his experience, the Sten was "NOT hard enough hitting," and that a "man can still fight after being hit" by the Sten.[98] Major Ostiguy pointed out the same thing about the lack of killing power, noting that the Sten was so widely mistrusted that "men preferred rifles."[99]

The officers gave detailed reports about other weapons that they found to be ineffective, though the Sten sub-machine gun was far and away considered the least usable weapon, and the rest varied considerably according to individual experience. For instance, Captain A.D. Willick, discussing the 6-pounder anti tank gun, noted: "[It] is only effective when right up with the [forward companies] and this is not always possible. Some 6-pounder crews fire very few if any rounds in action."[100] The No. 69 fragmentation grenade, which had been specifically designed to be less destructive than the popular No. 36, was derided by some officers for being a "useless weapon, [with] no killing power," and was simply "not lethal."[101] The officers' standard-issue .38 calibre pistol was also treated with a degree of scorn. It was the second-most frequently mentioned weapon for "ineffectiveness" in the surveys after the Sten, incurring twenty officer complaints, and seems generally to have been judged of "no use" in combat, and largely ceremonial.[102]

Relatively few weapons were considered to be uniformly ineffective, and even the Sten gun was listed as ineffective by fewer than one-third of all responding officers. It was more common for officers to note things such as: "All weapons are outstandingly effective when used properly [and] in the right circumstances."[103] What these surveys tell us, however, is that when weapons were ineffective in combat, for any reason – persistent mechanical issues, a lack of killing power, or simple disuse – Canadian officers noticed. With the notable exception of the Sten sub-machine gun and a few other weapons with which officers had individual problems, there is no indication at all of systemic weapon ineffectiveness or any general failure on the part of soldiers to make adequate use of their weapons. Fire from rifles and Bren light machine-guns, the most common weapons, was frequently described as "consistent, useful in all types of operations," "accurate and dependable," and having "great killing power."[104] The standard-issue infantry rifles were not among the top-ranked weapons for "outstanding effectiveness," according to the officer respondents, but no complaint was registered that rifles were thought to be "ineffective." They seem to have been a reliable weapon, whose use was typically efficient enough for most combat purposes. Even so, several officers did note that the rifle was particularly effective in battle. Major A.M. Hamilton made special note of his troops' skill with them: "Men [are] good shots, feel confident with rifle. Deadly accurate, made any enemy movement risky."[105] The rifle and the Bren gun were both singled out by Major Liddell as being effective in combat due to the "Shoot to kill attitude of t[roo]ps with good [fire discipline] training."[106] The rifle's accuracy and killing power were noted by several others, and while the weapon may not have been terribly glamorous, there is every indication that Canadian riflemen used them to satisfactory effect in battle.[107] That it was favoured by many officers over the automatic Sten gun, which could generate much higher volumes of fire when functioning correctly, is also noteworthy. As the standard-issue weapon of any infantry rifle company, the .303 calibre rifle was the most pervasive weapon in the Canadian Army; any systemic failure on the part of troops to make adequate use of it for mechanical, ballistic, or moral reasons would have been mentioned in the questionnaires. The lack of any such complaints, in conjunction with the many other comments on Canadian small arms effectiveness, strongly suggests that the officers did not perceive any notable difficulties with the firepower that their companies and platoons could generate.

In addition, the staple infantry heavy weapons all received considerable praise from the officers for their battlefield performance. Weapons that could produce large volumes of fire were typically well received, as were weapons that had lots of "killing effect" or a decisive impact upon the enemy's morale. The Bren light machine gun was noted as an "outstandingly effective" weapon by fifty-four officers. It was highly accurate, and several officers commented favourably on its "beaten zone," the area around it that could effectively be covered by its firepower.[108] Others, including Major Norman Wilson-Smith of the Royal Winnipeg Rifles, noted that the Bren was "accurate and if used well could 'shoot down' German [machine guns]," suppressing them as part of fire-and-movement actions.[109] Another officer wrote that his Bren guns were "effective [because] of handiness at close quarters + volumes of fire."[110] Sub-machine guns in general, though rarely the Sten specifically, were highly regarded for many of the same reasons. Captain Edward Brady praised the U.S.-issued Thompson sub-machine gun as having "great killing power, dependability, [and the effect of] lowering … enemy morale."[111] Flame throwers, though employed infrequently by the Canadians, were reportedly devastating to enemy morale: and were noted for their "good moral effect," their ability to "knock out the [enemy's] will to fight," and their deterent effect: "very effective and terrifying when properly used."[112] Grenades, particularly the No. 36 "Mills bomb," were also considered highly effective. Thirty-three officers found the No. 36 fragmentation grenade "outstandingly effective," highlighting it as one of the "essential" infantry arms and praising the grenade's "killing effect and faith of men in [the] weapon."[113]

While some individuals complainted about certain weapons, they represented less than 5 percent of responders for all but a select few armaments, such as the Sten gun or the .38 calibre pistol. No other weapons seemed to be particularly troublesome or useless in the Canadian experience.[114] Officers were either extremely pleased with the fire and killing effects of the small arms available to their troops, or else they were sufficiently satisfied with (or ambivalent toward) them not to believe they warranted comment either way. The officers as a group of respondents tended to be remarkably consistent in how they regarded weapon effectiveness: no weapon ranked as being "outstandingly effective" was cited as "ineffective" by more than two or three officers.[115] Weapons that were effective were, by and large, regarded as such across all the infantry officers being surveyed.

Significant comments also appear in the officers' addendum notes in response to the questionnaire's specific request to attach additional comments on the subject of the best infantry section weapons. Dozens of officers replied to this particular question, and while many had negative comments about the Sten gun, and occasionally about other weapons, the great majority indicated that they found the weapons carried by their infantry rifle sections to be "adequate," "satisfactory," and "effective."[116] "Infantry weapons," commented Captain Yuile, "are sufficient and very effective. The PIAT as we learnt by bitter experience should *always* be carried by platoon."[114] Recalling an episode at Ortona in Italy, Major John Clarke mentioned that his "Battalion [was] cut off and surrounded for 48 hrs. by paratroopers. [We] beat off several attacks by good use of infantry weapons, and [the] determination of [our] men."[118] Captain Leonard James Gouten of the Royal Canadian Regiment also commented that the weapons of the infantry section were "ideal for close-quarters + hand-to-hand fighting, easy to control – but for [company] attacks, additional men would give greater fire-power, especially for the fire [platoons] covering the attacking [platoons]."[119] And Captain Edward Maxted, also of the Royal Canadian Regiment, wrote that the weapons used and firepower produced were "quite adequate ... to meet any circumstances or situation."[120] The addendum comments on the surveys confirm the other data on weapons use and effectiveness: while a few officers had complaints about individual weapons (usually the Sten) most who took the time to comment expressed complete satisfaction with the effectiveness of the weapons and fire of their soldiers.

THE PROBLEM OF THE REPLACEMENT SOLDIER

While the battle experience questionnaires demonstrate the general tactical flexibility and capabilities of Canadian infantry, they also address a major problem that Canadian rifle companies faced. The losses sustained by infantry units in combat during the Second World War were appalling, and frequently equalled losses from equivalent stretches of time during the First World War. Casualties could easily exceed 100 percent of a unit's original numerical strength. The Calgary Highlanders battalion, which suffered more infantrymen killed and wounded than any other Canadian infantry battalion in Northwest Europe, began the Normandy campaign with an establishment size of 817 officers and men, and by May 1945 it had suffered 403 killed in action and 1,354 wounded, a casualty rate in excess of 200 percent. To keep the battalion at fighting strength, some 3,220 reinforcement soldiers joined it in the course of the campaign.[121] Every infantry battalion in the Canadian Army encountered a similar problem, and faced adversity caused by the lack of administrative foresight in planning for casualties on this scale. Although pre-Normandy casualty projections were reasonably accurate, all of the Western Allies woefully underestimated the disproportionate burden of killing and dying that would fall upon the infantry, and had overestimated casualties for other arms, including the Armoured Corps and anti-aircraft gunners. C.P. Stacey noted that the wrong lessons had been taken from earlier campaigns in North Africa and not enough attention had been paid to the more telling Italian experience, so that by late 1944 too many reinforcements had been prepared for artillery, armour, and support units, and far too few to sustain modern infantry combat.[122]

In order to compensate for the casualties and rapidly rebuild depleted infantry battalions, the training of reinforcement soldiers – who were parcelled out individually rather than deployed as part of the units they had trained with – necessarily became rushed, starting in the summer of 1944. To make good the shortfalls in infantrymen, soldiers from over-manned supporting arms (particularly the anti-aircraft artillerymen, who had very little to do in 1944) were put through rapid "re-allocation" programs and retrained as infantrymen.

While such measures, along with the eventual deployment of conscripted soldiers overseas, allowed Canada to sustain its infantry battalions at something resembling fighting strength through to the end of the war, they came at a price. Some of the bitterest and most pronounced complaints made by officers in the battle experience questionnaires were related to the poor quality of the men who were being sent to them as replacement soldiers. Few had flattering things to say about the degree of training that these soldiers received prior to being deployed to active infantry units, or about their fighting skills or efficiency. Several officers commented that the reinforcements – many of whom had been re-allocated and were doubtless none too pleased with this fact – generally lacked the will to fight. Although these remarks on reinforcements can be somewhat exaggerated, as Terry Copp has suggested, the questionnaires still highlight the replacement soldier problem as one of the most significant facing Canadian officers during the worst of the war's fighting. The respondents' comments to this effect therefore deserve our attention.

The Canadian infantry officers surveyed for the questionnaires clearly understood that the combat effectiveness of their units was seriously undermined by the heavy casualties they sustained in battle. Data from the surveys show that over 81 percent of the officer respondents reported having had infantry sections under their command go into battle under-strength due to combat losses. The numbers were roughly the same in the different campaigns, but were slightly higher for the Mediterranean theatre of operations (almost 83 %) than for Northwest Europe (80.8 %).[123] Clearly, there was recognition of the overall problem, although with the Canadian Army's losses (10,000 soldiers killed, wounded, and missing between 20 September and 7 November 1944 alone), the greater surprise would be if this problem was *not* widely reflected in the surveys. Given that Canadian infantry sections, the smallest formal level of combat organization, were endemically under-strength, the size of these sections was often greatly reduced out of necessity.[124] Many officers believed that the combat effectiveness of infantry sections was compromised as a direct result. In the surveys, 31 percent of responding officers noted that these under-strength infantry sections were not adequate for close-quarters fighting; the number was somewhat lower (26 %) in the Mediterranean, and slightly higher (33 %) in Northwest Europe.[125] The impact of heavy casualties was in part responsible for the uneven effectiveness of the army, as battalions frequently had to be rotated out of combat and be "rebuilt" with reinforcements when their losses began to detract from the ability of the unit to achieve its objectives, or even to function.

Unfortunately, the replacement soldiers brought in to help rebuild Canadian units were not highly regarded by the officers, and this attitude, according to the questionnaires, was widespread. The surveys included a question about the efficiency of "casualty replacement" soldiers, allowing answers of "High," "Moderate," or "Low." Only a small proportion of officers (5 %) rated the quality of their casualty replacements as high; this number was somewhat higher in the Sicilian and Italian campaigns (8 %) than in the Northwest Europe campaign (4 %).[126] The majority of officers rated reinforcements as being of "moderate" efficiency, although here a greater disparity between the two theatres existed. In the Mediterranean 65 percent of officers rated their replacement soldiers as "moderate" and only 16 percent as low, whereas in Northwest Europe 57 percent of officers chose moderate and 32 percent rated replacements as being low quality soldiers.[127] These evaluations no doubt reflect the reinforcement crisis, which was a function of the much higher casualty numbers in Northwest Europe (if only because of the greater scope of Canadian deployment there). Casualties in the Mediterranean, at least up to late 1944, were sustainable for the Canadian Army with its normal infantry replacement system; the casualties became overwhelming in Northwest Europe when the entire First Canadian Army was committed to action, and reinforcements had to be scavenged from unorthodox places and moved through training more rapidly than before. The quality, it seems, went down. Across all theatres replacement soldiers were only rarely regarded with complete satisfaction; usually they were regarded as merely adequate, and at worst as unfit for combat.

Officers who assessed the reinforcements in their addendum notes tended to take an unforgiving view of their personal qualities. As many of the "green" soldiers were re-allocated to the infantry from other supporting branches of the army, such as logistics, signals, or artillery, one of the most recurring and damning complaints had to do with their physical condition. "Reallocated troops were NOT hard physically," complained Major Thomas McCoy of the Essex Scottish Regiment. "They did NOT know the tremendous capabilities of the human body. They had NOT been taught hardships – did NOT know how to look after feet. Wanted to quit."[128] Captain Yuile observed much the same thing: "The physical condition of reinforcements generally speaking was poor and remustered personnel were unable to stand up to long marches and be expected to fight efficiently."[129] Major Carmichael, who fought in the same battalion as Yuile, remembered that "reinforcements that came to us in large numbers in August/September were [artillery] personnel and these men were willing – even determined – but they were *not* up to infantry standards in infantry work ... we nearly liquidated the lot by marching them 60 to 70 miles."[130] Captain W. Parker of the Royal Hamilton Light Infantry had a few words to say about the infantry reinforcements his company had received: "More care could be taken in sending men as reinforcements to an infantry [battalion]. Men who have spent all their time as clerks, or in other sedentary occupations, should be given more physical training in holding units. One man was received with a medical category under which was written "Unfit for marching" or words to that effect. No doubt this man could be used elsewhere, but not in a rifle [company] ... One poorly conditioned reinforcement can ruin a good section."[131]

Even though not every officer in the Sicilian and Italian campaigns rated their reinforcements highly, almost all the written complaints specifically about replacement soldiers' poor physical condition came from officers serving in Northwest Europe. Such complaints are in evidence even among officers who filled out their questionnaires after being wounded in Normandy as early as July and August 1944. The reinforcement problem was evidently being felt at the front long before it developed into a major crisis back in Ottawa.

While their not physically being able to keep up was a major hindrance, soldiers who were also not properly trained as infantrymen were a serious hazard. Too many reinforcements, many respondents believed, came to their units with little to no practical infantry training, particularly the re-allocated personnel. Captain Pariseault, fighting in Italy with Le Royal 22e Régiment, bitterly complained that some reinforcements "were ill-trained ... had never thrown a live grenade or fired a Tommy gun."[132] The Calgary Highlanders' Major Harrison likewise noted: "Many tradesmen were being used as straight riflemen [reinforcements] ... in many cases they knew very little or nothing about the PIAT and the Bren."[133] Major Carmichael added to his comments: "[Reinforcements] were unfamiliar with the PIAT, inexpert with the Bren, in many cases afraid of grenades ... In my opinion, unnecessary casualties were caused by their unfamiliarity with [infantry] weapons."[134] Lieutenant-Colonel E.T. Jacques also complained about a lack of weapons-handling skills among incoming reinforcements, and went as far as to say: "Some had absolutely no infantry training of any kind."[135]

More worrying than even a lack of weapons' skills, which could be learned, was the further perception that some reinforcements were unwilling to fight. Major Jock McLeod, fighting with the Algonquin Regiment, had a particularly penetrating indictment: "Reinforcements coming into battle, at first do not seem to realize that before one side can win there must be a fight. They never seem to be ready to start that fight."[136] Some officers noted that replacement infantrymen were poorly versed in battle procedures; in the assault, for example, many reinforcement soldiers would refuse to go forward ahead of the tanks, a normal mode of operation for the Canadian infantry.[137] Reinforcements who had been reallocated from other arms, according to both Major James Dandy and Captain Gordon A. Crutcher, "generally were in a poor mental condition" and were more likely to sustain heavy casualties, both physical and mental.[138] Some officers portrayed the reinforcements they received as extremely problematic, and reported that this issue became more pervasive and damaging the longer the war went on, as reinforcements were "poorer with each new draft."[139]

We must, however, consider a caveat. As historians C.P. Stacey and Terry Copp have both written, it is "a notorious fact of army life that no commanding officer ever admits that the reinforcements his unit receives have been properly trained," so there is a possibility that the negative comments on reinforcements may be unfair.[140] They were certainly balanced by positive comments on reinforcements. While no respondents made any comments praising the specific skills or abilities of their replacement soldiers, many suggested that even poor-quality reinforcements were better than none. Given the constant manpower wastage and attrition in front-line infantry units, there were, according to Major F.J. Hammond's Mediterranean experience, never sufficient reinforcements; rifle companies were constantly under-strength.[141] Captain Parker, reporting on his experiences in Normandy in July and August 1944, mentioned his observation that the men of his rifle company were in fact always eager for reinforcements, and that the lack of replacements was a constant topic of conversation and source of discontent. Although Parker, too, made negative comments about the quality of the reinforcements his unit received, he ended his survey on a positive note: "However, even poorly trained reinforcements were better for morale than no reinforcements at all."[142] Soldiers felt – and rightly so – that their risk of becoming a casualty was greater when the strength of their company, platoon, and section was severely compromised. In contrast to his disparaging comments on infantry replacements, Major Carmichael noted that officer replacements were of adequate quality, but that most units suffered from a want of good NCOs, probably a side effect of the best enlisted men being skimmed off the top to be commissioned as officers.[143] In answering questions on the survey relating to morale, twelve different officers listed the arrival of reinforcements, fully trained or not, as being one of the greatest morale boosters among the troops.[144]

In all, a considerable range of opinions was profferred on the reinforcement issue, but the battle experience questionnaires reflect predominantly negative or ambivalent attitudes toward the capabilities of those replacement soldiers. Although it is difficult to generalize from these results, where opinions in the surveys were given on reinforcements, they were clearly quite negative. This is perhaps to be expected. No matter how well trained, reinforcements who had never seen actual battle before could not be expected to hold up as well as the more experienced men in the units they were joining. Whether the reinforcements were as badly trained, or as completely untrained as some officers alleged, it would have taken time, learning, and experience to integrate replacements into an existent fighting unit. Chances are good that they would seem ineffective to some infantry commanders, if only by comparison.

At the least, it can be said that reinforcement soldiers represented a source of ineffectiveness to the Canadian infantry in that green soldiers with no battle experience were being parcelled into shattered fighting units, and would have to gain their experience the hard way. The alternative, though – that units *not* receive reinforcements but carry on the fight anyway – was simply not acceptable. While many officers expressed concern about the fighting qualities of the replacements they received, comments to that effect were in the minority, and the majority of respondents gave no indication of strong feelings about the training or abilities of the incoming manpower. Concerns about the lack of meaningful training being given to some replacements were likely legitimate, given the scale and cobbled-together nature of the Canadian Army's reinforcement system, but these were not the rule. Replacements were normally of adequate quality in relation to the infantrymen they were joining in the line.

An American study on combat psychology after the Second World War, carried out by Samuel Stouffer and his team, makes an interesting point about combat replacements. Stouffer's study was based on surveys of American GIs who were asked to identify combat errors frequently made by replacements. "Shooting before they are able to see their target" was perceived as an error far more prevalent in replacements than other contrasting errors such as "freezing" or "not being aggressive enough in combat." The psychologists commented: "Shooting before they are able to see their target, or being 'trigger happy,' is usually interpreted as a sign of improperly controlled anticipatory anxiety or nervousness, which was of course high among replacements." The study further indicated that "seasoned combat men made all these errors much less frequently."[145] In other words, excessive anticipatory firing of weapons was common in green soldiers; more experienced fighters knew the value of disciplining their fire. That survey was taken by American fighting men, of course, so we cannot automatically generalize to the Canadian experience. However, it serves as indirect evidence that Allied replacement soldiers made more errors simply because of their inexperience than veteran fighters, and that one of those errors may have been a tendency to fire off their weapons to panicked excess.

TOO MUCH FIRE AND NOT ENOUGH

The historical problem of how many soldiers in a given group would fire their weapons in battle has tantalized many who engage in discussions of military effectiveness: S.L.A. Marshall's "discovery" of the ratio of fire among American troops during the Second World War has prompted some historians and military analysts to regard this ratio as an accurate measure of a military force's success. Such a crude calculation of effectiveness is distasteful to some, since, as Roger Spiller put it in his famous critique of Marshall, it is "too frail a vessel to bear the weight of explaining a soldier's conduct in combat."[146] Unfortunately, this "crude vessel" has since served as a major theoretical underpinning for historical accounts of the Second World War (and other conflicts), particularly accounts that emphasize the ineffectiveness of American or Allied armies. As mentioned in chapter 1, until now very little primary documentary evidence has been available to either buttress or disprove Marshall's claims. The Canadian battle experience questionnaires, on the other hand, contain a wealth of first-hand tactical information that firmly addresses many unanswered questions about Marshall's ratio of fire from the Canadian perspective. A substantial amount of evidence about the application of firepower is contained in the questionnaires, and, given how privileged Marshall's argument has become in the historiography of the Second World War, it is important that this evidence be brought to the debate.

There is no "magic bullet" that proves or disproves Marshall's ratio of fire in one tidy document, and there almost certainly never will be. The questionnaires indicate, however, that Marshall's concern that not enough soldiers were making use of their firearms was not shared by Canadian officers who led their soldiers into battle; no mention is made in any infantry questionnaire of low volumes of small arms fire.[147] When any comments at all on the volume of fire produced by Canadian soldiers was offered, it was always to complain of too much firing of weapons, rather than not enough.

The battle experience questionnaires confirm that one of the most noteworthy difficulties facing Canadian officers was getting soldiers to *stop* firing, not getting them to start in the first place; many officers expressed concern that their troops were making excessive use of their weapons. Captain Bennett of the FSSF, for instance, commented: "Many people seem to favour too unreasoningly automatic fire in lieu of well-aimed rifle shots." Heavy automatic fire, he warned, quickly betrayed one's position to the enemy, allowing it to be singled out and destroyed. "The clever rifleman," he offered in contrast, "is difficult to discover and his careful shooting will demoralize the enemy."[148] Major C.K. Crummer, a company commander in the Lincoln and Welland Regiment, noted that his troops often took to "indiscriminate, very inaccurate firing of inf[antry] weapons to impress large numbers of enemy troops opposing them."[149] Enemies that troops could not visibly identify were often the cause of excessive, panicky fire. Major T.M. Lowe of the Cape Breton Highlanders wrote of an occasion at the crossing of the Liri River in Italy, when a few hidden German snipers were impeding the bridging process by picking off engineers. Six Bren machine gunners emptied multiple magazines worth of ammunition on the snipers' "general location" to try to flush them out.[150] Rampant "speculative shooting" was also noted by Captain Sinkewicz, an intelligence officer who carried out post-combat interviews with troops; and it was particularly evident when the Germans would counterattack a position that had just been taken by the Canadians, when close combat was likely and fire support from tanks and artillery was inconsistent.[151] As discussed earlier, laying down heavy fire was characteristic of some patrol actions; many officers reported that patrolling soldiers loaded up on automatic weapons to increase their organic firepower.[152] The tendency for patrols to lay down heavy fire could get Canadians into trouble, however: Captain Robert Mainprize commented in frustration that patrols would often get stuck exchanging fire with enemy machine-gun outposts, rather than try to find a different way to infiltrate or work around the strong-point.[153] Infantrymen were also sometimes very liberal when firing anti-tank weapons such as the PIAT, whose high-explosive bombs were frequently employed as suppressing fire against German infantry positions regardless of whether enemy tanks were around.[154]

Canadian soldiers would go to considerable lengths to ensure that they could generate sufficient volumes of fire on the battlefield, acquiring additional guns for themselves and making certain that their weapons would be ready for combat at any time. Major C.K. Crummer observed that his troops would try to salvage extra Bren guns from wrecked carriers, though he noted with concern: "[A] very close eye must be kept on ammunition in this respect."[155] Captain F.W. Grafton of the Algonquin Regiment noticed the same thing, commenting: "I saw one Platoon carrying four [Bren] guns and the [required] ammo for each even though [the platoon] was under-strength by seven men."[156] In a slightly different vein, Major A.M. Hamilton of the Stormont, Dundas and Glengarry Highlanders noted that his troops were constantly "zeroing" (adjusting the sights on) their rifles: "Even in battle area zeroing was carried on, two or three men at a time. Made all the difference to a man's confidence in the weapon to know it was zeroed."[157] Archived correspondence regarding the Courts of Inquiry held by the Calgary Highlanders Regiment in Northwest Europe indicated that friendly-fire shooting accidents, particularly at night, were relatively frequent. Commenting on an incident when a soldier was shot by his own rifle after leaving the rifle cocked and the safety catch off, the Calgaries' Lieutenant-Colonel Ellis noted: "Men who have fought in action leave the safety catches on their rifles off, due to the need for immediate actions, on many occasions. The accident was apparently caused due to this habit."[158] Having weapons ready for instant action on the front lines was evidently common enough for such accidental casualties to be seen as routine. The Calgaries' Courts of Inquiry also discussed incidents of sentries being over-zealous in using their weapons, and inflicting casualties on friendly troops who did not respond quickly enough to verbal challenges.[159]

Regardless of Marshall's claims, constant firing and the production of a large volume of fire was not always a positive force on the battlefield; when not controlled and directed properly, such shooting, as Captain

Bennett warned, could betray one's position and was seen as a terrible waste of ammunition. Ammunition shortages were not an inconsequential matter. In his book *The Soldier's Load and the Mobility of the Nation* Marshall declared that, due to the low ratio of fire in the Second World War, ammunition shortages practically never occurred in battle.[160] However, during the Northwest Europe campaign in particular, supply shortages were far more acute among the Allied armies than he acknowledged. The failure to open up the port of Antwerp meant that the torrent of supplies necessary to keep over fifty Allied divisions in France on the offensive had slowed to a trickle, as supplies had to come through the inadequate Normandy beachhead.[161] Fuel and ammunition were at times in particularly short supply. While the Americans were the worst hit, being furthest from their sources of supply, all the Allied army groups were desperate for supplies by the autumn of 1944.[162]

Canadian officers were queried about the ammunition situation in the battle experience questionnaires. About 25 percent of respondents indicated that their units had been caught short of ammunition while in battle, typically running low on mortars, grenades, PIAT rounds, and .303 rifle ammunition.[163] Shortages were especially acute for units subject to enemy counterattacks while on the offensive, when the only supplies available were those carried by the soldiers themselves.[164] Even in Italy, where the logistics situation had been less problematic, ammunition shortages could be a serious impediment: Major John Clarke, for example, advised that more automatic weapons *not* be adopted for the infantry section owing to ammunition shortages and the difficulty of rapidly transporting ammunition across the mountainous Italian countryside.[165] Supply shortages did not occur everywhere, of course, and should not be considered the norm for the materially overstocked Western Allies. Major Liddell remarked in his questionnaire that his company never needed more than 75 percent of its carried ammunition.[166] But, as Major G.P. Boucher of Le Régiment de la Chaudière wrote in his survey, when supply shortfalls did occur, it was "good fire control" that prevented shortage of ammunition.[167]

Officers were emphatic about the value of fire discipline and control, admiring it in their troops and making favourable reference when their German enemies possessed it. Fire discipline, as defined by the *Infantry Training 1937* manual used by Commonwealth armies, "entails strict attention to the signals and orders from the commander, correct adjustment of sights, correct recognition, deliberate aim and economy of ammunition. It demands of the men endurance of the enemy's fire even when no reply is possible, and a cool and intelligent use of their weapons when control by the fire unit commander can no longer be exercised."[168] Fire discipline was a check on the production of too much fire in battle: well-trained troops were not supposed to empty their magazines by employing their firepower lavishly unless the situation absolutely demanded it. As discussed earlier, the 1935 *Field Service Regulations* stressed the same training, demanding of soldiers a high degree of discipline in firing and in some places actively discouraging troops from firing.[169] The emphasis on fire discipline recognized that the reactions of inexperienced soldiers would be to fire their weapons blindly and in panic when frightened and under stress.

It was also widely acknowledged in the questionnaires that German infantrymen usually exercised better fire discipline than the Canadians they faced. "The Germans are very good," wrote Major G.E. Colgate, "at holding their fire until the last minute."[170] The best German units made a practice of allowing Canadian patrols and offensives to infiltrate past their camouflaged forward line, then hitting the unsuspecting Canadians from enfilade positions and causing grievous casualties, especially if the patrol had previously made its presence known through too much firing.[171] This seemed to be a common occurrence, particularly at night when the active Canadian patrols could easily walk right past the enemy in the dark without knowing it. Small groups of disciplined German soldiers would sometimes hold their fire until a Canadian unit had passed by them completely, and then open up with "murderous fire" from the rear.[172] Sometimes the Germans would use sporadic fire to lure Canadian soldiers in closer to an established kill-zone. Major Colgate recalled a particularly unnerving incident when the Germans lured his company into a trap: "On one night attack in a push on the bank of the Seine, we advanced until fired on by a sniper. A scout was sent out to silence him and was successful. We advanced another few yards until fired on by a [machine-gun]. This too was taken out, and then Jerry sprang up practically on all sides. He had at us."[173] This ability to achieve local surprise during an attack, particularly at night, was regarded by the Canadian officers as a hallmark of superior training. "The ... attack had not managed to draw the enemy out," commented Major Hamilton at another point in his notes. "The German will not give away his position by random firing; it takes a full scale attack to draw down the defensive power."[174] German tanks were observed to maintain a similar discipline and economy of fire: if they could, German tanks would wait for the Canadians to show themselves first before opening fire, and as Captain Sinkewicz noted: "The [tank] who moves first gets shot."[175] German fire discipline was not perfect, of course; particularly toward the end of the war, German divisions on all fronts were heavily infused with inexperienced soldiers. But Canadians in both Northwest Europe and in Italy fought a disproportionate number of battle-hardened, highly experienced *Wehrmacht* and *SS* divisions that were dug in on the defensive, and one of their most written-about traits in the battle experience questionnaires was excellent fire discipline and control.[176]

The superiority – in at least some cases – of German fire discipline stood in contrast to the Canadian tendency to enter battle with weapons blazing, at least in the minds of some of the officers who filled out the surveys. Cool, controlled fire discipline was an ideal that they strove to inculcate in their own troops but couldn't always achieve. When Canadian troops *did* achieve good fire discipline, though, it was viewed very favourably by the officers. When discussing night operations, Major R.G. Liddell, for example, spelled out the success his company achieved through training for rigorous fire discipline and surprise: "Absolute silence helped to demoralize enemy, who was only fired on at very close ranges."[177] Captain F.T. Rea, a Black Watch liaison officer, was of the opinion that, from his personal observations, infantry was better served through stealthy actions and fire discipline than through the laying down of heavy artillery and small-arms fire. "Infantry must be well-trained," Rea wrote, "in locating and stalking individual tanks, [machine-guns], and guns."[178] Captain Bennett of the FSSF also commented on the power of skilled marksmanship from hidden locations to demoralize the enemy, and how good fire control could keep the Germans off-balance and guessing, especially in the attack.[179]

Many more questionnaire responses expressed higher regard for German fire discipline than for Canadian restraint. On the other hand, many Canadian officers praised the large volume of fire created by their soldiers. Regardless of doctrine, there was a wide variety of opinions from officers on the proper application of fire; the reality was messy and contradictory. Different situations called for different tactics, as governed by the terrain, time of day, steadiness of the troops, and a legion of other factors. As established earlier, fire-and-movement tactics were integral to close combat fighting, and involved bringing heavy fire to bear on an enemy position, not to kill but to neutralize that position long enough to move other troops forward. Conversely, the likelihood that, when following a creeping barrage, soldiers who stopped to fire on an enemy position would be left behind by the artillery placed a premium on fire discipline. During major offensive operations, heavy fire could thus either be a necessity or an immense liability. Other officers in different times and circumstances advocated quieter infiltration tactics across difficult terrain, the better to achieve surprise and to the minimize the casualties that would inevitably be sustained once the troops' position was revealed. It seems that inexperienced soldiers were more likely to fire to excess, while fire discipline was a mark of more seasoned troops; but even this was not universally true, since some officers observed German units firing their weapons wildly as well. Terry Copp perhaps encapsulated these seeming contradictions best when he emphasized that the Canadian Army adopted a "problem-solving" approach: "A flexible approach to tactical problems encouraged officers to seek solutions based on specific battlefield conditions, especially analysis of the terrain."[180] There was no overall agreement among the surveyed officers on precisely how tightly fire was to be controlled. Generally, the majority of them seemed to value fire discipline, as advocated in training and tactical documentation, but this view was not shared universally or under all circumstances.[181] Sometimes more fire was necessary and advisable.

The battle experience questionnaires *do* indicate, however, that while there were debates on whether it was preferable to fire freely or to exercise tight fire discipline, the reality was that Canadian soldiers normally fired their small arms in great volume, and often to excess. Many officers indicated that they could stand to see their soldiers fire less, but there is not one recorded instance in the questionnaires of officers claiming that their soldiers did not fire their weapons enough, or that not enough soldiers fired at all. As established in chapter 3, such phenomena would certainly have been noticed by combat officers at the platoon and company level, and would have been written about in their questionnaires had it been happening. Given the opportunity, Canadian soldiers tended to make full use of their weapons; hence the cautions of the FSR and other training manuals and the pervasive emphasis upon controlling, regulating, and disciplining that fire so that it could be made more useful and less of a liability on the battlefield. Marshall's axioms on the supremacy of infantry small-arms fire are too simple, and there were many circumstances in which it was not beneficial to lay down heavy small arms fire. However, the Canadian soldiers, who were only committed to large-scale battle at the very end of the Second World War, generally lacked combat experience and may have had to discover the hard way that giving away your position to the enemy was unwise. If anything, a reduction in a unit's blind firing could well have been an indicator of discipline, experience, and solid training.

From a psychological perspective, this behaviour is in line with much of what is presently known about soldiers in battle: military analysts and historians have noted that the tendency of soldiers is to fire their weapons too much, rather than too little. Ben Shalit, an Israeli military psychologist and author of the excellent book *The Psychology of Conflict and Combat*, states in regard to Marshall's work:

> With Marshall's [ratio of fire] in mind, I have often sought to find corroboration for his finding that only 30 percent [*sic*] of the men fire at the enemy. Other reports from different wars give much higher figures, around 75–80 percent. My observation – carried out on ordinary infantry units, as well as in select commando units – left me with the impression that nearly 100 percent fired, when told to do so or when circumstances demanded. In fact, my very strong impression (as well as my own experience) is that firing is a very effective method of relieving tension and fear, and is often engaged in even when there is no need for it.[182]

Shalit continues: "Some people do react to danger by freezing; but, if one does react at all, it seems to me that the tendency is to fire excessively, rather than not to fire." He gives examples of his own experience with Israeli soldiers from the Six Day War, which included these soldiers' producing volumes of fire that could only be described as "overkill," but he concludes: "Like whistling and yelling in the dark, firing has a calming effect. The drumming and thudding of the weapon serves to cover up the throbbing fear within oneself. One often fires not so much to destroy and conquer ... as to overcome and control one's own fear. Such firing is often ineffective, and it requires learning and example by a good leader to control."[183]

Psychiatrist Theodore Nadelson also claims that firing a weapon, "excites, and can strangely soothe." As Nadelson explains in his book *Trained to Kill*, there is a power inherent in firing a weapon, wherein one engages in the destructive desire to unleash irresistible force: "The desire becomes an all-engrossing fact ... force is 'launched from the eyes' – the eye sees, the missile flies its trajectory, annihilates space, and the opponent who would kill you is dead ... Killing a man who wants to kill you erases the primal fear of death. The repetitive exercise of such control and dominance over terror becomes addictive, and other experience pales."[184] Even Dave Grossman, Marshall's most vocal advocate and the intellectual heir to the ratio-of-fire thesis, discusses the same phenomenon in his premier work. In *On Killing*, Grossman comments in some detail on how firing a gun is helpful in meeting a number of human psychological urges, most notably the deep-seated desire to posture in the face of aggression. Although he argues that posturing fire was meant to scare and not to kill, Grossman nonetheless tells us: "Soldiers in battle have a desperate urge to fire their weapons even when (perhaps especially when) they cannot possibly do the enemy any harm."[185]

A major reason that soldiers will fire their weapons so much, aside from the inherent power, is that shooting also constitutes an effective action that soldiers can take in hostile circumstances. In examining the roots of mass violence, renowned psychologist Ervin Staub outlined two of the most basic needs of human beings: the need to feel as though one's actions are effective, and the need for security. According to Staub, the ability to effect change in the environment constitutes the "need to know or believe that we have the capacity to protect ourselves from harm (danger, attack, etc.), to engage with the world and accomplish things we set out to do."[186] The basic needs of security, effectiveness, and control are fundamentally linked. By taking effective action, human beings feel as though they can protect themselves from harm and pursue favourable outcomes. Staub goes on to say: "The belief that we have control, the illusion of control, is essential for humans."[187] Some evidence of this can also be found in the questionnaires. Many officers, when discussing physical and mental fatigue, wrote that their soldiers were generally able to withstand any physical hardship and not crack under the pressure as long as they were able to take effective action to protect themselves and fulfill their objectives. However, as Major Kemp wrote in his battle experience questionnaire:

"When we were in defensive positions under heavy mortar and artillery fire and the men were unable to hit back at anything, mental fatigue became very noticeable and had to be watched carefully."[188] This seems to have been true in most companies, at least among the many officers who commented on it: nothing was as liable to cause soldiers to mentally break down as being shelled, since there was literally nothing they could do to stop it or, if a shell landed near enough to them, even protect themselves.[189] It was always when no effective action could be taken to stop the enemy or protect themselves that soldiers were most stressed. Notably, several officers reported finding that the best way to stave off mental fatigue in their units was to keep them busy doing something: constantly on the move, as Lieutenant-Colonel Petch suggested, or, in the words of Captain Crutcher, "digging alternative positions, improving living quarters, intensive patrolling to familiarize them with the surroundings."[190] Major W.C. Allan would have agreed: "Mental Fatigue was always noticeable under heavy shelling during periods of inactivity. Only relief seemed to be to keep on the move, even if by moving nothing was gained."[191] Major John Clarke, on the other hand, suggested a more proactive, bloody-minded approach, and from his experience the best antidote to mental fatigue was "killing Germans at close quarters."[192] Other officers also noted that taking effective action and achieving success in battle were primary elements in keeping morale high among soldiers. When surveyed about morale, forty-six officers specifically wrote down "success" and "knowledge of own effectiveness" (or variations thereof) as factors contributing to the raising of morale. Beyond material factors such as hot food and regular mail from home, one of the top determinants to morale was "success."[193] The common denominator was that giving soldiers something to do so that they would feel they were taking effective action – and better yet, having that action be successful – was the best way to avoid mental breakdown in combat and low morale. Firing a weapon could, if nothing else, fulfill a basic psychological need in many stressful circumstances. Stan Whitehouse, a British soldier in Northwest Europe, reacted to a night ambush with blind self-defence: "I felt I was about to be killed and there was nothing I could do about it. To combat my 'bomb-happiness' I stood up and hosed another magazine down the road, this time finding relief by shouting 'Come on you bastards, come on.'"[194] If a soldier could do something to make himself believe he was in control of a small part of his environment, the mental strain was considerably reduced.

Intimately connected with effectiveness and control in Staub's outline of basic needs, and rather more straightforward, was the human need for security, "the need to know or believe that we are and will continue to be free of physical and psychological harm (of danger, attack, injury to body or dignity)."[195] Humans and animals, Staub continues, have a tendency to respond strongly to signals of potential harm, and "attack and threat of attack, which frustrate the need for security (but can also frustrate other needs), are the strongest, most reliable instigators of aggression" in human beings.[196] The ramifications for military action are obvious. Historian David Bercuson has written that there is no need to inculcate a "will to kill" or a "killer mentality" in army recruits, since, "the 'killer mentality,' or hate for the enemy, will develop soon enough in soldiers under fire when their comrades are being killed and maimed beside them. But they will kill mostly because they know that the only way to be safe on a battlefield is to destroy those who are trying to destroy them."[197]

The evidence on small arms fire from the battle experience questionnaires therefore makes sense within the context of basic human needs; soldiers, particularly inexperienced ones who have not learned better, are likely to fire their weapons excessively to satisfy both their need for effective action and their need for personal security. While this issue requires further investigation and nuance, it seems to be reinforced by the historical evidence from the Second World War. At no point in the surveys are there any complaints about inadequate fire on the part of infantrymen; there are only complaints about *too much* indiscriminate fire. Even these come from only a minority. Most officers seem to have been content with the high volume of fire that their soldiers were producing with small arms, and used it to their advantage in battle. While the ideal of tighter, more disciplined control over troops' firepower had been established by doctrine, as that ideal sometimes went unrealized in practice and was more observable in the Germans than it was in the Canadians. Instead, Canadian officers commanded soldiers who tended to act on the very human urge to make too much use of their firearms rather than not enough, in spite of Marshall's claims to the contrary.

CONCLUSION

As a prelude to the official history of the Canadian Army in the Second World War, army historian Colonel C.P. Stacey wrote in a 1948 historical summary that the Canadian troops "were soldiers, and very good ones; but they were citizen soldiers ... The typical Canadian fighting man of 1939–45 was a volunteer, who came forward of his own free will to do a duty he did not find pleasant but which, he knew, had to be done." Stacey continued:

> Nevertheless, it would be erroneous to suggest that the men who broke the Adolf Hitler Line or cleared the Hochwald were simply civilians in uniform. Nothing could be more undesirable than to foster in the minds of Canadians the dangerous delusion that any Canadian citizen can merely put on military costume and thereby find himself immediately a first-class soldier ... The Canadian Army of 1939–45, by the time it went into action, was better trained than any peacetime regular troops had ever been. Even so, its units found that they still had something to learn on the battlefield. Regiments, and Armies, are not made overnight, however excellent the raw material (and the Canadian raw material was the best possible); they are formed, as Kipling once remarked, by the expenditure of time, money and blood.[1]

It was an accurate portrait, albeit tinged with national pride in the heady aftermath of victory. The Canadian Army in the Second World War was a citizen force, made up overwhelmingly of volunteers who trained intensively for years before being sent into combat against the battle-hardened German Army. The spearhead of the Canadian Army – the "sledgehammer," as General Simonds phrased it – was its solid corps of infantrymen, who carried out the most difficult fighting and sustained the most casualties during the war. The army won a string of hard-fought victories in the Mediterranean, Normandy, the Low Countries, and Germany on the capabilities and combat effectiveness of its infantry rifle companies. That effectiveness was not uniform, and no matter how much training they received, the Canadians needed the experience of bloody combat to become a powerful fighting force. The constant erosion of fighting strength and its replenishment by green reinforcements meant that battlefield learning had to be a continuous, cyclical process rather than an ascending curve, but Canadian riflemen typically fought capably, exhibiting both tactical skill and initiative.

The battle experience questionnaires provide a new perspective on how Canada's Second World War was fought at that tactical level. Rather than being dominated by artillery and armour, Canadian warfare was grounded in the same close-quarters infantry combat that had earned the Canadian Corps its victory during the First World War. But rather than being utterly subordinate to this artillery-based doctrine and experiencing tactical arthritis as a consequence, the Canadian riflemen, as indicated by the questionnaires, were capable of flexible responses to the problems presented by the battlefield. Canadians frequently attacked at night, when centralized control was impossible and sub-unit initiative was at a premium; they patrolled and raided the enemy lines aggressively, often dominating the no-man's land along the front; they exercised fire-and-movement tactics in battle and followed a conservative doctrinal policy of bite-and-hold fighting meant to defeat the strong German counterattacks. They followed in the wake of creeping barrages to reach their objectives during set-piece attacks, but were not slaves to them and were still capable combatants when the artillery failed to support them adequately.

There were setbacks and disasters, of course, and grievous losses were suffered by the Canadian Army. Even the best tactics in the Second World War would ultimately cause the deaths of hundreds, or even thousands, of friendly troops: this was the toll of mechanized warfare, and a tremendous burden of command fell upon those who led these soldiers into battle. But given the difficult terrain that the Canadian Army had to contend with, to say nothing of the entrenched *Wehrmacht* and *SS* divisions waiting for them, few better alternatives could be found. Regardless of the successes or failures of those in positions of high command, Canadian infantrymen proved themselves to be effective in combat against the Germans. If the *Wehrmacht* was as consistently superior in qualitative fighting ability to the Canadians and Allies as has been indicated by scholars like Trevor Dupuy, there is little evidence of it in the battle experience questionnaires. The Canadians did not always succeed, of course, and the personnel turmoil that they constantly had to contend with – on top of the stresses of battle and clear flaws in combined-arms doctrine – was an ongoing source of difficulty.

At the same time, owing to the challenges presented by the terrain, the equipment, the enemy, and the doctrine, spectacular success was rarely achieved. Infantry bite-and-hold tactics privileged consolidation over exploitation, making it more probable that objectives would be successfully seized and held but less likely that success could be turned into the consummate breakthrough or major rout. It was a doctrine well suited to tearing apart German counterattacks and seizing limited ground, but it is difficult to imagine it resulting in the spectacular breakthrough success of the American COBRA offensive in Normandy. Whether this doctrine was the one best suited for the fighting that was encountered will likely remain an ongoing debate. What I have tried to stress in study, however, is that, in all the campaigns they were involved in, Canadian soldiers put their doctrine to work and managed to tactically out-fight the Germans on many occasions. Against a battle-hardened *Wehrmacht* and *SS*, this was a major feat.

Just as interesting are the ramifications of the battle experience questionnaires for the ratio-of-fire observations of S.L.A. Marshall. The officers who responded to the questionnaires were normally well situated on the battlefield to observe the actions of their troops, and their comments in the questionnaires reflect observations on the fighting and detailed commentary on the use (or lack of use) of infantry weapons. Remarkably, not one officer recorded the slightest complaint about volumes of fire being too low, or about large-scale non-participation in battle. A few made scattered comments about inadequate combat motivation, but these were infrequent and all in reference to replacement soldiers. In notable contrast to Marshall's ratio-of-fire theory, Canadian officers considered their troops' making *too much* use of their firearms to be a more pervasive and dangerous problem than their not shooting enough or at all. Fire discipline was a virtue on the modern battlefield, where excessive firing could betray one's position and call down enemy retaliation, a reality of combat that Marshall's *Men Against Fire* neglects in favour of simplistic notions about the weight of fire winning battles. Officers admired restrained use of small arms where they saw it; this restraint, however, seems, in the Canadian case, to have been the exception rather than the rule. It required highly trained and well-disciplined soldiers to not engage in the psychologically-comforting use of their weaponry when under pressure in combat. Inexperienced soldiers tended to fire to nervous excess; trained and experienced veterans possessed a greater degree of control in battle and had a better chance of surviving a fight. If anything, Marshall's axiom had it backward when it comes to Canadians: it was the experienced soldiers who fired less frequently but more carefully, and the green troops who were more likely to blaze away with their weapons.

There is no evidence in the questionnaires to support the contention that only 15 to 20 percent of riflemen were firing their weapons; and there is little support for the concept of an innate or culturally developed "resistance to killing" in Canadian soldiers. It is an unpleasant fact to contemplate, but a generation of Canadian soldiers fought effectively and killed their enemies in battle. These soldiers had, in overwhelming numbers, volunteered for duty overseas specifically with that intention. Most had trained for many years in Canada and Britain precisely in order to be able to kill, wound, or capture Germans when they reached continental Europe. Once the fighting on the ground began in Sicily, Italy, and Northwest Europe, they were not always courageous or effective. Many suffered from battle exhaustion and even complete mental collapse from the stress of battle. A steady stream of replacements had to be taught how to fight almost from scratch, particularly if they came in poorly trained. The Canadian Army was not a perfect military formation, and it had many problems and difficulties to overcome between 1943 and 1945. But nothing in the questionnaires indicates that any of those problems included the widespread failure of infantry riflemen to take an active, aggressive role in the fighting.

The ramifications of this new perception for the study of military history may be modest, but will, I hope, be important nonetheless. It would be going too far to say that the evidence from the battle experience questionnaires completely disproves Marshall's ratio-of-fire theory. Marshall, after all, was exclusively chronicling American rifle companies with his after-action interviews, and although he met C.P. Stacey and was acquainted with the Canadian Army's historical officers, to the best available knowledge he never interviewed Canadian soldiers.[2] The battle experience questionnaires say nothing about the American experience (beyond one Canadian officer having served in the First Special Service Force) and it is possible that the conscription-based U.S. Army did indeed have problems with soldiers not firing their weapons; American General George S. Patton was said to have commented on this phenomenon in Sicily.[3] More research is needed on this subject from an American perspective and in American archives. If there were problems with infantry fire, the reasons need to be explored in more detail. However, the battle experience questionnaires show that this was not a problem facing the Canadian Army, which fought in all the same European theatres as the Americans. By association this means that S.L.A. Marshall was demonstrably incorrect in stating that his ratio-of-fire data were universally applicable to all armies. Marshall, and particularly his later disciples, elevated the ratio-of-fire thesis into a basic principle of war, claiming that only a handful of soldiers would do any real fighting or killing in close combat. This evokes the ancient Homeric warfare of mythology, where stylized duels between elite warriors characterized the "honourable" battlefield and dominated the fates of all lesser soldiers. Although fantasies of Homeric-style warfare run deep in many military traditions, they now constitute an anachronistic interpretation of military history.[4] The Canadian experience of the Second World War strongly suggests that the phenomenon of only a few soldiers fighting while the rest hold back is *not* a fundamental principle of war and should not be privileged as such. Perhaps American rifle companies were having difficulty generating sufficient firepower to sustain themselves in battle, but this was not a universal experience, and this supposition should be explored and properly historicized.

Even Marshall's correctness in formulating his ratio-of-fire thesis on the basis of U.S. soldiers must be questioned, since it would mean that Canadian soldiers were fighting much more effectively and consistently than the Americans were. While such a thought may appeal to Canadian nationalist sentiment, there is no evidence whatsoever that the Canadian Army was significantly more effective in infantry combat than the U.S.

Army. Certainly the Americans achieved more conspicuous success than the Canadians in Northwest Europe. This line of questioning takes us back to the well-founded criticisms of Marshall's reliability as a witness to historical events, and his credibility as a primary source. Especially when placed against a documented historical source such as the battle experience questionnaires, "SLAM" Marshall's arguments about the ratio of fire seem to lack credible grounding.

Perhaps it is past time, then, for military historians to move beyond Marshall's ratio of fire in the continuing dialogue on human behaviour in combat. Historians have been reluctant to make this move owing to a previous lack of challenging documentary evidence, and, if we are honest, owing to the ease with which the ratio-of-fire numbers supposedly allowed scholars "access" to aspects of human behaviour normally shrouded by the fog of war. Taking Marshall's belief that hardly any soldiers actually fought in combat as a truism, some scholars have tried to craft corollary arguments about human nature, behavioural conditioning, and military effectiveness. In the past Marshall's work has provided an appealing academic shortcut: a simple proposition – that most soldiers will not fight – seemingly backed up by hard data and numbers. However, the evidence uncovered in the course of the present study strongly suggests that Marshall's work on this point was not based upon hard data or even, it seems, on any accurate recording of the facts on the ground. Marshall's ratio-of-fire data are unreliable and cannot be generalized as any sort of universal law of combat.

S.L.A. Marshall authored many fine works, and his journalistic inquiries into the nature of combat have left modern historians with a number of excellent records of battles in the Second World War. His overall contribution to the field should not be minimized. Whether Marshall deliberately lied about his ratio of fire to prove a point or was simply incorrect in his observations will never be known, and this line of inquiry is fruitless and injurious. All that can be definitively stated is that Marshall's claims about the ratio of fire are inconsistent with the documentary evidence gathered from Canada's experience of the Second World War. Any pretense to universality that Marshall or his successors claimed for his ratio-of-fire numbers is demonstrably false in the case of Canada. In the fierce fighting in the Mediterranean and Northwest European fronts there were, as Stacey himself observed, no more effective soldiers to be pitted against enemy fire than those of the Canadian Army.

SAMPLE QUESTIONNAIRES

The following are reproductions of the original battle experience questionnaire documents from Library and Archives Canada. They have been reproduced for this volume as faithfully as possible, and include all particulars from the originals, though the spacing has been changed in places to accommodate publication. All wording and language is that of the original battle experience questionnaire documents.

Also included are reproductions of the cover letters sent to officers along with the letters, as well as a reproduction of the CFA-276 form that was distributed to all returning army officers to determine who would be sent a battle experience questionnaire.

SAMPLE FORM CFA-276

This form will be issued to and completed by all officers, NOT below the rank of Capt, on arrival in the UK from any theatre of operations.

(BLOCK CAPITALS, PLEASE)

Rank   Surname
_____

Christian Names
_____

Corps or Arm of Service
_____

In what theatre have you been serving?
_____

_____

Have you had actual Battle Experience?
_____

In what capacity have you served?
_____

In a unit and/or on the staff
_____

Give approximate dates (but NOT the actual name of unit)
_____

_____

Address which will find you during next ten days
_____

_____

Signature of officer
_____

Date
_____

This form, when completed, should be folded as indicated and mailed via Field Post Office.

Source: "Tactical investigation questionnaires, routine requests." LAC RG4-C-2 vol. 9824.

SAMPLE COVER LETTER SENT TO OFFICERS
NOT IN HOSPITAL

6 Apr 45

Dear

Thank you for completing Form CFA-276 which has been received here and from which we note that you have returned to this country from your service in Europe. The purpose of the form was to make it possible to reach you quickly in order that we can extract from you as much information as possible concerning your recent employment.

Questionnaires are attached which you are now asked to consider and complete in as much detail as possible. For security reasons, it is necessary that you return them in the enclosed secret envelope.

I hope this will not take up too much of your time or interfere with your personal arrangements, but you will appreciate that it is important for all of us to make available as much information as possible concerning recent experience in order that we may keep all concerned fully informed as to the necessities of training in the light of operational requirements.

I may add that any notes, especially on Armoured–Infantry intercommunication, you might care to send on any subject outside the scope of the questionnaire would also be highly appreciated and that material received in this way frequently constitutes a most valuable supplement to information derived from official and other sources.

It may be necessary to have you come here for an interview to supplement or amplify the information you send in. Therefore, it will assist us considerably if you keep us acquainted with any change of address in order that we may reach you quickly if required.

Yours most sincerely,

(E.C. Baker) Major.

Source: "Tactical investigation questionnaires, routine requests." LAC RG4-C-2 vol. 9824.

SAMPLE COVER LETTER SENT TO OFFICERS
IN HOSPITAL

2/Tact Invest/1 (Trg)
5 Oct 44

Dear

I attach an official memorandum which indicates the high value we hope to obtain from information derived from Questionnaires addressed to officers returning from theatres of war.

I hope you will forgive me for bothering you while in hospital, but no doubt you will readily appreciate that the sooner we can get from you any useful information you may have, the more valuable it will be in helping us to make our training fit with operational requirements.

Therefore, if you will be good enough, I would be most grateful if you would complete the Questionnaires and return them as early as possible in the secret envelopes provided for the purpose.

I may add that any notes you might care to send on any subject outside the scope of the Questionnaires, would also be highly appreciated. I can assure you that frequently such notes form a most valuable supplement to information derived from official sources.

I hope that you make a speedy recovery and will soon be enjoying good health again.

Yours most sincerely,

RECIPIENT NAME
No. 23 Cdn General Hospital,
Canadian Army, England.

Source: "Completed Battle Experience Questionnaires" LAC RG24-C-2 vol. 9879

BATTLE EXPERIENCE QUESTIONNAIRE "A"
GENERAL

Note – This questionnaire is intended to ensure that the best use is made of your practical experience in the field during the present war.

(a) Please be quite frank. Your replies will be treated as confidential.

(b) Except where you are specifically asked for an opinion, please base your replies only on *what you personally have done or seen in your unit*. Do not include anything which you have merely been told by others.

(c) Please answer every question. If you have no information on any particular question insert the letters N.K. (Not Known.) Do not leave it unanswered.

(d) If you have opinions and/or experiences of value which are not covered by the questionnaire, please attach them to the questionnaire on separate sheets. It will be helpful if you will give as much factual evidence for your views as possible.

Name

Present Rank　　　　　　　　Personal No.

Age Last Birthday

Regular, T.A. or Temp. Commission

Arm　　　　　　　　Unit

Theatre(s) of War in which your Experience has been gained (with Dates):

Theatre	Dates From	To	Rank	Job in Unit	Unit if different from above

Actual Operations on which your information is based (with Dates):

_____

_____

_____

_____

_____

_____

_____

_____

1. (a) Please complete the following table in respect of the enemy weapons which have been used against your unit.

In Col. (2) insert an estimate of the number of times the weapon in Col. (1) has been used against your unit. (For example, if your unit has been dive bombed three times, put a 3 in Col. (2) beside Dive Bomber. If many times (e.g. Rifle) insert "often.")

In Col. (3) insert the figure "1" against the weapon which in your view had the greatest adverse effect on the morale of your unit, the figure "2" against the weapon which had the next greatest adverse effect on the morale of your unit, and the figure "3" against the weapon which had the next greatest adverse effect on morale.

Serial No.	Weapon. (1)	Used Against You (2)	Greatest Moral Effort (3)
1	Rifles		
2	Sub-Machine Guns		
3	Machine Guns		
4	Mortars		
5	A/T Guns		
6	Other Artillery		
7	Bayonets		
8	Grenades		
9	Flame Throwers		
10	Land Mines		
11	Booby Traps		

Serial No.	Weapon. (1)	Used Against You (2)	Greatest Moral Effort (3)
12	Tanks		
13	Armoured Cars		
14	Dive Bombers		
15	High Level Bombers		
16	Aerial Machine Guns		
17	Aerial Cannons		

(b) Please give your view of the main reason for the adverse moral effectiveness of the weapons you have marked in Col. (3).

(1) Weapon with greatest adverse moral effect, ie.
effective because

(2) Weapon with next greatest adverse moral effect, ie.
effective because

(3) Weapon with next greatest adverse moral effect, ie.
effective because

2. (a) List any weapon whose effect upon morale in your unit appeared to *decrease* with experience

(b) List any weapons whose effect upon morale in your unit appeared to *increase* with experience

3. Please list in order of importance factors which, in your unit, appeared to have the effect of raising morale

_____

_____

_____

4. Please list in order of importance factors which, in your unit, appeared to have the effect of lowering morale

_____

_____

_____

Signature _____ Rank _____

Date _____

Present address _____

_____

_____

BATTLE EXPERIENCE QUESTIONNAIRE "H"
INFANTRY

Name

Present Rank   Personal No.

Unnit Served with

1. Underline the weapon which your unit has actually used in action (add any not listed):

Rifle	Med. Machine Gun	Sticky Grenade
Sub-machine Gun	A/T Rifle	36 Grenade
Bren Gun	2-in. Mortar	69 Grenade
Pistol	3-in. Mortar	68 Grenade
20mm. Gun	Twin A.A. M.G.s	Bayonet
		2-pdr.
		6-pdr.
		P.I.A.T.

2. Have you found any of these weapons outstandingly effective? If so, which and why?

Weapon (1)	Chief Reason(s) for Effectiveness (2)
1	
2	
3	
4	
5	

3. Have you found any of these weapons ineffective? If so, which and why?

Weapon (1)	Chief Reason(s) for Ineffectiveness (2)
1	
2	
3	
4	
5	

4. (a) Has your unit ever undertaken mine clearance?
If so (b) What equipment was used?
(c) Was smoke used for clearance?
(d) Was night used for clearance?
(e) If you have experience of both, which do you prefer?
(f) Have you had experience of operating in an area containing anti-personnel mines?
(g) If so were they actuated by trip wire, pressure, or both?
(h) Based on your experience, what percentage of casualties may be expected in crossing an anti-personnel minefield?

5. (a) Has your unit undertaken mine-laying?
If so (b) What types of mines were laid?
(c) How were mines marked?
(d) How were mines recorded?
(e) Did you have R.E. Assistance?
(f) Do you regard R.E. Assistance as necessary? If so, why?
(g) When moving forward, did you clear your own mines?

6. (a) Did your unit take part in Night Operations?

If so (b) Were they specially trained for Night Operations?

(c) What methods did you use for keeping direction?

(d) Were these effective?

If not, why not?

(e) What distances did you cover?

7. (a) Did you ever receive Direct Air Support?

If so (b) How were targets indicated to Air?

(c) Was the support effective?

If not, why not?

8. (a) Did you ever have to organise rapid defence against counter-attack?

If so (b) What equipment and gear were used? (e.g. Wire, sandbags, mines, etc.)

(c) Did the R.E. bring it forward?

(d) What necessary equipment and gear were not available?

9. (a) What methods did you use for indicating objectives and targets in battle?

(b) What signals (whistles, etc.) did you use in battle? Were they effective? If not, why not?

(c) Have you ever used coloured smoke?

(d) If so, for what?

(e) Was it effective? If not why not?

(f) Have you ever used coloured flares?

If so (g) For what purpose?

(h) Were they effective? If not, why not?

10. (a) Did your section go into battle under W.E. strength?

If so (b) What was the average number of ors in the section?

(c) Please list, in order of importance, the cause of wastage

(d) In your view, did your sections at the strength given under (b) prove adequate for close quarters fighting?

(e) At this strength, did they prove adequate for carrying sufficient ammunition for platoon weapons into battle?

(f) From where did you get casualty replacements?

Was their general standard of efficiency high, moderate or low?

(g) Did you detach "Left out of Battle" personnel before going into action?

11. Were you able to put the tactical principles of fire and movement, taught as battle drill before going overseas, into practice?

Often, fairly often, or seldom?

12. (a) Did your unit carry out an attack under an artillery barrage?

(b) If so, did they have preliminary training?

(c) Did they keep up with the barrage effectively? If not, why not?

(d) Was the attack by day or by night?

(e) If by night, were any special aids used to help troops lean on the barrage?

(f) If so, give details

13. List the main tasks carried out by your Pioneer platoon in battle

_____

_____

14. (a) Was your unit ever short of ammunition in battle?
If so (b) Of what natures of ammunition and how frequently?

_____

Serial	Nature of Ammunition	Frequency of Shortage (Often, fairly often, or seldom)
	(1)	(2)

(c) From where did you get ammunition replenishments when in action?
_____

(d) Who brought the ammunition to this point?
(e) Who brought it forward to you?
(f) Did this system work efficiently?
If not, why not?

_____

15. (a) Have you ever co-operated with Infantry Tanks?
If so (b) Did you move in front of, behind, or amongst the tanks?
(c) If either in front or behind, what distances were maintained behind you and the tanks? (yards)
(d) If the tanks led, please estimate the time interval between the tanks and yourselves reaching the objective? (minutes)
(e) Please estimate the time between your arrival at objective and releasing the tanks to forward rally (minutes).

16. With what wireless sets was your unit equipped?

17. Into what groups were stations netted?

18. Give details of any difficulties experienced when working two wireless sets in one vehicle

19. Give data as to any use made of:
(a) Remote control
(b) Re-broadcast
(c) Relay stations

20. What use respectively was made of: (a) R.T.?
(b) W.T.?
(c) Line?

21. Was assault cable used?
If so, how?

22. Are line-laying facilities adequate?
If not, state in what respect they are inadequate

23. Did you have any battery or charging troubles?
If so, give details

24. Was visual signalling used?
If so, how?

25. Is knowledge of semaphore considered to be desirable?

26. How were communications arranged with:
(a) Artillery?
(b) Armour
(c) Air

27. Give details of any improvised methods of communication or signalling equipment

28. Have you any complaints about the nature or scale of issue of signalling equipment?
If so, give details

29. Have you any experience of jamming or deception by the enemy?
If so give details

30. Any other remarks on communications, particularly as regards failures or outstanding success?

Note – Please attach, on accompanying separate sheets (a) any answers for which there is not sufficient room above, and (b) any notes on matters not covered by your answers to the questionnaire. Information is particularly required on:
(a) Detailed description of any night operation in which you have been engaged.
(b) Incidence of physical and mental fatigue under battle conditions.
(c) The best size and weapons for an infantry section.
(d) Details of any operation in which you have co-operated with infantry tanks.

(e) Details of use of smoke to cover an operation and how it was used (Arty, Mortars 4.2 in., 3 in. or 2 in., generator or 77 grenades).

(f) Details and comments on systems of patrolling in your Unit.

(g) Detailed account of any particular operation in which tactical lessons of outstanding importance emerged or in which any original ruse or new use of weapons proved successful.

Signature   Rank

Date

Present address

SELECTED QUESTIONNAIRE STATISTICS

The following are statistics derived from responses given by the Canadian infantry officers whose battle experience questionnaires are stored at Library and Archives Canada, RG 24, volume 10450. A total of 161 infantry surveys were located in this collection and compiled as part of this study. All the questions of particular relevance to this present volume are reproduced here with the statistical breakdown of the officers' answers.

Note that despite the instructions on the questionnaire, not every officer gave an answer to every question. An officer who specifically wrote "Not Known" or "N.K." to a question was categorized as "No Answer." Those who did not answer a question at all and left it blank were not included when compiling the statistics, so the total number of officers who responded to most questions does not equal 161. It was thought better to gather the data based only upon answered questions, rather than taking the leap of interpreting questions left blank even as "No Answer," since we cannot know the respondents' motives for omitting certain survey questions.

Percentages have been rounded to the nearest tenth of a percent.

"Underline the weapons which your unit has actually used in action."

Weapon	Surveys reporting use
Rifle	153
Sub-machine Gun	149
Bren Gun	152
Pistol	115
20 mm Gun	14
Medium Machine Gun	77
A/T Rifle	5
2-inch Mortar	139
3-inch Mortar	140
Twin A.A. Machine Guns	2
Sticky Grenade	3
No. 36 Grenade	142
No. 69 Grenade	52
No. 68 Grenade	16
Bayonet	81
2-pounder	6
6-pounder	125
P.I.A.T.	141
No. 77 Grenade*	57
No. 75 Grenade*	26
Flame Thrower*	24
Rifle Grenade*	2
Hawkins Grenade*	2
Anti-Personnel Mines*	1
Anti-Tank Mines*	5
No. 88 Grenade*	1
"Crocodiles"*	1
Bangalore Torpedo*	1
Booby Traps*	1
U.S. .30 Carbine*	1
4.2-inch Mortar*	3

*indicates a write-in; all others were options provided on the questionnaire.

SURVEY "H": QUESTION 2

"Have you found any of these weapons outstandingly effective?"

Weapon	Surveys reporting "outstandingly effective"
Bren Gun	54
P.I.A.T.	74
6-pounder	15
No. 36 Grenade	33
No. 77 Grenade	24
2-inch Mortar	10
Sub-machine Gun**	17
3-inch Mortar	44
Rifle	15
Browning Light Machine Gun	1
No. 88 Grenade	1
Rifle Grenade	2
No. 75 Grenade	1
Medium Machine Gun	13
No. 69 Grenade	1
No. 68 Grenade	1
Bayonet	1
20mm Gun	1
Flame Thrower	15

*includes reports of both Sten and Thompson sub-machine guns.

SURVEY "H": QUESTION 3

"Have you found any of these weapons ineffective?"

Weapon	Surveys reporting "ineffective"
Sten Sub-machine Gun	45
2-inch Mortar	17
Bayonet	2
Pistol	20
No. 69 Grenade	11
6-pounder	3
3-inch Mortar	1
Bren Gun	2
Rifle	1
Sticky Grenade	2
P.I.A.T.	3
No. 68 Grenade	1
Flame Thrower	1
20mm Gun	2

SURVEY "H": QUESTION 6(a)

"Did your unit take part in Night Operations?"

	Total	Percentage
ALL OFFICERS		
Yes	133	87.5
No	16	10.5
No Answer	3	1.97
OFFICERS		
IN MEDITERRANEAN		
Yes	49	92.4
No	4	7.6
No Answer	0	0
OFFICERS		
IN NORTHWEST EUROPE		
Yes	84	84.9
No	12	12.1
No Answer	3	3.0

SURVEY "H": QUESTION 6(b)

"Were they specially trained for Night Operations?""

	Total	Percentage
ALL OFFICERS		
Yes	46	34.6
No	80	60.2
No Answer	7	5.3
OFFICERS		
IN MEDITERRANEAN		
Yes	26	53.1
No	18	36.7
No Answer	5	10.2
OFFICERS		
IN NORTHWEST EUROPE		
Yes	20	23.8
No	62	73.8
No Answer	2	2.4

SURVEY "H": QUESTION 6(c)

"Were [Night Operations] effective?"

	Total	Percentage
ALL OFFICERS		
Yes	122	91.7
No	4	3.0
No Answer	7	5.3
OFFICERS		
IN MEDITERRANEAN		
Yes	46	93.8
No	1	2.0
No Answer	2	4.1
OFFICERS		
IN NORTHWEST EUROPE		
Yes	76	90.5
No	3	3.6
No Answer	5	6.0

SURVEY "H": QUESTION 7(a)

"Did you receive Direct Air Support?"

	Total	Percentage
ALL OFFICERS		
Yes	100	66.2
No	39	25.8
No Answer	12	8.0
OFFICERS		
IN MEDITERRANEAN		
Yes	33	63.5
No	15	28.9
No Answer	4	7.7
OFFICERS		
IN NORTHWEST EUROPE		
Yes	67	67.7
No	24	24.2
No Answer	8	8.1

SURVEY "H": QUESTION 7(C)

"Was the [Air Support] effective?"

	Total	Percentage
ALL OFFICERS		
Yes	81	80.2
No	3	3.0
Partially	16	15.8
No Answer	1	1.0
OFFICERS		
IN MEDITERRANEAN		
Yes	26	76.5
No	1	2.9
Partially	7	20.6
No Answer	0	0
OFFICERS		
IN NORTHWEST EUROPE		
Yes	55	82.1
No	2	3.0
Partially	9	13.4
No Answer	1	1.5

SURVEY "H": QUESTION 10(a)

"Did your section ever go into battle under W.E. strength?"

	Total	Percentage
ALL OFFICERS		
Yes	123	81.5
No	23	15.2
No Answer	5	3.3
OFFICERS		
IN MEDITERRANEAN		
Yes	43	82.7
No	7	13.5
No Answer	2	3.9
OFFICERS		
IN NORTHWEST EUROPE		
Yes	80	80.8
No	16	16.2
No Answer	3	3.0

SURVEY "H": QUESTION 10(d)

"Generally speaking, did your section [size] prove adequate for close-quarters fighting?"

	Total	Percentage
ALL OFFICERS		
Yes	81	55.5%
No	45	30.8%
No Answer	20	13.7%
OFFICERS		
IN MEDITERRANEAN		
Yes	31	59.6
No	14	26.9
No Answer	7	13.5
OFFICERS		
IN NORTHWEST EUROPE		
Yes	50	53.2
No	31	33.0
No Answer	13	13.8

SURVEY "H": QUESTION 10(f)

"Was the general standard of efficiency [of casualty replacements] high, moderate, or low?"

	Total	Percentage
ALL OFFICERS		
High	8	5.6
Moderate	85	59.9
Low	38	26.8
No Answer	11	7.8
OFFICERS		
IN MEDITERRANEAN		
High	4	8.2
Moderate	32	65.3
Low	8	16.3
No Answer	5	10.2
OFFICERS		
IN NORTHWEST EUROPE		
High	4	4.3
Moderate	53	57.0
Low	30	32.3
No Answer	6	6.5

SURVEY "H": QUESTION II

"Were you able to put the tactical principles of fire and movement, taught as battle drill before going overseas, into practice?"

	Total	Percentage
ALL OFFICERS		
Yes	128	84.8
No	15	9.9
No Answer	8	5.3
OFFICERS		
IN MEDITERRANEAN		
Yes	45	86.5
No	5	9.6
No Answer	2	3.9
OFFICERS		
IN NORTHWEST EUROPE		
Yes	83	83.8
No	10	10.1
No Answer	6	6.1

SURVEY "H": QUESTION II

"[If Yes,] Often, Fairly Often, or Seldom?"

	Total	Percentage
ALL OFFICERS		
Often	34	26.6
Fairly Often	48	37.5
Seldom	46	35.9
OFFICERS		
IN MEDITERRANEAN		
Often	10	22.2
Fairly Often	18	40.0
Seldom	17	37.8
OFFICERS		
IN NORTHWEST EUROPE		
Often	24	28.9
Fairly Often	30	36.1
Seldom	29	34.9

SURVEY "H": QUESTION 12(a)

"Did your unit carry out an attack under an artillery barrage?"

	Total	Percentage
ALL OFFICERS		
Yes	115	80.4
No	19	13.3
No Answer	9	6.3
OFFICERS		
IN MEDITERRANEAN		
Yes	42	85.7
No	3	6.1
No Answer	4	8.2
OFFICERS		
IN NORTHWEST EUROPE		
Yes	73	77.7
No	16	17.0
No Answer	5	5.3

SURVEY "H": QUESTION 12(b)

"If so, did they have preliminary training?"

	Total	Percentage
ALL OFFICERS		
Yes	58	49.6
No	54	46.2
No Answer	5	4.3
OFFICERS		
IN MEDITERRANEAN		
Yes	21	48.8
No	21	48.8
No Answer	1	2.3
OFFICERS		
IN NORTHWEST EUROPE		
Yes	37	50.0
No	33	44.6
No Answer	4	5.5

SURVEY "H": QUESTION 12(c)

"Did they keep up with the barrage effectively?"

	Total	Percentage
ALL OFFICERS		
Yes	87	75.0
No	21	18.1
No Answer	8	6.9
OFFICERS		
IN MEDITERRANEAN		
Yes	29	67.4
No	10	23.3
No Answer	4	9.3
OFFICERS		
IN NORTHWEST EUROPE		
Yes	58	79.5
No	11	15.1
No Answer	4	5.5

SURVEY "H": QUESTION 12(d)

"Was the attack by day or night?"

	Total	Percentage
ALL OFFICERS		
Day	60	51.7
Night	12	10.3
Both	32	27.6
No Answer	12	10.3
OFFICERS		
IN MEDITERRANEAN		
Day	23	53.5
Night	4	9.3
Both	11	25.6
No Answer	5	11.6
OFFICERS		
IN NORTHWEST EUROPE		
Day	37	50.7
Night	8	11.0
Both	21	28.8
No Answer	7	9.6

SURVEY "H": QUESTION 15(a)

"Have you ever co-operated with Infantry Tanks?"

	Total	Percentage
ALL OFFICERS		
Yes	114	79.2
No	26	18.1
No Answer	4	2.8
OFFICERS		
IN MEDITERRANEAN		
Yes	38	77.6
No	10	20.4
No Answer	1	2.0
OFFICERS		
IN NORTHWEST EUROPE		
Yes	76	80.0
No	16	16.8
No Answer	3	3.2

SURVEY "H": QUESTION 15(b)

"Did you move in front of, behind, or amongst the tanks?"

	Total	Percentage
ALL OFFICERS		
In Front	49	41.5
Amongst	16	13.6
All	30	25.4
No Answer	9	7.6
OFFICERS		
IN MEDITERRANEAN		
In Front	15	38.5
Amongst	2	5.1
All	15	38.5
No Answer	3	7.7
OFFICERS		
IN NORTHWEST EUROPE		
In Front	34	43.0
Amongst	14	17.7
All	15	19.0
No Answer	6	7.6

LIST OF OFFICER RESPONDENTS

The following is a complete list of the names of the infantry officers whose battle experience questionnaires were tabulated as a part of this present work; 161 officers are listed, ranging in rank from captain to lieutenant-colonel. Each officer's entry is filled out according to his self-identification on his battle experience questionnaire, and includes questionnaire number, first and surname (though many used initials), regiment, and theatre(s) of operations. For ease of consultation with the text, they are organized according to questionnaire number.

Note that the questionnaires are numbered based according to numerical order given to the documents in Library and Archives Canada, and that these numbers are not sequential. The infantry questionnaires were interspersed with questionnaires from engineers, artillery, and armour officers, which account for the gaps.

In terms of theatre of operations, "NW Europe" refers to operations in France, Germany, and the Low Countries, beginning with Normandy in June 1944 and extending to the end of hostilities in May 1945. "Italy" refers to operations that took place in Sicily and Italy, beginning in July 1943 and lasting until Canadian units were withdrawn from Italy and redeployed to Northwest Europe in early 1945.

LIST OF OFFICER RESPONDENTS

# RANK AND NAME	REGIMENT	THEATRE
8 A/Major I.H. Louson	1 Royal Highlanders of Canada	NW Europe
15 Captain Donald Findlay	1/6 Queen's Royal	NW Europe
16 A/Major Thomas McCoy	Essex Scottish Regiment	NW Europe
17 Captain W.D. Parker	Royal Hamilton Light Inf.	NW Europe
18 Captain M. Pariseault	Royal 22e Regiment	Italy
27 Major Herbert Fulleston	Cape Breton Highlanders	Italy
28 A/Major J.P.G. Kemp	1 Royal Highlanders of Canada	NW Europe
29 A/Major C.K. Crummer	Lincoln and Welland Regiment	NW Europe
30 A/Captain Yuile	1 Royal Highlanders of Canada	NW Europe
31 Captain A.V. Malone	Queen's Own Rifles of Canada	NW Europe
32 Captain A.C. MacCallum	North Shore Regiment	NW Europe
33 Captain Edward J. Brady	Hastings and Prince Edward Regiment	Italy
34 A/Captain J.A.D. Graham	Queen's Own Cameron Highlanders	NW Europe
35 Major A.M. Hamilton	Stormont, Dundas and Glengarry	NW Europe
36 A/Major John Irvin Mills	Queen's Own Rifles of Canada	NW Europe
48 A/Captain Sinkewicz	HQ, 3rd Cdn Infantry Division	NW Europe
54 Lt.-Colonel T.P. Gilday	1st Cdn Special Service Battalion	Italy
55 Captain A.M. Matheston	South Saskatchewan Regiment	NW Europe

#RANK AND NAME	REGIMENT	THEATRE
56 Captain Samuel Lerner	Royal Canadian Regiment	Italy
57 Major Ryall	Royal Regiment of Canada	NW Europe
58 Captain Donald Clair Smith	Hastings and Prince Edward Regiment	Italy
59 Major F.J. Hammond	Hastings and Prince Edward Regiment	Italy
60 Major A.C. Ross	Cape Breton Highlanders	Italy
61 Lt.-Colonel G.H. Christiansen	Stormont, Dundas and Glengarry	NW Europe
62 Captain A.H. Maclean	West Nova Scotia Regiment	Italy
63 Major Jeff A. Nicklin	1st Cdn Parachute Battalion	NW Europe
64 Major D.J. Wilkins	1st Cdn Parachute Battalion	NW Europe
65 Major D.W. Drennan	Lorne Scots	Italy
66 Major D. McG. Archibald	West Nova Scotia Regiment	Italy
67 Major J.C. Allan	Seaforth Highlanders	Italy
68 Major Cyril Wrightman	Canadian Scots	NW Europe
69 A/Captain F.T. Rea	Black Watch of Canada	NW Europe
70 Lt.-Colonel Autin M. Young	Royal Regiment of Canada	NW Europe
71 A/Captain William Doheny	1 Royal Highlanders of Canada	NW Europe
72 Captain F.W. Oxley	West Nova Scotia Regiment	NW Europe
73 Captain Armstrong	Saskatoon Light Infantry	Italy
74 Major R. Rutherford	Camerons of Canada	NW Europe
75 Major John Campbell	Calgary Highlanders	NW Europe
76 Major W.E. Allan	West Nova Scotia Infantry	Italy

#RANK AND NAME	REGIMENT	THEATRE
77 Captain V.E. Traversy	Black Watch of Canada	NW Europe
78 Captain T.H. Burdett	Royal Canadian Regiment	Italy
79 Major Allister MacMillan	West Nova Scotia Regiment	Italy
80 Lt.-Colonel D.B. Buell	North Shore Regiment	NW Europe
81 Lt.-Colonel P.W. Bennett	Essex Scottish Regiment	NW Europe
82 Major J.D. Learment	North Nova Scotia Highlanders	NW Europe
83 A/Major D.M. Ripley	North Nova Scotia Highlanders	NW Europe
84 Major G.E. Lockwood	North Shore Regiment	NW Europe
85 A/Major F.H. Bonnell	Seaforth Highlanders	Italy
86 A/Major A.H.M. Carmichael	1 Royal Highlanders of Canada	NW Europe
87 Captain Louis Francois	North Shore Regiment	NW Europe
88 Captain A.J. Baker	Unknown	NW Europe
89 Captain G.A. Marron	Royal Hamilton Light Inf.	NW Europe
90 Captain V.L. Chapin	Queen's Own Cameron Highlanders	NW Europe
99 Major Charles Bellavance	Royal 22e Regiment	Italy
100 Lt.-Colonel Charles Petch	North Nova Scotia Highlanders	NW Europe
110 A/Captain Henry Sorenson	H.Q. 1st Cdn. Army	NW Europe
112 Captain H.G.G. Tolchard	Princess of Wales' Own Regiment	NW Europe
113 Major Norman Wilson-Smith	Royal Winnipeg Rifles	NW Europe
114 A/Major D. Cowans	1 Royal Highlanders of Canada	NW Europe
115 Major David Durward	Highland Light Infantry	NW Europe
116 A/Major G.E. Colgate	South Saskatchewan Regiment	NW Europe
118 Captain A.J. Willick	5 Wilts	NW Europe

# RANK AND NAME	REGIMENT	THEATRE
119 Captain S.D. Smith	West Nova Scotia Regiment	Italy
120 Captain Pollin	Highland Light Infantry	NW Europe
121 Captain J.R. Laliberte	Régiment de la Chaudière	NW Europe
122 Captain B.F. Kearns	Highland Light Infantry	NW Europe
123 Captain G. Fawcett	Essex Scottish Regiment	NW Europe
124 Captain Orest Dutchak	Algonquin Regiment	NW Europe
125 A/Captain P.A.R. Blaker	Argyll and Sutherland Highlanders	NW Europe
126 Captain Charles Aubrey Bean	Highland Light Infantry	NW Europe
127 A/Major R.J. Orr	Regina Rifles	Italy
128 A/Major Jock McLeod	Algonquin Regiment	NW Europe
129 A/Major T.M. Lowe	Cape Breton Highlanders	Italy
130 A/Major Elbert Louis Froggett	Royal Hamilton Light Infantry	NW Europe
131 Major John Wesley Burgess	Essex Scottish Regiment	NW Europe
143 Major L.P. Coderre	South Saskatchewan Regiment	NW Europe
144 Captain S.E. Cameron	Irish Regiment of Canada	Italy
145 Captain F.W. Grafton	Algonquin Regiment	NW Europe
146 Captain Reginald Smith	Stormont, Dundas, and Glengarry Highlanders	NW Europe
147 Captain Robert Mainprize	Princess Patricia's Canadian Light Infantry	NW Europe
148 Captain L.G. Norman-Din	Les Fusiliers Mont-Royal	NW Europe
149 Captain M.D. Guy Levesque	Les Fusiliers Mont-Royal	NW Europe
150 A/Captain H.G. McKinley	Irish Regiment of Canada	Italy
151 Major M.B. John	Royal Canadian Regiment	Italy
156 Major W.G. Stashart	West Nova Scotia Regiment	Italy

# RANK AND NAME	REGIMENT	THEATRE
157 Captain B.R. Howard	Cameron Highlanders	NW Europe
158 Captain R. Benuais	Les Fusiliers Mont-Royal	NW Europe
159 Captain H.S. Lamb	The Black Watch	NW Europe
160 Captain A. Rathbone	Argyll and Sutherland Highlanders	NW Europe
161 A/Captain Thomas D. Murray	Cameron Highlanders	NW Europe
169 Major T.M. Powers	Royal Canadian Regiment	Italy
170 Major T.E. O'Reilly	H.Q. 1st Canadian Army	NW Europe
171 Captain Duchaitel de Montrouge	1 Royal Highlanders of Canada	NW Europe
172 Captain N.R. Edwards	Regina Rifles	NW Europe
173 A/Captain J.C. Watts	Royal Winnipeg Rifles	NW Europe
176 A/Major William Ewing	1 Royal Highlanders of Canada	NW Europe
177 Major R.A. Cottrill	Queen's Own Rifles of Canada	NW Europe
178 Major John C. Clarke	48th Highlanders	Italy
180 Captain Warren G. Harvey	North Shore Regiment	NW Europe
181 Captain J. Pender Mollison	Canadian Scottish Regiment	NW Europe
182 Captain S.R. Lambert	South Saskatchewan Regiment	NW Europe
186 Lt.-Colonel E.T. Jacques	Régiment de Maisonneuve	NW Europe
187 Major D. Campbell	Royal Winnipeg Rifles	NW Europe
188 A/Major Harold M. Cunningham	North Nova Scotia Highlanders	NW Europe
189 Major H.G. Dawson	Lake Superior Regiment	NW Europe
190 Major T.S. Ketcheson	Hastings and Prince Edward	Italy
191 A/Major Harrison	Calgary Highlanders	NW Europe

# RANK AND NAME	REGIMENT	THEATRE
192 Major J.W. Ostiguy	Régiment de Maisonneuve	NW Europe
193 Major J.E. Tipler	Perth Regiment	Italy
194 Captain J.R. Learn	Essex Scottish Regiment	NW Europe
204 A/Major Jean-C. Closson	Régiment de Châteauguay	NW Europe NW Europe
205 Major J.G. Stothart	Stormont, Dundas, and Glengary Highlanders	NW Europe
206 Captain Leonard James Gourten	Royal Canadian Regiment	Italy
207 Captain Gordon A. Crutcher	Carleton and York Regiment	Italy
208 Captain William R. Bennett	First Special Service Force	Italy
209 Captain Mark Tennant	Calgary Highlanders	NW Europe
224 Major G.P. Boucher	Régiment de la Chaudière	NW Europe
225 Major George A. Cooper	Regina Rifles	NW Europe
226 Major James L. Dandy	Lincoln and Welland Regiment	NW Europe
227 Major Herald Hudson Usher	Hastings and Prince Edward	Italy
228 Captain G.F. Johnston	West Nova Scotia Regiment	Italy
229 Captain L. LeClerc	Régiment de la Chaudière	NW Europe
234 Major D.S. Beatty	Royal Regiment of Canada	NW Europe
235 Major A.L. Saunders	West Nova Scotia Regiment	Italy
236 Captain W.D. MacDougal	Princess Patricia's Canadian Light Infantry	Italy
237 Captain Wettlaufer	Perth Regiment	Italy
241 Major D.G. Duncan	Seaforth Highlanders	Italy
242 Major H. Tellier	Royal 22e Regiment	Italy

# RANK AND NAME	REGIMENT	THEATRE
243 A/Major Daniel Tremblay	Régiment de Maisonneuve	NW Europe
244 Major Fernand Trudeau	Royal 22e Regiment	Italy
245 Captain John Earl Harry	Saskatoon Light Infantry	Italy
246 Captain D.A.J. Pare	Régiment de la Chaudière	NW Europe
255 Major C.M. McDougall	Princess Patricia's Canadian Light Infantry	Italy
256 Captain L.P. Beech	Queen's Own Cameron Highlanders	NW Europe
257 Captain James Douglas Cooper	Stormont, Dundas, and Glengarry Highlanders	NW Europe
258 Captain G.A. Fortin	Royal 22e Régiment	Italy
259 Captain Charles E. Lévesque	Royal 22e Régiment	Italy
260 Captain D.C. Menzies	The Black Watch	NW Europe
261 Captain G. Rosa	Fusiliers Mont-Royal	NW Europe
268 Major F.J. Chauvin	Essex Scottish Regiment	NW Europe
269 A/Major Donald Hogarth	Queen's Own Rifles of Canada	NW Europe
270 A/Major Leslie Edward Pope	Lake Superior Regiment	NW Europe
271 Major R.D. Medland	Queen's Own Rifles of Canada	NW Europe
272 Major J.K. Rhodes	West Nova Scotia Regiment	Italy
273 Major Thompson	Saskatoon Light Infantry	Italy
274 Captain W.R. Burnett	North Nova Scotia Highlanders	NW Europe
275 Captain Ian Scott Waldie	Queen's Own Rifles of Canada	NW Europe
280 Major R.C. Graves	North Nova Scotia Highlanders	NW Europe
281 Major R.G. Liddell	Royal Canadian Regiment	Italy
282 Captain R.D. Bacon	Calgary Highlanders	NW Europe

#RANK AND NAME	REGIMENT	THEATRE
283 Captain James Bulloch	Royal Winnipeg Rifles	NW Europe
284 Captain W.L. Lyster	Calgary Highlanders	NW Europe
290 Major Froggett	Royal Hamilton Light Infantry	NW Europe
291 Major A.F. Mitchell	Royal Canadian Regiment	Italy
292 Major F.H. McDougall	Loyal Edmonton Regiment	Italy
293 Major Ray Styffe	Lake Superior Regiment	NW Europe
294 Captain Arthur Kendall Gale	Cape Breton Highlanders	Italy
295 Captain Edward Kenneth Maxted	Royal Canadian Regiment	Italy
296 A/Major R.L. Boulanger	Régiment de la Chaudière	NW Europe
297 Captain Norman C. Root	Perth Regiment	Italy
298 Captain J.A. MacDonald	Princess Louise Fusiliers	Italy

NOTES

INTRODUCTION

1 Bernardete, *The Argument of the Action*, 34–58.

2 Hayward, "The Measurement of Combat Effectiveness," 316.

3 Sarkesian, *Combat Effectiveness*, 9.

4 Millett, "The Effectiveness of Military Organizations," 2–3.

5 Sarkesian, *Combat Effectiveness*, 9.

6 Walsh, "Inadequacy of Cost per 'Kill,'" 750. For some more recent works that include such measurements, see: Mosier, *The Myth of the Great War*; Ferguson, *The Pity of War*.

7 English, *On Infantry*, 143.

8 Ibid., 139.

9 Dupuy, *Numbers, Prediction, and War*.

10 For recent commentary on these perceptions, see Smelser, *The Myth of the Eastern Front*.

11 Marshall, *Men Against Fire*, 54.

12 Doubler, *Closing with the Enemy*, 60.

13 Williams, *SLAM*, 80.

CHAPTER ONE

1 Quoted in Keegan, *The Face of Battle*, 117.

2 Ellis, *The Sharp End of War*, 109–11.

3 Keegan, *The Face of Battle*, 36.

4 Audoin-Rouzeau, *14–18*, 11–12.

5 Ibid., 16.

6 Spiller, "S.L.A. Marshall and the Ratio of Fire," 65.

7 Marshall, *Bringing Up the Rear*, 67.

8 Williams, *SLAM*, 26. The number of interviews that Marshall conducted is a matter of some controversy. In *Men Against Fire* Marshall claimed that he interviewed "approximately 400 infantry rifle companies," but by 1952 the number had grown to 603; five years later it was "something over 500." As Roger Spiller has demonstrated, however, given the time Marshall claimed he needed to carry out a detailed interview – at least three days – then, even by the most generous allowance, there is no physical way that he could have carried out anywhere near that number. See Spiller, "S.L.A. Marshall," 68.

9 Marshall, *Night Drop*, xi.

10 Spiller, "S.L.A. Marshall," 63.

11 Marshall, *Men Against Fire*, 54.

12 Ibid., 56–7.

13 Ibid., 58.

14 Ibid., 59.

15 Ibid., 60–1.

16 Ibid., 78.

17 Ibid., 79.

18 For example, in F.D.G. Williams's official U.S. Army publication defending S.L.A. Marshall. See Williams, *SLAM*, 84–5.

19 Marshall, *Men Against Fire*, 53.

20 Spiller, "S.L.A. Marshall," 69.

21 Strachan, "Training, Morale and Modern War," 213.

22 Marshall, *Men Against Fire*, 51, 53.

23 Ibid., 56. Marshall claimed: "The trail of this same question was followed through many companies with varying degrees of battle experience, in the Pacific and in Europe. The proportions varied little from situation to situation."

24 Spiller, "S.L.A. Marshall," 67.

25 John Marshall, *Reconciliation Road*, 23.

26 S.L.A. Marshall to B.H. Liddell Hart, 8 February 1950. Quoted in Spiller, "S.L.A. Marshall," 64.

27 Marshall, *Infantry Operations and Weapons Usage in Korea*, 4–8.

28 Williams, *SLAM*, 84. More controversy has been generated on Marshall's experience in Vietnam that almost anything else, due to accusations penned by Colonel David Hackworth, Marshall's aide and companion during his work in Vietnam.

29 Keegan, *The Face of Battle*, 74.

30 In Canada two articles were published in the *Canadian Army Journal* in the 1950s that for all purposes repeat S.L.A. Marshall's arguments for a Canadian audience. These are: Chamberlain, "Training the Functional Rifleman," and Garber, "Every Rifleman Must Be an Aggressive Fighter."

31 Keegan, *The Face of Battle*, 74.

32 A few particularly well-known works have accepted Marshall's numbers and used them as evidence to buttress their own arguments. Some of the most widely cited are: Holmes, *Acts of War*; Shalit, *The Psychology of Conflict and Combat*; Janowitz, *Sociology and the Military Establishment*; Sarkesian, *Combat Effectiveness*; Ashworth, *Trench Warfare, 1914–1918*; John English, *On Infantry*. Note that only the first edition of English's *On Infantry* makes serious reference to Marshall's ratio of fire; the updated second edition excises virtually all of the material on Marshall.

33 Spiller, "S.L.A. Marshall," 64.

34 Weigley, *Eisenhower's Lieutenants*.

35 Stouffer, *The American Soldier*.

36 It needs to be mentioned that there were anecdotal reports of Allied soldiers not firing their weapons, particularly among green soldiers.

37 Spiller, "S.L.A. Marshall," 68–9.

38 Smoler, "The Secret of the Soldiers Who Didn't Shoot."

39 Spiller, "S.L.A. Marshall," 68; Chambers, "S.L.A. Marshall's *Men Against Fire*," 118–20.

40 Hackworth, *About Face*, 548–86.

41 S.L.A. Marshall's grandson, a journalist named John Marshall, investigated many of the allegations levelled against his grandfather. According to his account, Hackworth's savage recounting of his time as Marshall's assistant in *About Face* was largely based upon a personal grudge, and bore little resemblance to what actually took place. See John Marshall, *Reconciliation Road*, 120–9. It seems unlikely that all of Hackworth's unflattering allegations – which include some extremely damaging remarks about Marshall spending time in Vietnamese brothels – are true. On

the other hand, Hackworth's testimony regarding Marshall's character and self-interested incompetence as a military observer are somewhat harder to dismiss.

42 Marshall, *Bringing Up the Rear*, 15.

43 John Marshall, *Reconciliation Road*, 53, 69. In some personal documents Marshall indicated that he had been standing five yards away from his best friend in the AEF, Charly Jones, when Charly took three machine-gun bullets in the face. John Marshall later discovered documentation that proved his grandfather had in fact been away from his unit in training for a commission for weeks before and after his friend had been killed. Coincidentally, he had also been away training for that commission when the war ended, and could not have been on the front lines on 11 November 1918 as he had frequently claimed.

44 Mansoor, *The G.I. Offensive in Europe*, 259–60.

45 Williams, *SLAM*, 3.

46 Ibid., 28.

47 Letter to F.D.G. Williams, quoted in Williams, *SLAM*, 30. John Westover, while apparently willing to entertain some criticisms of his old boss before the worst of the Marshall controversy unfolded, later retreated on many of his prior comments and claimed not to remember any specifics, as John Marshall found to his frustration. See John Marshall, *Reconciliation Road*, 22–40.

48 Marshall, *Bringing Up the Rear*, 70.

49 Ferguson, *The War of the World*, 521.

50 Bourke, *An Intimate History of Killing*, 63–4, 73–5.

51 Dyer, *War: The New Edition*, 53–7.

52 Horn, "'But … It's Not My Fault!,'" 175.

53 Wessely, "Twentieth-century Theories on Combat Motivation and Breakdown," 275.

54 Grossman, *On Killing*, 333.

55 Canadian Forces Leadership Institute, *A Guide to Reading on Professionalism and Leadership*, 26.

56 Grossman, *On Killing*, 4.

57 Grossman, "Trained to Kill."

58 Grossman, *On Combat*, 74–5.

59 Grossman, "On Killing II," 142. Grossman makes a similar and more recent comment in *On Combat*: "Everything you think you know about war is based on 5,000 years of lies." Grossman, *On Combat*, 10.

60 For an example, see the work of Major David S. Pierson, published for the U.S. Army's Command and General Staff College, which is heavily derived from both Grossman and Marshall. Pierson, "Natural Killers."

CHAPTER TWO

1 The documents are stored in Record Group 24, volume 10450 in the Library and Archives Canada (LAC) collection, and complete reproductions of the survey templates have been included in Appendix A of the present work.

2 Sample cover letter, from "Tactical investigation questionnaires, routine requests," LAC RG 24, vol. 9824.

3 British National Archives Catalogue Research Guides, "Second World War: British Army Operations 1939–1945," catalogue reference WO 232. Administrative/biographical background.

4 Most of the archived memoranda on the administrative side of the battle experience questionnaires can be found in: "Completed Battle Experience Questionnaires," LAC RG 24, vol. 9879; and "Tactical investigation questionnaires, circulation and disposal," LAC RG 24, vol. 9823.

5 Memo from Brigadier M.H.S. Penhale, General Staff CMHQ, to Colonel F.F. Fulton, CMHQ, 18 March 1944, LAC RG 24, vol. 9879.

6 Memo from Deputy Director of Tactical Investigation, British War Office, to CMHQ, 11 May 1945, LAC RG 24, vol. 9823.

7 A sample CFA-276 form can be found in Appendix A. Hundreds of filled-out and returned CFA-276 forms can be found in LAC, though their nature as a preliminary survey limits their usefulness, and thus they are not included in this present study in any meaningful way.

8 Memo from Captain E.C. Baker, GSO III (Training Misc.) CMHQ, 12 April 1944, LAC RG 24, vol. 9879.

9 Ibid.

10 "Statistics Covering Battle Exp. Questionnaires," LAC RG 24, vol. 9823. According to CMHQ statistics, thirty battle experience questionnaires were permanently retained by the British War Office. In all likelihood they can be found in catalogue WO 232 at the British National Archives along with the rest of the Directorate of Tactical Investigation files, though the author has, unfortunately, not had the opportunity to find out.

11 Ibid. It should be noted, however, that these numbers may not be completely accurate, as some questionnaires were returned either before or after the July 44–April 45 timeframe that bracketed the statistics.

12 More battle experience questionnaires may be stored in other locations, with equally important information. At present, and to my best knowledge, no other questionnaires have surfaced beyond those ones in Record Group 24 at LAC.

13 Both questionnaires "A" and "H" are reproduced in Appendix A.

14 Memo from Lieutenant-General K. Stuart, Chief of Staff CMHQ, to Directorate of Tactical Investigation, 26 April 1944, LAC RG 24, vol. 9879. Stuart confirms the received instruction: "The distribution of this form is to be made … to Cdn officers NOT below the rank of Captain, by British Movement Control."

15 See Copp, *Battle Exhaustion*, 99. Bill McAndrew mentions them again five years later in a chapter published for a compilation, though the mention is again a passing one. See McAndrew, "The Soldier and the Battle," in Granatstein, *The Good Fight*, 134. More substantive use of these documents may have been made in other historical works, but I am unaware of any instances.

16 Stacey, *A Date With History*, 229–30.

17 For a good discussion, see John English, *The Canadian Army and the Normandy Campaign*, 2–3.

18 John Marshall, *Reconciliation Road*, 190–4. Leinbaugh and John D. Campbell carried out interviews with U.S. Second World War veterans four decades after the end of the war, asking them to recall their actions. While it may make for an interesting account, John Marshall is correct in asserting: "It has definite shortcomings as a way to capture history." See Leinbaugh, *The Men of Company K*.

19 For a good example, see Krauss, "Factors Affecting Veterans' Decisions to Fire," 105–11. While the goal of the article – to determine whether social education can influence soldiers to differentially regard the cue to fire their weapons – was commendable, its central weakness was its reliance on the memories of veterans who had not seen combat in 15–20 years for precise details on weapons use.

20 CFA-276 forms, "Completed Battle Experience Questionnaires," LAC RG 24, vol. 9879.

21 Curtis, *The Politics of Population*, 25.

22 Ibid., 29.

23 Labaw, *Advanced Questionnaire Design*, 1.

24 Oppenheim, *Questionnaire Design*, 101.

25 Labaw, *Advanced Questionnaire Design*, 13.

26 Oppenheim, *Questionnaire Design*, 6.

27 Ibid., 9. Emphasis added.

28 Labaw, *Advanced Questionnaire Design*, 37.

29 Oppenheim, *Questionnaire Design*, 102.

30 Ibid., 102.

31 Actually, this is not entirely true. A select few officers whose questionnaires had been judged to be "particularly valuable" and had been sent to the War Office by CMHQ were later brought in for face-to-face interviews with Directorate of Tactical Investigation researchers. However, this sample was extremely small, approximately one face-to-face interview for every hundred questionnaires sent in to the War Office (apparently this number was consistent for both Canadian and British officers being surveyed), and the transcripts of the interviews were not released back to Canada, so they were not accessible for the present study.

32 Labaw, *Advanced Questionnaire Design*, 61–2.

33 Ibid., 26, 62–3. Labaw uses the following definition of "consciousness" for her book: the process by which a person is able to arrange events and ideas together within his head as they may have never actually been. A person who is able to imagine outcomes, plot, plan, and visualize the outcomes of future behaviour in a given situation can be said to be conscious of that situation.

34 Ibid., 67.

35 Ibid., 68, 88.

36 Ibid., 68.

37 For more information on survey design from a more technical and mathematical perspective, see Saris, *Design, Evaluation, and Analysis*.

38 Cover letter to officers in hospital, from "Completed Battle Experience Questionnaires," LAC RG 24, vol. 9879.

39 Memo from Deputy Director of Tactical Investigation to CMHQ, 16 Sept. 1944, LAC RG 24, vol. 9879.

40 Directorate of Tactical Investigation reports, "Illumination of the Battlefield," and "Wireless Communication within the Infantry Battalion," LAC RG 24, vol. 9823.

41 Memorandum from Deputy Director of Tactical Investigation to CMHQ, "Canadian Officers Returning from Overseas," 16 Aug. 1944, LAC RG 24, vol. 9879.

42 Memorandum from Directorate of Tactical Investigation to CMHQ, "Information required from officers returning from active theatres of operations," 9 February 1945, LAC RG 24, vol. 9823.

43 From the last page of questionnaire "H" - Infantry, LAC RG 24, vol. 10450. Reproduced in entirety in Appendix A. Information was "particularly required on" topics such as infantry-tank co-operation, night operations, battle fatigue, patrolling, and others.

44 Memorandum from Deputy Director of Tactical Investigation to CMHQ, "Canadian Officers Returning from Overseas," 16 August 1944, LAC RG 24, vol. 9879.

45 Memorandum from Lt.-General J.C. Murchie to British Under-Secretary of State, 23 March 1946, LAC RG 24, vol. 9823. It is not known if this information was ever received by CMHQ after this memo was sent out.

46 Memorandum from Lt.-Colonel F.S. Wilder, to SD&T section CMHQ, "Battle Experience Questionnaires," 14 Oct. 1944, LAC RG 24, Vol. 9879.

47 Granatstein, Canada's Army, 181.

48 "Statistics Covering Battle Exp. Questionnaires," LAC RG 24, vol. 9823.

49 Oppenheim, Questionnaire Design, 102.

50 Memorandum from Directorate of Tactical Investigation to CMHQ, "Canadian Officers Returning from Overseas," 16 Aug. 1944, LAC RG 24, vol. 9879.

51 Labaw, Advanced Questionnaire Design, 87.

52 Battle Experience Questionnaire "A" - General, LAC RG 24, vol. 10450. Reproduced in Appendix A.

53 Ibid.

54 Labaw, Advanced Questionnaire Design, 87. Labaw writes that a fundamental operating reality of opinion polling is that people will answer questions, on any topic, regardless of whether or not they know anything about it. She places very little faith in the efficacy of including a "don't know" category on questionnaires.

55 CFA-276 form, "Battle Experience Questionnaires Routine Requests," LAC RG 24, vol. 9824.

56 Allan English, Understanding Military Culture, 31–8.

57 Granatstein, Canada's Army, 297.

58 Bercuson, Significant Incident, 36–7.

59 Battle Experience Questionnaire cover letter, "Battle Experience Questionnaires Routine Requests," LAC RG 24, vol. 9824.

60 Of course, not every officer with combat experience would have returned to England from their unit while the war was being fought. But
given ordinary rotations, leave, and extremely high casualty rates among
officers (discussed in much more detail in the next chapter), it is likely
that over the nine-month period in which the battle experience questionnaires were being circulated that a majority of Canadian captains,
majors, and lieutenant-colonels with combat experience would have
at some point been handed a CFA-276 form.

61 Curtis, *Politics of Population*, 29.

62 Ibid., 30.

63 As mentioned earlier, attempts on the part of CMHQ to collate the data
from the Canadian battle experience questionnaires came to nothing.
Given that only a very small number of the Canadian questionnaires
were retained by the DTI for their assessments, there is evidence that
the great majority of the information contained in the battle experience
questionnaires, at least those filled out by Canadian officers, was not
utilized to any extent even during the Second World War.

64 Lists of the officers whose questionnaires were forwarded to DTI can
be found in: "Tactical investigation questionnaires, circulation and
disposal," LAC RG 24, vol. 9823.

65 See sample questionnaires provided in Appendix A. Specifically:
Weapons effectiveness – survey "H" question 1; tactical fire and movement – survey "H" question 11; German counter-attacks – survey "H"
question 8; artillery and air support – survey "H" questions 12 and 7
respectively; troop morale – survey "A" questions 1, 2, and 3; average
section strength – survey "H" question 10(a); close-quarters fighting –
survey "H" question 10(d).

66 According to Terry Copp, around 100,000 men were on the strength
of First Canadian Army preparing for Operation Overlord, the invasion
of France. Fewer than 30,000 of these, including both officers and men,
would be involved in close combat in any way. Copp, *Fields of Fire*, 15.

67 See Appendix A, survey "A" question 1(a).

CHAPTER THREE

1 The Canadian Army's official histories corroborate this account of the
attack on Catenanuova. The town was evidently taken with surprising
ease, as the German 923rd Fortress Battalion failed to offer much resistance inside Catenanuova itself. The fighting inside the town, which

seemed to involve the killing of POWs, was thus a "mopping-up" affair, though the Germans put up more of a fight later in the night outside of Catenanouva. See Stacey, *The Canadian Army*, 104; and Nicholson, *The Canadians in Italy*, 137–42.

2 LAC RG 24, vol. 10450, Battle Experience Questionnaire (hereafter BEQ), 62, Captain A.H. Maclean.

3 For an excellent critical discussion of how these perceptions and assumptions are interwoven with Western culture and its use of violence, see: Asad, *On Suicide Bombing*.

4 Marshall, *Men Against Fire*, 78.

5 Chamberlain, "Training the Functional Rifleman," 26.

6 Some of these include: Grossman, *On Killing*; Ehrenreich, *Blood Rites*; Dyer, *War*. David French's otherwise excellent *Raising Churchill's Army* seems to subscribe to it in places as well. Connected to this is the literature on "just war," particularly when read as an artifact of Western humanist ideology rather than taken as a moral absolute. See Walzer, *Just and Unjust Wars*. For a critique, see Asad, *On Suicide Bombing*.

7 Neither work is a cultural study, of course, but no attempt is made to define what is meant by "Western" and whether the phenomenon of ineffectiveness they speak of applies to "non-Western" societies as well.

8 See in particular Audoin-Rouzeau, *14–18*; Canning, *Power, Violence and Mass Death*.

9 Allan English, *Understanding Military Culture*, 19.

10 There has been substantial criticism of these categories, and elaboration of them, but going into them in more detail is unnecessary for the sake of this study. For a more detailed breakdown, see English, *Understanding Military Culture*, Ibid., 17–21.

11 Walzer, *Just and Unjust Wars*.

12 Even the idea of international peacekeeping, so close to the hearts of Canadians as the ultimate expression of humanitarian values, has been attacked on these grounds. For a good recent example dealing with the inherent racism and peacekeeping violence, see Razack, *Dark Threats and White Knights*.

13 Copp, *Fields of Fire*, 15. Also see Granatstein, *Canada's Army*, 296–7.

14 Morton, *When Your Number's Up*, 181.

15 Vance, *Death So Noble*, 4.

16 Ibid., 11–13.

17 Ibid., 17.

18 Mosse, *Fallen Soldiers*, 6–7.

19 Vance, *Death So Noble*, 12–13.

20 Ibid., 35–72. For more on the religious aspects of the war and memory, from an American point of view, see Gamble, *The War for Righteousness*.

21 Winter, *Sites of Memory*, 8.

22 Sheffield, "The Shadow of the Somme," in Addison, *Time to Kill*, 36–7.

23 Mosse, *Fallen Soldiers*, 159.

24 Ibid., 160.

25 Audoin-Rouzeau, *14–18*, 34.

26 Winter, *Remembering War*, 82.

27 Grosse, *Fallen Soldiers*, 160.

28 Audoin-Rouzeau, *14–18*, 35.

29 Ibid., 159, 174.

30 Vance, *Death So Noble*, 22–5. For more on this subject, see Horne, *German Atrocities, 1914*.

31 Quoted in: Vance, *Death So Noble*, 25.

32 Thompson, *Canada 1922–1939*, 141–2.

33 Heron, *The Workers' Revolt in Canada*, 27.

34 For an excellent recent history of the Regina Riots and the On-to-Ottawa trek, see Waiser, *All Hell Can't Stop Us*.

35 Copp, *Fields of Fire*, 16.

36 Audoin-Rouzeau, *14–18*, 33.

37 Winter, *Sites of Memory*, 8. It is important to note, though, that while the Canadian army had no lack of volunteers, a manpower crisis was nonetheless observable from 1943 onward, due almost entirely to the army's poor allocation of its volunteers. Support services were heavily overstaffed while the combat infantry – which sustained the great bulk of the war's casualties – were chronically under-strength once Canadian divisions were committed to battle. Re-allocation of support troops to the combat ranks was implemented as a quick-fix long before conscription, and will be discussed in greater depth later. See Copp, *Fields of Fire*, 16–17.

38 Asad, *On Suicide Bombing*, 34–8.

39 For an excellent counterpoint and discussion of the interwar development of Canadian pacifism, which stood in opposition to the dominant way of viewing the war, see Socknat, *Witness Against War*.

40 Förster, "The Ultimate Horror," in Chickering, *A World of Total War*, 67–8.

41 It is worth noting, though, that there *was* some restraint, particularly in the use of chemical weapons, which all combatants had but which none of them used, creating a curious paradox given the seemingly unrestricted warfare being waged otherwise. For more, see Lagrou, "Representations of War in Western Europe," in Canning, *Power, Violence and Mass Death*, 175–83.

42 Mosse, *Fallen Soldiers*, 200.

43 Winter, *Sites of Memory*, 9.

44 Bercuson, *Maple Leaf Against the Axis*, 2–5.

45 Bercuson, *Significant Incident*, 61–5; Stacey, *Arms, Men and Governments*, 420–4.

46 Granatstein, *Canada's Army*, 181; Copp, *Fields of Fire*, 15.

47 Granatstein, "Canadian Generals in the Second World War," in Horn, *Generalship and the Art of the Admiral*, 71. For one of the classic discussions of this process, among many other things, see John English, *The Canadian Army and the Normandy Campaign*, 125–37.

48 Copp, *Fields of Fire*, 15.

49 Stacey, *Canadian Army Historical Summary*, 235. The decision to send conscripts overseas was forced upon Mackenzie King "by the army's initial ignorance of manpower implications involved in building a six-division army and its subsequent failure to monitor casualty rates accurately." Harris, *Canadian Brass*, 211. For more on the conscription crisis, see Dawson, *The Conscription Crisis of 1944*; Dexter, *Conscription Debates of 1917 and 1944*.

50 Bercuson, *Significant Incident*, 26.

51 See, for example: Cohen, *Citizens and Soldiers*.

52 Dunnigan, *How to Make War*, 485–6. While not an academic source, Dunnigan tends to be well informed about military affairs and offers some prescient commentary on present-day military events.

53 Place, *Military Training in the British Army*, 53.

54 Admittedly this needs to be problematized. Conscripts were put into the forward lines in 1945. Perhaps more relevant, by the summer of 1944 the Canadian army was forced to pursue a policy of re-allocating soldiers from top-heavy support branches – particularly anti-aircraft units, since the *Luftwaffe* had been largely swept from the sky – and re-training them as infantry reinforcements. While these men had, of course,

initially volunteered to join the armed forces, calling their re-allocation to the incredibly dangerous infantry arm voluntary would be stretching credibility. Perhaps it is no coincidence, though, that there were widespread complaints about the performance of such reinforcement soldiers. This will be discussed further in chapter 5.

55 South Africa comes closest, sporting an all-volunteer army of 334,000, although only white soldiers – two-thirds of the force – were allowed to actually fight. For a good overview, see Orpen, *South African Forces*. Over 700,000 Australians served in the Australian army during the war and many were volunteers. The country had effectively re-introduced conscription alongside voluntary service in 1942 after a series of military setbacks. See Long, *Australia in the War of 1939–1945*.

56 French, *Raising Churchill's Army*, 126.

57 Cohen, *Citizens and Soldiers*, 81. For the original numbers on Canada's prewar military, see Stacey, *Six Years of War*, 34.

58 Stacey, *Six Years of War*, 129–31.

59 Copp, *Cinderella Army*, 6. Note that, while originally an Officer Cadet Training Unit attached to the Canadian Army Overseas in Great Britain, this was dissolved in early 1942, and all officer candidates from the ranks of soldiers overseas were subsequently transported *back* to Canada for officer training. It was a rather burdensome system. Stacey, *Six Years of War*, 138.

60 The numbers should be understood and elaborated upon a little. From April 1941 to May 1945, 10,929 officers were also commissioned directly (not from the ranks), but as Stacey goes to some effort to point out, these commissions were mostly accounted for by exceptions made for cerain specialists, "primarily those having technical university degrees or other specialized training suitable for appointments to the Engineers, Judge-Advocate General's Branch, the Pay or Ordnance Corps or the Chaplain Service." After April 1941, virtually all officers for the non-technical combat arms, like the infantry, were commissioned from the ranks. Stacey, *Six Years of War*, 129, 132.

61 Allan English, *The Cream of the Crop*, 8.

62 Crang, *The British Army and the People's War*, 22–3.

63 Stacey, *Six Years of War*, 129–30.

64 Ibid., 130–1.

65 Crang, *British Army and People's War*, 31–3.

66 Dickson, *A Thoroughly Canadian General*, 158–9.

67 Stacey, *Six Years of War*, 131.

68 English, *Cream of the Crop*, 4.

69 Crang, *British Army and People's War*, 33, 37; Stacey, *Six Years of War*, 131.

70 Crang, *British Army and People's War*, 28.

71 Dickson, *Thoroughly Canadian General*, 160.

72 Ibid., 23.

73 Brooks, "The Impact of Culture," in Brooks, *Creating Military Power*, 21.

74 Marshall, *Men Against Fire*, 53–4.

75 Ibid., 54.

76 As laid out in War Office, *Infantry Section Leading, 1938*, 6–8. The British and Canadian armies were initially structured along identical lines to allow for rapid integration and co-operation, and became even more so as the Second World War progressed.

77 The responsibilities of each rank seem to have been somewhat fluid, however, likely owing to heavy casualties among officers. For more on responsibilities within a battalion, see Ewing, "Tacticians to House-mothers," in Horn, *In the Breach*.

78 Some works involving detailed discussion of doctrine most pertinent to this present study are John English, *Canadian Army in Normandy*; Doubler, *Closing with the Enemy*; John English, *On Infantry*; Place, *Military Training in the British Army*.

79 Several versions of the British War Office's *Infantry Training, Infantry Section Leading*, and *Field Service Regulations* were issued between 1920 and 1939, and each one represented a continued negotiation of doctrinal realities. Generally speaking, doctrinal manuals released from 1937 through 1939 seem to have been in effect, although frequently updated, for most of the Second World War. For one of the best recent studies of the impact of doctrine upon the British (and, by association, Canadian) army in the war, see French, *Raising Churchill's Army*, 12–47.

80 War Office, *Infantry Training 1937*, 125–30.

81 Ibid., 61.

82 *Infantry Section Leading 1938* lists the following components for a Company Headquarters: "Company commander; Second-in-command; Company serjeant-major; Company quarter-master-serjeant; Corporal motor-mechanic; 7 Privates – 2 batmen, 1 clerk, 1 storeman, 3 orderlies." War Office, *Infantry Section Leading 1938*, 6.

83 French, *Raising Churchill's Army*, 19.

84 War Office, *Infantry Training 1937*, 131.
85 Allan English, "The Masks of Command," in Allan English, *The Operational Art*, 5.
86 Copp, *Montgomery's Scientists*, 425.
87 The number drops off steadily from there. Second-in-command officers for rifle companies suffered 20.1 percent casualties every month; battalion commanding officers 18 percent; support platoon commanders anywhere from 14.8 to 9.8 percent; and support company commanders 6.2 percent. It is also mentioned in the original report that, owing to the late arrival of some divisions, "casualty rates were probably higher than they appear [from these figures], but it is not possible to make any allowance for this." Ibid., 426.
88 Ibid., 427–8.
89 Weekly Reports, Canadian Small Arms Liaison Officer Overseas, 1941–1945, LAC, microfilm reel c-5167. On the same subject, also see BEQ 186, Lt.-Colonel E.T. Jacques; BEQ 192, Major J.W. Ostiguy. Both of these officers were from the Régiment de Maisonneuve.
90 Ibid.
91 BEQ 173, A/Captain G.C. Watt.
92 BEQ 224, Major G.P. Boucher; BEQ 259, Captain Charles E. Lévesque.
93 BEQ 209, Captain Mark Tennant.
94 BEQ 118, Captain A.J. Willick.
95 For other commentary on officers leading patrols and other forward actions in the battle experience questionnaires, see: BEQ 16, A/Major Thomas McCoy; BEQ 29, A/Major C.K. Crummer; BEQ 35, Major A.M. Hamilton; BEQ 150, Captain H.G. McKinley; BEQ 208, Captain William R. Bennett; BEQ 58, Captain Donald Clair Smith. Captain Smith demonstrates the point about the great variety of experience by complaining about *too much* patrolling by junior officers and platoon commanders.
96 BEQ 191, A/Major Harrison (no first name given).
97 The Operational Research report admits that while the troops believed that mortars inflicted over 70 percent of all casualties upon them, the reality was that "the estimate of 70% may be appreciably in error, and that the figure … includes a large number of captured." But it was still their belief that mortars and *Nebelwerfers* had inflicted over 25,000 casualties among British Canadian troops in the first seven weeks of fighting in Normandy. Copp, *Montgomery's Scientists*, 428, 437.

98 Marshall, *Men Against Fire*, 58.

99 Grossman, *On Killing*, 141–8.

100 Marshall, *Men Against Fire*, 57–8.

101 Stacey, *Six Years of War*, 131–2.

102 English, *Canadian Army and Normandy*, 130.

CHAPTER FOUR

1 Some of the most-cited works advocating these positions are Ellis, *Brute Force*; Dupuy, *A Genuis for War*; van Creveld, *Fighting Power*; Stolfi, *Hitler's Panzers East*.

2 Stolfi, *Hitler's Panzers East*, x.

3 Dupuy, *A Genuis for War*, 4–5, 253–4.

4 Weigley, *Eisenhower's Lieutenants*, 10–14.

5 D'Este, *Decision in Normandy*.

6 The United States military began a German Military History Program very soon after the end of the Second World War, interrogating and even hiring former *Wehrmacht* officers to prepare reports for the Historical Division of the U.S. Army's European Command. The subject for most of these studies was, not surprisingly, the German war against the Red Army on the eastern front, which was of tremendous interest to the Americans once the Cold War began and ensured a sympathetic and attentive audience. Bizarrely, the key proponent of this program, German General Franz Halder, later received the U.S. Meritorious Civilian Service Award for his work on this project. A collection of 213 reports culled from some 2,500 manuscripts in the U.S. National Archives was produced as a 24-volume series in the late 1970s. Detwiler, *World War II German Military Studies*, vol. 1, 1–4.

7 Bonn, *When the Odds Were Even*, 3.

8 Weigley, *Eisenhower's Lieutenants*, 26–8.

9 Mansoor, *The G.I. Offensive in Europe*, 2. For an excellent discussion of how the German perspective on their own failure became so widely accepted and credible in Western military circles following 1945, see Smelser, *The Myth of the Eastern Front*.

10 For a few criticisms, see Brown, "Colonel Trevor N. Dupuy and the Mythos of *Wehrmacht* Superiority"; Brown, "The *Wehrmacht* Mythos Revisited"; Mansoor, *G.I. Offensive in Europe*, 7–8; Bonn, *When the Odds Were Even*, 6–8. For a good overview, particularly as the debate

relates to the Normandy campaign, see Johnston, "D +20,000," 49.

11 Overy, *Why the Allies Won*, 4–6.

12 Canadian military historian Terry Copp has led the way on bringing this to light. See Copp, *Montgomery's Scientists*.

13 McAndrew, "Soldiers and Technology," 21.

14 Ibid., 21. McAndrew claims that: "One persistent theme in post-action questionnaires completed by combat officers concerning morale was their lack of opportunity to exercise initiative." Presumably he is writing of the same battle experience questionnaires employed in this study, since he has referenced them before, but a careful reading shows that this does not seem to have been a noteworthy trend in the BEQs. Officers sometimes expressed frustration with not being able to exercise initiative, but this was certainly not endemic in the BEQs.

15 Copp, *Cinderella Army*, 5–6.

16 Doubler, *Closing with the Enemy*, 286.

17 For a good discussion, particularly from a German perspective, see Corum, *The Roots of Blitzkrieg*.

18 For a decent, if somewhat incomplete discussion of the continuities of Canadian doctrine, see McAndrew, "Canadian Doctrine: Continuities and Discontinuities."

19 Corum, *The Roots of Blitzkrieg*, 7–8.

20 Callahan, "Two Armies in Normandy," 273. It is also important to note that some German officers who fought mostly or exclusively on the Western Front in the First World War adopted similar ways of thinking about warfare as their Allied counterparts, particularly General Walther Reinhardt. See Corum, *The Roots of Blitzkrieg*, 56.

21 Ibid. Corum goes to great length to attack the idea that Germany's interwar tactical innovations were all imports from other countries, and is largely successful in proving his case. The greater part of German tactical thinking appears to have evolved through hard work and a dedication to learning the lessons of the war, rather than from foreign military theorists.

22 Brown, "Not Glamorous, But Effective," 422. Germany's vaunted Spring Offensives of 1918 mostly succeeded in hastening its own demise; they resulted in the loss of nearly 1 million men, including practically all of Germany's elite stormtroop divisions.

23 Rawling, *Surviving Trench Warfare*, 114–15.

24 For further discussion of the creeping barrage and ways in which it was sometimes unsuccessful, particularly earlier in the war, see Keegan, *The First World War*, 291–3.

25 Godefroy, "Canadian Military Effectiveness in the First World War," in Horn, *The Canadian Way of War*, 187.

26 Brown, "Not Glamorous, But Effective," 422.

27 Schreiber, *Shock Army of the British Empire*, 9–12; Curtis, "The Elastic Defence," 53–7. The doctrine of the elastic defence and counter-attack remained a central part of German tactical doctrine throughout the interwar years and the Second World War, with relatively minor variations.

28 Rawling, *Surviving Trench Warfare*, 140–2; Godefroy, "Canadian Military Effectiveness," 188–9; Schreiber, *Shock Army of the British Empire*.

29 Brown, "Not Glamorous," 426–7.

30 John English, *Canadian Army and Normandy*, 16.

31 Rawling, *Surviving Trench Warfare*, 165; English, "Lessons from the Great War," 56.

32 Interestingly, the inherent strength of the defensive posture gives some insight into why the Germans generally killed more Entente and Allied soldiers in the First World War than they sacrificed of their own. The Germans were generally on the defensive in the west throughout the war. They suffered some of their greatest casualties when they elected to take the offense instead, particularly in 1918. For the numbers on casualties broken down by nation, see Ferguson, *The Pity of War*, 295.

33 McAndrew, "Canadian Doctrine," 45.

34 French, *Raising Churchill's Army*, 12–14.

35 Ibid., 19.

36 War Office, *Field Service Regulations 1935*, 124.

37 Ibid., 124–6.

38 Corum, *The Roots of Blitzkrieg*, 32.

39 Callahan, "Two Armies in Normandy," 273–4.

40 French, *Raising Churchill's Army*, 19–20. Also see English, *Canadian Army and Normandy*.

41 Schreiber, *Shock Army of the British Empire*, 3–4.

42 Godefroy, "Canadian Military Effectiveness," 188–9.

43 Lt.-General Guy Simonds, Operational Policy – 2 Cdn Corps, 17 Feb. 1944, reproduced in Copp, *Fields of Fire*, 269–76.

44 McAndrew, "Canadian Doctrine," 42–3.

45 The Canadian Corps of the First World War was regarded to have a particularly "pronounced artillerist bent." English, *Canadian Army and Normandy*, 18.

46 Ferguson, *The War of the World*, 515.

47 Overy, *Why the Allies Won*, 316–18.

48 Ferguson, *War of the World*, 520.

49 French, *Raising Churchill's Army*, 12–14.

50 Some German sources believed that his approach of "Equipment Saves Lives" was a stark contrast to the German approach, which imbued rigorous tactical training with the utmost importance, typified in the saying "Sweat Saves Blood." Fritz, *Frontsoldaten*, 61.

51 English, *Canadian Army and Normandy*, 174–5.

52 McAndrew, "Fire or Movement?," 140.

53 Fritz, *Frontsoldaten*, 62–3.

54 Quoted in: Copp, *Cinderella Army*, 92.

55 Statistics compiled are based on answers to survey "H" question 12(a): "Did your unit carry out an attack under an artillery barrage?" Overall: "Yes" 115 surveys, "No" 19 surveys, "No Answer" 9. The difference between the Mediterranean and Northwest Europe campaigns can possibly be accounted for by the broken terrain of the Italian peninsula, which limited the use of armoured vehicles and maximized the responsibility of infantry in co-operation with artillery.

56 LAC RG 24, vol. 10450, BEQ 15, Captain Donald Findlay.

57 BEQ 182, Captain S.R. Lambert.

58 BEQ 205, Major J.G. Stothart.

59 BEQ 36, A/Major John Irvin Mills.

60 Statistics compiled based on answers to survey "H" question 12(c): "Did [troops] keep up with the barrage effectively?" Overall: "Yes" 87 surveys; "No" 21 surveys; "No Answer" 8 surveys. See Appendix B.

61 BEQ 173, A/Captain G.C. Watt.

62 BEQ 180, Captain Warren G. Harvey.

63 Statistics compiled based on answers to survey "H" question 12(b): "did [troops] have preliminary training [in attacking under a barrage]?" Overall: "Yes" 58 surveys; "No" 54 surveys; "No Answer" 5 surveys. See Appendix B.

64 Statistics based on answers to survey "H" question 12(b), compiled according to the number of months an officer had served in the theatre of operations. See Appendix A.

65 Copp, *Fields of Fire*, 43, 124–6.

66 Copp, *Cinderella Army*, 189.

67 Ibid., 290–1.

68 For critiques of wireless communications in particular, see BEQ 146, Captain Reginald Harvey Smith; BEQ 192, Major J.W. Ostiguy. Fully half of the questions (nos. 16 through 30) on survey "H" of the questionnaires ask questions about the effectiveness of communications and signalling in battle, so it was clearly an area in which the surveyors felt there was room for improvement.

69 The distinction should be made here that there is every indication that good systems were worked out for calling down *observed* fire with reasonable accuracy, particularly when thwarting German counter-attacks. But Forward Observation Officers (FOOs) tended to sustain casualties equal to those of the infantry with whom they normally operated, and communications between FOOs and their artillery batteries could sometimes be unreliable. See Copp, *Fields of Fire*, 28.

70 BEQ 78, Captain T.H. Burdett.

71 BEQ 192, Major J.W. Ostiguy.

72 BEQ 83, A/Major D.M. Ripley.

73 BEQ 54, Lt.-Colonel T.P. Gilday.

74 BEQ 48, A/Captain Sinkewicz.

75 BEQ 246, Captain D.A.J. Paré.

76 BEQ 290, Major Froggett.

77 Copp, *Cinderella Army*, 291.

78 BEQ 75, Major John Campbell.

79 BEQ 205, Major J.G. Stothart.

80 BEQ 191, A/Major Harrison.

81 Based on answers to survey "A" question 4: "Please list in order of importance factors which, in your unit, appeared to have the effect of lowering morale." See Appendix A.

82 BEQ 243, A/Major Daniel Tremblay.

83 Based on compiled answers to survey "H" questions 12(a), 12(b), 12(c). See Appendix A.

84 English, *Canadian Army and Normandy*, 26.

85 Bercuson, *Maple Leaf Against the Axis*, 220.

86 Copp, *Cinderella Army*, 291.

87 Callahan, "Two Armies in Normandy," 272.

88 For one of the definitive discussions of this issue, see English, *Canadian*

Army and Normandy, 163–71. Also see French, *Raising Churchill's Army*, 96–106.

89 Callahan, "Two Armies in Normandy," 272–3.

90 Copp, *Fields of Fire*, 133–54.

91 Overy, *Why the Allies Won*, 223.

92 English, *Canadian Army and Normandy*, 166.

93 BEQ 129, A/Major T.M. Lowe; BEQ 186, Lt.-Colonel E.T. Jacques.

94 Statistics compiled based on answers to survey "A" question 3: "Please list in order of importance factors which, in your unit, appeared to have the effect of raising morale."

95 English, *Canadian Army and Normandy*, 240; Copp, *Fields of Fire*, 106, 260.

96 Morton, *A Military History of Canada*, 216; Perrun, "Best-Laid Plans," 139; Keegan, *Six Armies in Normandy*, 197–8.

97 Copp, *Montgomery's Scientists*, 397.

98 BEQ 177, Major R.A. Cottrill.

99 Extracts from War Diaries and Memoranda, June–October 1944, reprinted in: Copp, *Cinderella Army*, 319. Also see English, *Canadian Army and Normandy*, 207.

100 Bercuson, *Maple Leaf Against the Axis*, 219. The Firefly was congruent with the Operational Research Section's conclusions, which suggested compensating for the Sherman's vulnerability by mounting a larger gun, "to make German tanks more vulnerable," rather than adding additional armour to the Sherman. Copp, *Montgomery's Scientists*, 397.

101 Copp, *Fields of Fire*, 129.

102 Operation GOODWOOD was a perfect example of an armoured attack breaking against an anti-tank screen. See Callahan, "Two Armies in Normandy," 276–8.

103 English, *Canadian Army and Normandy*, 164.

104 French, *Raising Churchill's Army*, 94–6.

105 BEQ 159, Captain H.S. Lamb.

106 French, *Raising Churchill's Army*, 89; Zuehlke, *Ortona*, 393. Zuehlke in particular mentions the PIAT as being an "unpopular" weapon, an opinion that the battle experience questionnaires would seem to contradict.

107 Statistics compiled based on answers to survey "H" question 2: "Have you found any of these weapons outstandingly effective? If so, which and why?" The top weapons mentioned by the officers are as follows: PIAT (74 mentions), Bren gun (54 mentions), 3-inch mortar (44 mentions),

No. 36 grenade (33), No. 77 grenade (24), Rifles (15). In contrast, the following question, survey "H" question 3, is: "Have you found any of these weapons ineffective? If so, which and why?" The PIAT received only three mentions as an *ineffective* weapon. It is possible that much of the perceived effectiveness was derived from the weapon's unconventional applications. See Appendix B.

108 Statistics compiled based on answers to survey "H" question 15(a): "Have you ever co-operated with Infantry Tanks?" Overall results: "Yes" 114 surveys; "No" 26 surveys; "No Answer" 4 surveys. See Appendix B.

109 BEQ 178, Major John C. Clarke.

110 BEQ 208, Captain William R. Bennett.

111 BEQ 243, A/Major Daniel Tremblay.

112 BEQ 209, Captain Mark Tennant; BEQ 115, Major David Durward. The failure of tanks to perform well in their supporting role is also listed in several surveys in answer to survey "A" question 4: "Please list in order of importance factors which, in your unit, appeared to have the effect of lowering morale." See Appendix A.

113 BEQ 54, Lt.-Colonel T.P. Gilday.

114 BEQ 186, Lt.-Colonel E.T. Jacques.

115 English, *Canadian Army and Normandy*, 167, 171.

116 BEQ 192, Major J.W. Ostiguy.

117 BEQ 131, Major John Wesley Burgess. Major Burgess appears to have gotten the dates wrong; the Canadian offensives against Verriers and Rocquancourt took place in mid-July, not mid-June.

118 BEQ 243, A/Major Daniel Tremblay.

119 BEQ 246, Captain D.A.J. Paré.

120 BEQ 280, Major R.C. Graves.

121 Statistics compiled based on answers to survey "H" question 15(b): "Did you move in front of, behind, or amongst the tanks?" Overall results: "In Front" 49 surveys; "Behind" 14 surveys; "Amongst" 16 surveys; "All" 30 surveys; "No Answer" 9 surveys. See Appendix B.

122 BEQ 281, Major R.G. Liddell.

123 BEQ 295, Captain Edward Kenneth Maxted; BEQ 209, Captain Mark Tennant; BEQ 192, Major Ostiguy.

124 BEQ 177, Major R.A. Cottrill.

125 BEQ 146, Captain Reginald Harvey Smith.

126 BEQ 235, Major A.L. Saunders.

127 BEQ 177, Major R.A. Cottrill.

128 BEQ 235, Major A.L. Saunders; BEQ 67, Major J.C. Allan; BEQ 78, Captain T.H. Burdett.

129 BEQ 125, A/Captain P.A.R. Blaker.

130 BEQ 178, Major John C. Clarke.

131 BEQ 120, Captain Pollin; BEQ 178, Major John C. Clarke.

132 Compiled from answers to survey "A" question 4. See Appendix A.

133 BEQ 89, Captain G.A. Marron.

134 BEQ 130, A/Major Elbert Louis Froggett.

135 BEQ 143, Major L.P. Coderre.

136 Neillands, *The Bomber War*, 309–10.

137 See Bonn, *When the Odds Were Even*; Doubler, *Closing with the Enemy*.

138 Statistics compiled based on answers to survey "H" question 7(a): "Did you receive Direct Air Support?" Overall results: "Yes" 100 surveys; "No" 39 surveys; "No Answer" 12 surveys. See Appendix B.

139 Statistics compiled based on answers to survey "H" question 7(c): "Was this support effective?" Overall results: "Yes" 80 surveys, "No" 3 surveys; "Partially" 16 surveys; "No Answer" 1 survey. See Appendix B.

140 BEQ 29, A/Major C.K. Crummer.

141 Statistics compiled based on answers to survey "A" question 3: "Please list in order of importance factors which, in your unit, appeared to have the effect of raising morale." See Appendix A.

142 Officially the RAF term was "direct support," but none of the infantry officers in the surveys use that term, opting instead for "air support" or "close air support." See Johnston, "Tactical Air Power Controversies," 62.

143 BEQ 32, Captain A.C. MacCallum.

144 BEQ 68, Major Cyril Wrightman.

145 BEQ 100, Lt.-Colonel Charles Petch.

146 Johnston, "Tactical Air Power Controversies," 63.

147 Ibid., 63–9.

148 Copp, *Cinderella Army*, 292.

149 Copp, *Fields of Fire*, 43. Admittedly, the weather was poor, but the sheer scope of the damage that was *not* inflicted on Juno Beach despite the application of a tremendous aerial bombardment is staggering.

150 Millett, "The United States Armed Forces," in Millett, *Military Effectiveness: Volume III*, 78.

151 Johnston, "Tactical Air Power Controversies," 69–70.

152 Keegan, *The Face of Battle*, 287–8.

153 English, *On Infantry*, 274.

154 Copp, *Fields of Fire*, 73.

155 Erickson, *The Road to Berlin*, 83.

156 English, *Canadian Army and Normandy*, 164–7.

157 Copp, *Fields of Fire*, 106.

CHAPTER FIVE

1 Hart, *Clash of Arms*, 187. Hart offers a decent, if somewhat curt, assessment of some of First Canadian Army's administrative problems in the context of the wider Allied campaign in Normandy.

2 Admittedly, where the Canadians did engage in large-scale mobile warfare, they tended to do poorly. The Canadian pursuit of German forces to the Seine River following the breakout of Normandy, for example, was nothing short of a fiasco. But few opportunities really presented themselves to Canadians during the war. See Copp, *Cinderella Army*, 15–56.

3 Ibid., 287.

4 Copp, *Fields of Fire*, 27.

5 Ibid., 27–9.

6 Ibid., 28.

7 McAndrew, "Canadian Doctrine," 42–5.

8 Statistics compiled based on answers to survey "H" question 8a, "Did you ever have to organise rapid defence against counter-attack?" Overall: "Yes" 109 surveys, "No" 34 surveys, "No Answer" 9 surveys. See Appendix B.

9 LAC RG 24, vol. 10450, Battle Experience Questionnaire (hereafter "BEQ") 48, A/Captain Sinkewicz. According to German doctrine on both the eastern and western fronts of the war, reserves being held back for counterattacks needed maximum firepower and mobility: armoured Panzer divisions came closest to meeting these requirements, and were employed extensively in this role once the Germans were thrown onto the defensive. See U.S. Department of the Army, "German Defense Tactics against Russian Break-Throughs," 3–4, in Detwiler, *World War II German Military Studies, Vol. 17.*

10 BEQ 76, Major W.C. Allan.

11 BEQ 60, Major A.C. Ross.

12 BEQ 290, Major Froggett. Major Froggett appears to be the only officer to have filled out *two* battle experience questionnaires, the first one in

October 1944, after which he returned to duty, and the second one in March 1945. Also see BEQ 130, A/Major Elbert Louis Froggett.

13 BEQ 76, Major W.C. Allan.

14 BEQ 258, Captain G.A. Fortin; BEQ 280, Major R.C. Graves; BEQ 59, Major F.J. Hammond; BEQ 130, A/Major Elbert Louis Froggett; BEQ 178, Major John C. Clarke.

15 BEQ 178, Major John C. Clarke; BEQ 36, A/Major John Irvin Mills.

16 BEQ 76, Major W.C. Allan.

17 BEQ 258, Captain G.A. Fortin; BEQ 73, Captain Armstrong.

18 BEQ 282, Captain R.D. Bacon; BEQ 178, Major John Clarke.

19 BEQ 36, A/Major John Irvin Mills.

20 BEQ 191, A/Major Harrison.

21 BEQ 16, A/Major Thomas McCoy.

22 Copp, *Fields of Fire*, 27.

23 War Office, *Field Service Regulations 1935*, 131.

24 Place, *Military Training in the British Army*, 67.

25 Ibid., 69-75.

26 Statistics compiled based on answers to survey "H" question 11, "Were you able to put the tactical principles of fire and movement, taught as battle drill before going overseas, into practice?" Overall: "Yes" 128 surveys, "No" 15 surveys, "No Answer" 8 surveys." See Appendix B.

27 Statistics compiled based on answers to survey "H" question 11, "Were you able to put the tactical principles of fire and movement, taught as battle drill before going overseas, into practice? Often, fairly often, or seldom?" Overall: "Often" 34 surveys, "Fairly Often" 48 surveys, "Seldom" 46 surveys. See Appendix B.

28 BEQ 147, Captain Robert B. Mainprize. There seems to be an irregularity in this questionnaire, since the PPCLI fought in the Mediterranean and did not arrive in Northwest Europe until early 1945, while Mainprize is recounting events from Normandy. It seems likely that he served with a different unit in Normandy, which he does not name.

29 BEQ 99, Major Charles Bellavance; BEQ 67, Major J.C. Allan. Major Bellavance talks about a lack of artillery support, and that fact that the Canadian tanks were torn apart by strong German anti-tank defences before they could be of much use. Major Allan concurs that all of their supporting tanks were knocked out several hundred yards short of the objective, forcing the infantry to go in alone.

30 BEQ 191, A/Major Harrison. The "pepper-pot" method of fire and

movement was taught to Commonwealth soldiers in training, and was fire-and-movement in a very rudimentary form, with an emphasis upon forward movement toward an objective rather than opportunistic maneuvre. For more details, see Place, *Military Training in the British Army*, 72–3.

31 BEQ 29, A/Major C.K. Crummer.

32 BEQ 271, Major R.D. Medland.

33 See in particular McAndrew, "Fire or Movement?: Canadian Tactical Doctrine, Sicily – 1943."

34 For some good recent overviews of Canadian trench raiding and infantry doctrine in the First World War, see Haynes, "The Development of Infantry Doctrine"; Jones, "The Role of Trench Raiding in Combat Motivation."

35 Ellis, *The Sharp End of War*, 53.

36 War Office, *Infantry Section Leading 1938*, 52–3.

37 Ibid., 55.

38 Ibid., 58.

39 Ibid., 58-60.

40 Bonn, *When the Odds Were Even*, 31–3; Condell, *On the German Art of War*.

41 U.S. War Department, *Field Service Regulations: Operations, 1941*, chapters 5 and 6.

42 BEQ 209, Captain Mark Tennant; BEQ 54, Lt.-Colonel T.P. Gilday; BEQ 27, Major Herbert R. Fullerston.

43 BEQ 207, Captain Gordon A. Crutcher.

44 BEQ 182, Captain S.R. Lambert.

45 BEQ 62, Captain A.H. Maclean; BEQ 15, Captain Donald Findlay; BEQ 28, A/Major J.P.G. Kemp.

46 BEQ 30, A/Captain Yuile.

47 BEQ 209, Major G.P. Boucher; BEQ 186, Lt.-Colonel E.T. Jacques. Also see BEQ 15, Captain Donald Findlay.

48 BEQ 234, Major D.S. Beatty. Also see BEQ 182, Captain S.R. Lambert.

49 BEQ 67, Major J.C. Allan.

50 BEQ 16, A/Major Thomas McCoy.

51 BEQ 36, A/Major John Irvin Mills.

52 BEQ 226, Major James L. Dandy.

53 BEQ 284, Captain W.L. Lyster; BEQ 123, A/Captain P.A.R. Blaker.

54 BEQ 76, Major W.C. Allan.

55 BEQ 281, Major R.G. Liddell.

56 BEQ 66, Major D. Archibald.

57 BEQ 59, Major F.J. Hammond; BEQ 208, Captain William R. Bennett.

58 BEQ 173, A/Captain G.C. Watt.

59 BEQ 161, A/Captain Thomas D. Murray; BEQ 34, A/Captain J.A.D. Graham.

60 BEQ 186, Lt.-Colonel E.T. Jacques; BEQ 79, Major Allister Myles MacMillan.

61 BEQ 227, Major Harold Hudson Usher.

62 BEQ 76, Major W.C. Allan.

63 BEQ 281, Major R.G. Liddell.

64 BEQ 54, Lt.-Colonel T.P. Gilday.

65 Overy, *Why the Allies Won*, 227.

66 For patrols constituting only night experience: BEQ 27, Major Herbert R. Fulleston.

67 Statistics compiled based on answers to survey "H" question 6a, "Did your unit take part in Night Operations?" Overall: "Yes" 133 surveys, "No" 16 surveys, "No Answer" 3 surveys. See Appendix B.

68 Also based on answers to survey "H" question 6a, differentiated by theatre of operations. Mediterranean: "Yes" 49 surveys, "No" 4 surveys, "No Answer" 0 surveys. NW Europe: "Yes" 84 surveys, "No" 12 surveys, "No Answer" 3 surveys. See Appendix B.

69 Statistics compiled based on answers to survey "H" question 6c: "Were [Night Operations] effective?", differentiated by theatre of operations. Mediterranean: "Yes" 46 surveys, "No" 1 surveys, "No Answer" 2 surveys. Northwest Europe: "Yes" 76 surveys, "No" 3 surveys, "No Answer" 5 surveys. See Appendix B.

70 BEQ 176, A/Major William Ewing.

71 BEQ 282, Captain R.D. Bacon. For examples of other re-positioning movements at night, see BEQ 150, Captain H.G. McKinley; BEQ 27, Major Herbert R. Fulleston; BEQ 62, Captain A.H. Maclean.

72 BEQ 151, Major M.B. John.

73 BEQ 182, Captain S.R. Lambert. According to Copp's account of the Rocquancourt; "Here the South Saskatchewan Regiment, which had been completely rebuilt since its devastating losses on 20 July, leaned into the barrage and swept through the village, clearing houses and establishing a defensive perimeter almost as if on exercise." See Copp, *Fields of Fire*, 202.

74 BEQ 54, Lt.-Colonel T.P. Gilday.

75 BEQ 75, Major John Campbell. For an account, see Copp, *Fields of Fire*, 157–69.

76 McAndrew, "Fire or Movement?," 141–4. McAndrew mentions some examples of successful infiltration attacks at night during Canadian operations in Sicily, but also claims that infiltration tactics were largely abandoned, at least by 1st Canadian Division.

77 BEQ 178, Major John Clarke.

78 BEQ 208, Captain William Bennett.

79 BEQ 241, Major D.G. Duncan; BEQ 209, Captain Mark Tennant. Captain Tennant's account is particularly noteworthy, since he was the commander of the anti-tank support platoon for the Calgary Highlanders and had much to say about fighting German tanks.

80 BEQ 281, Major R.G. Liddell.

81 BEQ 293, Major Roy Styffe.

82 BEQ 243, A/Major Daniel Tremblay.

83 On problems with command and control, see BEQ 34, A/Captain J.A.D. Graham; BEQ 36, A/Major John Irvin Mills; BEQ 100, Lt.-Colonel Charles Petch; BEQ 226, Major James L. Dandy; BEQ 259, Captain Charles E. Levesque.

84 BEQ 58, Captain Donald Clair Smith.

85 BEQ 62, Captain A.H. Maclean. On a similar note, see BEQ 27, Major Herbert R. Fulleston.

86 Statistics compiled based on answers to survey "H" question 6b: "Were [your troops] specially trained for Night Operations?", differentiated by theatre of operations. Mediterranean: "Yes" 26 surveys, "No" 18 surveys, "No Answer" 5 surveys. NW Europe: "Yes" 20 surveys, "No" 62 surveys, "No Answer" 2 surveys. See Appendix B.

87 BEQ 58, Captain Donald Clair Smith.

88 BEQ 209, Captain Mark Tennant.

89 See Appendix "A": Survey "A" questions 1(a)(b), 2(a)(b); Survey "H" questions 1, 2, 3.

90 All statistics on weapons use compiled from survey "H" question 1: "Underline the weapon which your unit has actually used in action (add any not listed)." Most of the major infantry small arms were listed underneath, and space was given for any additional weapons that officers could think off. See Appendix A.

91 Marshall was very disparaging of the grenade, based upon his "observa-

tions" in the Second World War: "With all hands carrying eight grenades, the number of men making *any use of the weapon at all* was consistently less than six per cent of the total in any general action. Research showed further that the grenade was rarely put to any practical use in the initial stage of an amphibious attack. This was also true in Europe." While the wording and lack of specificity in the battle experience questionnaire cannot allow any firm conclusions, the fact remains that close to 90 percent of Canadian officers indicated in their questionnaires that they had witnessed grenades being used in action. Therefore, Marshall's correctness on this point should be brought into question. Marshall, *The Soldier's Load*, 13–14.

92 All statistics on weapons effectiveness compiled from survey "H" question 2: "Have you found any of these weapons particularly effective? If so, which and why?" and survey "H" question 3: "Have you found any of these weapons ineffective? If so, which and why?" See Appendix B.

93 BEQ 159, Captain H.S. Lamb.

94 Statistics compiled from survey "H" question 3. See Appendix A.

95 BEQ 81, Lt.-Colonel P.W. Bennett; BEQ 68, Major Cyril Wrightman.

96 BEQ 145, Captain F.W. Grafton.

97 BEQ 124, Captain Orest P. Dutchak.

98 BEQ 209, Captain Mark Tennant.

99 BEQ 192, Major J.W. Ostiguy. The preference for carrying rifles over the Sten was also noted in: BEQ 8, A/Major I.H. Louson.

100 BEQ 118, Captain A.J. Willick.

101 BEQ 157, Captain B.R. Howard; BEQ 187, Major H.G. Dawson. The No. 69 grenade was cited as "ineffective" by 11 officers and as "outstandingly effective" by only one.

102 BEQ 190, Major T.S. Ketcheson. Also, while the pistol was listed as "ineffective" by 20 officers, it was not listed as "outstandingly effective" by anyone.

103 BEQ 208, Captain William R. Bennett.

104 BEQ 123, Captain G. Fawcett; BEQ 129, A/Major T.M. Lowe; BEQ 33, Captain Edward Brady.

105 BEQ 35, Major A.M. Hamilton.

106 BEQ 281, Major R.G. Liddell.

107 For additional comments on the rifle, see BEQ 192, Major J.W. Ostiguy; BEQ 74, Major R. Rutherford; BEQ 66, Major D. McG. Archibald.

108 BEQ 18, Captain M. Pariseault; BEQ 60, Major A.C. Ross.

109 BEQ 113, Major Norman Wilson-Smith. Also: BEQ 78, Captain T.H. Burdett.

110 BEQ 31, Captain A.V. Malone.

111 BEQ 33, Captain Edward Brady.

112 Only twenty-four officers reported having ever seen the flame-thrower employed in action by their units. Survey "H" question 1. Of these, fifteen found the weapon to be "outstandingly effective," and no officers at all found it to be "ineffective." See BEQ 173, Captain J.C. Watt; BEQ 188, A/Major Harold Mortimer Cunningham. For more on the use of flame throwers, see Copp, *Cinderella Army*, 191.

113 BEQ 79, Major Allister Myles MacMillan; BEQ 127, Major R.J. Orr.

114 See Appendix B for a more detailed break-down of the questionnaire data.

115 See Appendix B. There are two possible exceptions to this. First is the 2-inch mortar. Ten officers rated the 2-inch mortar as "outstandingly effective," and 17 rated it as "ineffective." The second is the sub-machine gun. While 45 officers specifically rated the Sten SMG as "ineffective," 17 officers rated the "SMG" as "outstandingly effective." Of these, however, only a bare handful specifically noted the *Sten* as being an effective weapon – most who rated the SMG highly were either referring to other SMG designs, such as the U.S. Thompson SMG, or else were just referring to it as a broad category.

116 For a few of the comments on the adequacy of section weapons, see BEQ 36, A/Major John Irvin Mills; BEQ 35, Major A.M. Hamilton; BEQ 79, Major Allister Myles MacMillan; BEQ 83, A/Major D.M. Ripley; BEQ 120, Captain Pollin; BEQ 100, Lt.-Colonel Charles Petch; BEQ 129, A/Major T.M. Lowe; BEQ 151, Major M.B. John; BEQ 209, Captain Mark Tennant; BEW 283, Captain James Bulloch.

117 BEQ 30, A/Captain Yuile.

118 BEQ 178, Major John C. Clarke.

119 BEQ 206, Captain Leonard James Gouten.

120 BEQ 295, Captain Edward Kenneth Maxted.

121 Bercuson, *Battalion of Heroes*, 247.

122 For a concise and readable account of an otherwise extremely complicated issue, see Stacey, *The Canadian Army*, 232–5.

123 Statistics compiled from survey "H" question 10(a): "Did your section go into battle under W.E. strength?" Overall: "Yes" 123 surveys (81.26%), "No" 23 surveys (15.23%), "No Answer" 5 surveys (3.31%).

Mediterranean campaign: "Yes" 43 surveys (82.69%), "No" 7 surveys (13.46%), "No Answer" 2 surveys (3.85%). NW Europe campaign: "Yes" 80 surveys (80.81%), "No" 16 surveys (16.16%), "No Answer" 3 surveys (3.03%). See Appendix B.

124 According to statistics compiled from Survey "H" question 10(b): "What was the average number of [other ranks] in your section?" The average taken from all responding officers was 5.63. Average taken from all officers in the Mediterranean theatre was 5.463. Average taken from all officers in the Northwest Europe theatre was 5.714. These numbers should be taken with a grain of salt, as they likely are compilations based on officers' rough estimates, rather than hard statistical research. See Appendix A.

125 Statistics compiled from survey "H" question 10(d): "In your view, did your sections at the strength given under (b) prove adequate for close quarter fighting?" Overall: "Yes" 81 surveys (55.48%), "No" 45 surveys (30.82%), "No Answer" 20 surveys (13.7%). The unusually high percentage of officers who gave no answer to the question likely has to do with those who answered "No" to question 10(b) not bothering to provide an answer. See Appendix B.

126 Statistics compiled from survey "H" question 10(f): "Was their [the casualty replacements'] general standard of efficiency high, moderate, or low?" Overall: "High" 8 surveys (5.63%), "Moderate" 85 surveys (59.86%), "Low" 38 surveys (26.76%), "No Answer" 11 surveys (7.75%). See Appendix B.

127 Also compiled from survey "H" question 10(f). Mediterranean theater: "High" 4 surveys (8.16%), "Moderate" 32 surveys (65.31%), "Low" 8 surveys (16.33%), "No Answer" 5 surveys (10.2%). Northwest Europe theatre: "High" 4 surveys (4.3%), "Moderate" 53 surveys (56.99%), "Low" 30 surveys (32.26%), "No Answer" 6 surveys (6.45%). See Appendix B.

128 BEQ 16, A/Major Thomas McCoy.

129 BEQ 30, A/Captain Yuile.

130 BEQ 86, A/Major A.H.M. Carmichael.

131 BEQ 17, Captain W. Parker.

132 BEQ 18, Captain M. Pariseault.

133 BEQ 191, A/Major Harrison.

134 BEQ 86, A/Major A.H.M. Carmichael.

135 BEQ 186, Lt.-Colonel E.T. Jacques.

136 BEQ 128, A/Major Jock McLeod.

137 BEQ 156, Major W.B. Stashart; BEQ 16, A/Major Thomas McCoy.

138 BEQ 226, Major James L. Dandy; BEQ 207, Captain Gordon A. Crutcher.

139 BEQ 35, Major A.M. Hamilton.

140 Copp, *Cinderella Army,* 178–9; Stacey, *Arms, Men, and Governments,* 440.

141 BEQ 59, Major F.J. Hammond.

142 BEQ 17, Captain W. Parker.

143 BEQ 86, A/Major A.H.M. Carmichael.

144 Compiled from answers to survey "A" question 3. See Appendix A.

145 Stouffer, *The American Soldier, Vol. II,* 282–4.

146 Spiller, "S.L.A. Marshall and the Ratio of Fire," 69.

147 One questionnaire mentions the rifle as being an ineffective weapon due to "indifferent marksmanship," but no elaboration is offered, and nothing similar appears in any other questionnaire. See BEQ 207, Captain Gordon A. Crutcher.

148 BEQ 208, Captain William R. Bennett. Captain Bennett receives passing mention in one of the newer histories of the First Special Service Force. See Nadler, *A Perfect Hell.*

149 BEQ 29, A/Major C.K. Crummer.

150 BEQ 129, A/Major T.M. Lowe. Captain Armstrong of the Saskatoon Light Infantry recounted much the same thing, only employing medium machine guns instead of Brens. See BEQ 73, Captain Armstrong.

151 BEQ 48, A/Captain Sinkewicz.

152 BEQ 151, Major M.B. John.

153 BEQ 147, Captain Robert B. Mainprize. See also BEQ 36, A/Major John Irvin Mills.

154 BEQ 275, Captain Ian Scott Waldie.

155 BEQ 29, A/Major C.K. Crummer.

156 BEQ 145, Captain F.W. Grafton.

157 BEQ 35, Major A.M. Hamilton.

158 Glenbow Archives, M1961, File 18, Calgary Highlanders Courts of Inquiry, 26 Nov. 1944.

159 Glenbow Archives, M1961, File 18, Calgary Highlanders Courts of Inquiry, 6 March 1945.

160 As Marshall put it: "The soldier who is always willing and eager to use his weapon has a reserve in the duty belt of the man next to him who

will go along into battle *but will not fire.*" Marshall, *The Soldier's Load,* 19. Emphasis in original.

161 Ellis, *One Day in a Very Long War,* 21–2; Copp, *Cinderella Army,* 59.

162 Mansoor, *The GI Offensive in Europe,* 182–3.

163 Statistics compiled based on answers to survey "H" question 14a, "Was your unit ever short of ammunition in battle?" Overall: "Yes" 38 surveys, "No" 106 surveys, "No Answer" 10 surveys. See Appendix B.

164 Copp, *Fields of Fire,* 28.

165 BEQ 178, Major John C. Clarke. Similar notes were recorded in BEQ 76, Major W.C. Allan; BEQ 290, Major Froggett.

166 BEQ 281, Major R.G. Liddell.

167 BEQ 224, Major G.P. Boucher.

168 War Office, *Infantry Training 1937,* 4. Also see War Office, *Infantry Section Leading 1938,* 19–31.

169 War Office, *Field Service Regulations 1935,* 131.

170 BEQ 116, A/Major G.F. Colgate.

171 BEQ 115, Major David Durward; BEQ 34, A/Captain J.A.D. Graham.

172 BEQ 129, A/Major T.M. Lowe; BEQ 100, Lt.-Colonel Charles Petch.

173 BEQ 116, A/Major G.E. Colgate.

174 BEQ 35, Major A.M. Hamilton.

175 BEQ 48, A/Captain Sinkewicz.

176 Gregory Liedtke has mentioned that, in Normandy, the Canadian II Corps "faced the most powerful German defence arrangement encountered by any of the Allied armies throughout the Normandy campaign." Liedtke, "Canadian Offensive Operations in Normandy Revisited."

177 BEQ 281, Major R.G. Liddell.

178 BEQ 69, Captain F.T. Rea.

179 BEQ 208, Captain William R. Bennett.

180 Copp, *Fields of Fire,* 29.

181 War Office, *Field Service Regulations 1935,* 131.

182 Shalit, *The Psychology of Conflict and Combat,* 141. Shalit accidentally misquotes Marshall by placing the ratio of fire as high as 30 percent: Marshall claimed it was usually around half that.

183 Ibid., 142. Also see Glass, "The Problems of Stress in Combat Zones."

184 Nadelson, *Trained to Kill: Soldiers at War,* 46.

185 Grossman also quotes historian Paddy Griffith's work on the Civil War: "Time and again we read of regiments [in the Civil War] blazing away uncontrollably, once started, and continuing until all ammunition was

gone or all enthusiasm spent. Firing was such a positive act, and gave the men such a physical release from their emotions, that instincts easily took over from training and from the exhortations of officers." Grossman, *On Killing*, 9–10.

186 Staub, *The Psychology of Good and Evil*, 56.

187 Ibid., 57.

188 BEQ 28, A/Major J.P.G. Kemp.

189 For a few examples, among others, of shelling being the cause of mental fatigue: BEQ 293, Major Roy Styffe; BEQ 284, Captain W.L. Lyster; BEQ 209, Captain Mark Tennant; BEQ 206, Captain Leonard James Gouten; BEQ 129, A/Major T.M. Lowe.

190 BEQ 100, Lt.-Colonel Charles Petch; BEQ 207, Captain Gordon A. Crutcher.

191 BEQ 76, Major W.C. Allan.

192 BEQ 178, Major John Clarke.

193 Data compiled from survey "A" question 3. See Appendix A.

194 Quoted in: French, *Raising Churchill's Army*, 152.

195 Staub, *Psychology of Good and Evil*, 56.

196 Ibid., 56.

197 Bercuson, *Significant Incident*, 34.

CONCLUSION

1 Stacey, *The Canadian Army*, 310.

2 Cook, *Clio's Warriors*, 110–11.

3 Historian Michael Doubler quotes General Patton as saying that: "It is the general consensus of opinion of all officers who have actually participated in battle that our men do not shoot enough." Quoted in: Doubler, *Closing with the Enemy*, 14.

4 Allan English, *Understanding Military Culture*, 65.

BIBLIOGRAPHY

ARCHIVAL SOURCES

Glenbow Archives, Calgary, Alberta
  Calgary Highlanders Fonds, M1961
  MacKinnon/Sage Family Fonds, M7699
  Prairie Command Headquarters Fonds, M8039
  Ross Ellis Fonds, M6743

Library and Archives Canada
  Record Group 24
    Volume 9823 – Tactical investigation questionnaires, circulation
      and disposal
    Volume 9824 – Tactical investigation questionnaires, routine
      requests
    Volume 9879 – Completed battle experience questionnaires
    Volume 10450 – Battle experience questionnaires
    C-5167   Weekly reports, Canadian Small Arms Liaison Officer
      Overseas, 1941–45

OTHER PRIMARY SOURCES

Copp, Terry (Ed.). *Montgomery's Scientists: Operational Research in Northwest Europe.* Waterloo, Ontario: Laurier Centre for Military, Strategic and Disarmament Studies, 2000.

Great Britain, War Office. *Field Service Pocket Book, 1940.* Ottawa: His Majesty's Stationery Office, 1940.

Great Britain, War Office. *Field Service Regulations, vol. II – Operations – General, 1935.* Ottawa: King's Printer, 1939.

Great Britain, War Office. *Infantry Section Leading, 1938.* London: 1938.

Great Britain, War Office. *Infantry Training (Training and War) 1937.* London: 1937.

Great Britain, War Office. *Notes from Theatres of War,* nos. 1 through 19. London: 1942–1945.

United States, War Department. *Field Service Regulations: Operations, 1941.* FM 100-5. Washington, DC: Government Printing Office, 22 May 1941.

SECONDARY SOURCES

Addison, Paul, and Angus Calder (eds.). *Time to Kill: The Soldier's Experience of War in the West 1939–1945.* London: Pimlico, 1997.

Asad, Talal. *On Suicide Bombing (The Wellek Library Lectures).* New York: Columbia University Press, 2007.

Ashworth, Tony. *Trench Warfare, 1914–1918: The Live and Let Live System.* New York: Holmes & Meier, 1980.

Audoin-Rouzeau, Stéphane, and Annette Becker. *14–18: Understanding the Great War.* Trans. Catherine Temerson. New York: Hill and Wang, 2002.

Bercuson, David J. *Battalion of Heroes: The Calgary Highlanders in World War II.* Calgary: The Calgary Highlanders Regimental Funds Foundation, 1994.

– *Maple Leaf Against the Axis: Canada's Second World War.* Toronto: Stoddart Publishing, 1995.

– *Significant Incident: Canada's Army, the Airborne, and the Murder in Somalia.* Toronto: McClelland & Stewart, 1996.

Bernardete, Seth. *The Argument of the Action: Essays on Greek Poetry and Philosophy.* Chicago and London: University of Chicago Press, 2000.

Bonn, Keith E. *When the Odds Were Even: The Vosges Mountains Campaign, October 1944 to January 1945.* Novato, California: Presidio Press, 1994.

Bourke, Joanna. *Dismembering the Male: Men's Bodies, Britain, and the Great War.* Chicago: University of Chicago Press, 1996.

– *Fear: A Cultural History.* Emeryville, California: Shoemaker & Hoard, 2005.

Brooks, Risa A., and Elizabeth A. Stanley (eds.). *Creating Military Power: The Sources of Military Effectiveness.* Stanford: Stanford University Press, 2007.

Brown, Ian M. "Not Glamorous, But Effective: The Canadian Corps and the Set-Piece Attack, 1917–1918." *Journal of Military History,* 58, no. 3 (July 1994).

Brown, John Sloan. "Colonel Trevor N. Dupuy and the Mythos of *Wehrmacht* Superiority: A Reconsideration." *Military Affairs* 50, no. 1 (January 1986).

– "The *Wehrmacht* Mythos Revisited: A Challenge for Colonel Trevor N. Dupuy." *Military Affairs,* 51, no. 3 (July 1987).

Bull, Stephen. *World War II Infantry Tactics: Company and Battalion.* Oxford: Osprey Publishing, 2005.

– *World War II Infantry Tactics: Squad and Platoon.* Oxford: Osprey Publishing, 2004.

Callahan, Raymond. "Two Armies in Normandy: Weighing British and Canadian Military Performance." In Wilson, *D-Day 1944.*

Canning, Joseph, Hartmut Lehmann, and Jay Winter (eds.). *Power, Violence and Mass Death in Pre-Modern and Modern Times.* Aldershot: Ashgate Publishing, 2004.

Chamberlain, W.R. "Training the Functional Rifleman." *Canadian Army Journal,* 4, no. 9 (February 1951).

Chambers, John Whiteclay. "S.L.A. Marshall's *Men Against Fire*: New Evidence on Fire Ratios." *Parameters* (autumn 2003).

Chickering, Roger, Stig Förster, and Bernd Greiner (eds.). *A World at Total War: Global Conflict and the Politics of Destruction, 1937–1945.* Cambridge: Cambridge University Press, 2005.

Cohen, Eliot A. *Citizens and Soldiers: The Dilemmas of Military Service.* Ithaca and London: Cornell University Press, 1985.

Condell, Bruce, and David T. Zabecki (eds.). *On the German Art of War: Truppenführung.* Boulder: Lynne Rienner Publishers, 2001.

Cook, Tim. *Clio's Warriors: Canadian Historians and the Writing of the World Wars*. Vancouver: UBC Press, 2006.

Copp, Terry. *Cinderella Army: The Canadians in Northwest Europe, 1944–1945*. Toronto: University of Toronto Press, 2007.

– *Fields of Fire: The Canadians in Normandy*. Toronto: University of Toronto Press, 2004.

Copp, Terry, and Bill McAndrew. *Battle Exhaustion: Soldiers and Psychiatrists in the Canadian Army, 1939–1945*. Montreal and Kingston: McGill-Queen's University Press, 1990.

Corum, James S. *The Roots of Blitzkrieg: Hans von Seeckt and German Military Reform*. Lawrence, Kansas: University Press of Kansas, 1992.

Crang, Jeremy A. *The British Army and the People's War 1939–1945*. Manchester: Manchester University Press, 2000.

Curtis, Bruce. *The Politics of Population: State Formation, Statistics, and the Census of Canada, 1840–1875*. Toronto: University of Toronto Press, 2001.

Curtis, Vincent J. "The Elastic Defence, 1917–1943." *Canadian Army Journal*, 8, no. 1 (winter 2005).

Dawson, Robert MacGregor. *The Conscription Crisis of 1944*. Toronto: University of Toronto Press, 1961.

D'Este, Carlo. *Decision in Normandy*. New York: Dutton, 1983.

Detwiler, Donald S. (ed.). *World War II German Military Studies*. New York and London: Garland Publishing Inc., 1979.

Dexter, Grant. *Conscription Debates of 1917 and 1944: An Analysis*. Winnipeg: Free Press, 1944.

Dickson, Paul Douglas. *A Thoroughly Canadian General: A Biography of General H.D.G. Crerar*. Toronto: University of Toronto Press, 2007.

Doubler, Michael D. *Closing with the Enemy: How GIs Fought the War in Europe, 1944–1945*. Lawrence, Kansas: University Press of Kansas, 1994.

Dunnigan, James F. *How to Make War*. 4th Edition. New York: HarperCollins, 2003.

Dupuy, Trevor N. *A Genius for War: The German Army and General Staff, 1807–1945*. London: Macdonald & Jane's, 1977.

– *Numbers, Prediction, and War: Using History to Evaluate Combat Factors and Predict the Outcome of Battles*. New York: Bobbs-Merrill, 1979.

Ellis, John. *Brute Force: Allied Strategy and Tactics in the Second World War*. London: A. Deutsch, 1990.

– *One Day in a Very Long War: Wednesday 25th October 1944*. London: Jonathan Cape, 1998.

– *The Sharp End of War: The Fighting Man in World War II*. Newton Abbot: David & Charles, 1980.

English, Allan. *The Cream of the Crop: Canadian Aircrew, 1939-1945*. Montreal and Kingston: McGill-Queen's University Press, 1996.

– (ed.). *The Operational Art: Canadian Perspectives – Leadership and Command*. Kingston, Ontario: Canadian Defence Academy Press, 2006.

– *Understanding Military Culture: A Canadian Perspective*. Montreal and Kingston: McGill-Queen's University Press, 2004.

English, John A. *Lament for an Army: The Decline of Canadian Military Professionalism*. Toronto: Irwin Publishing, 1998.

– "Lessons from the Great War." *Canadian Military Journal*, 4, no. 2, (summer 2003).

– *On Infantry*. New York: Praeger, 1984.

– *The Canadian Army and the Normandy Campaign: A Study of Failure in High Command*. New York: Praeger, 1991.

Erickson, John. *The Road to Berlin: The Continuing Story of Stalin's War with Germany*. Boulder, Colorado: Westview Press, 1983.

Ferguson, Niall. *The Pity of War: Explaining World War I*. London: Basic Books, 1998.

– *The War of the World: Twentieth-Century Conflict and the Descent of the West*. New York: Penguin Press, 2006.

French, David. *Raising Churchill's Army: The British Army and the War Against Germany, 1919–1945*. Oxford: Oxford University Press, 2000.

Fritz, Stephen G. *Frontsoldaten: The German Soldier in World War II*. Lexington: The University Press of Kentucky, 1995.

Gamble, Richard M. *The War for Righteousness: Progressive Christianity, the Great War, and the Rise of the Messianic Nation*. Wilmington: ISI Books, 2003.

Garber, W.E. "Every Rifleman Must Be an Aggressive Fighter." *Canadian Army Journal*, 6, no. 6 (January 1963), 21–5.

Glass, A.L. "The Problems of Stress in Combat Zones." Symposium on Stress. Washington, DC: Army Medical Service Graduate School, 1953.

Godefroy, Andrew. "Canadian Military Effectiveness in the First World War." In Horn, *The Canadian Way of War*.

Granatstein, J.L. *Canada's Army: Waging War and Keeping the Peace*. Toronto: University of Toronto Press, 2002.

Granatstein, J.L., and Peter Neary (eds.). *The Good Fight: Canadians and World War II.* Toronto: Copp Clark Ltd., 1995.

Grossman, Dave. *On Combat: The Psychology and Physiology of Deadly Combat in War and in Peace.* PPCT Research Publications, 2004.

– *On Killing: The Psychological Costs of Learning to Kill in War and Society.* New York: Back Bay Books, 1996.

– "On Killing II: The Psychological Cost of Learning to Kill." *International Journal of Emergency Mental Health*, 3, no. 3 (2001), 137–44.

– "Trained to Kill." *Christianity Today*, (10 August 1998).

Hackworth, David H. and Julie Sherman. *About Face: The Odyssey of an American Warrior.* New York: Simon and Schuster, 1989.

Harris, Stephen J. *Canadian Brass: The Making of a Professional Army, 1860–1939.* Toronto: University of Toronto Press, 1988.

Hart, Russell A. *Clash of Arms: How the Allies Won in Normandy.* Boulder: Lynne Reinner Publishers, 2001.

Haynes, Alex D. "The Development of Infantry Doctrine in the Canadian Expeditionary Force: 1914–1918." *Canadian Military Journal*, 8, no. 3 (autumn 2007).

Hayward, Philip. "The Measurement of Combat Effectiveness." *Operations Research*, 16, no. 2 (March–April 1968).

Heron, Craig (ed.). *The Workers' Revolt in Canada, 1917–1925.* Toronto: University of Toronto Press, 1998.

Holmes, Richard. *Acts of War: The Behavior of Men in Battle.* New York: Free Press, 1986.

Horn, Bernd (ed.). *In the Breach: Perspectives on Leadership in the Army Today.* Kingston, Ontario: Land Combat Development, 2004.

– (ed.). *The Canadian Way of War: Serving the National Interest.* Toronto: Dundurn Press, 2006.

Horn, Bernd, and Stephen J. Harris (eds.). *Generalship and the Art of the Admiral: Perspectives on Canadian Senior Military Leadership.* St Catharines, Ontario: Vanwell Publishing Limited, 2001.

Horne, John, and Alan Kramer. *German Atrocities, 1914: A History of Denial.* New Haven and London: Yale University Press, 2001.

Huebner, Andrew J. *The Warrior Image: Soldiers in American Culture from the Second World War to the Vietnam Era.* Chapel Hill: University of North Carolina Press, 2008.

Janowitz, Morris. *Sociology and the Military Establishment.* Beverly Hills: Sage Publications, 1974.

Johnston, Paul. "D +20,000: Still Fighting the Normandy Campaign." *The Army Doctrine and Training Bulletin*, 3, no. 1 (Spring 2000).

– "Tactical Air Power Controversies in Normandy: A Question of Doctrine." *Canadian Military History*, 9, no. 2 (spring 2000).

Jones, Michael Patrick. "The Role of Trench Raiding in Combat Motivation in the Canadian Corps on the Western Front." Kingston, Ontario: Queen's University, unpublished paper, 2007.

Keegan, John. *Six Armies in Normandy: From D-Day to the Liberation of Paris, June 6th–August 25th, 1944.* New York: Viking Press, 1982.

– *The Face of Battle: A Study of Agincourt, Waterloo and the Somme.* London: Pimlico, 2004.

– *The First World War.* Toronto: Vintage Canada, 2000.

Krauss, Beatrice J., et al. "Factors Affecting Veterans' Decisions to Fire Weapons in Combat Situations." *International Journal of Group Tensions*, 3, no. 3–4, (1974).

Labaw, Patricia J. *Advanced Questionnaire Design.* Cambridge, Massachusetts: Abt Books, 1982.

Leinbaugh, Harold P., and John D. Campbell. *The Men of Company K.* New York: Morrow, 1985.

Liedtke, Gregory. "Canadian Offensive Operations in Normandy Revisited." *Canadian Military Journal*, 8, no. 2, (summer 2007).

Long, Gavin. *Australia in the War of 1939–1945, Army: The Final Campaigns.* Canberra: Australian War Memorial, 1963.

Mahon, John K., and Romana Danysh. *Infantry, Part I: Regular Army.* Washington, DC: Office of the Chief of Military History, 1972.

Mansoor, Peter R. *The G.I. Offensive in Europe: The Triumph of American Infantry Divisions, 1941–1945,* (Lawrence, Kansas: University Press of Kansas, 1999.

Mantle, Craig Leslie (ed.). *The Unwilling and the Reluctant: Theoretical Perspectives on Disobedience in the Military.* Kingston: Canadian Defence Academy Press, 2006.

Marshall, John Douglas. *Reconciliation Road: A Family Odyssey of War and Honor.* Syracuse: Syracuse University Press, 1993.

Marshall, S.L.A. *Bringing Up the Rear: A Memoir.* Cate Marshall (ed.). San Rafael, California: Presidio Press, 1979.

– *Infantry Operations and Weapons Usage in Korea.* London: Greenhill Books, 1988.

– *Men Against Fire: The Problem of Battle Command in Future War.* New

York: William Morrow and Company, 1968.

– *Night Drop: The American Airborne Invasion of Normandy.* Boston: Little, Brown and Company, 1962.

– *The Soldier's Load and the Mobility of a Nation.* Washington, DC: Combat Forces Press, 1950.

Massey, Hector J. *The Canadian Military: A Profile.* Copp Clark, 1972.

McAndrew, Bill. "Canadian Doctrine: Continuities and Discontinuities." *The Army Doctrine and Training Bulletin,* 4, no. 3 (fall 2001).

– "Fire or Movement?: Canadian Tactical Doctrine, Sicily – 1943." *Military Affairs,* 51, no. 3 (July 1987).

– "Soldiers and Technology." *The Army Doctrine and Training Bulletin,* 2, no. 2 (May 1999).

Millett, Allan R. "The Effectiveness of Military Organizations." In Allan R. Millett and Williamson Murray (eds.). *Military Effectiveness: Volume I – The First World War.* Boston: Allen & Unwin, 1988.

– "The United States Armed Forces in the Second World War." In Allan R. Millett and Williamson Murray (eds.). *Military Effectiveness: Volume III – The Second World War.* Boston: Allen & Unwin, 1988.

Morton, Desmond. *A Military History of Canada: From Champlain to the Gulf War.* Toronto: McClelland & Stewart, 1992.

– *When Your Number's Up: The Canadian Soldier in the First World War.* Toronto: Random House of Canada, 1993.

Mosier, John. *The Myth of the Great War: A New Military History of World War I.* New York: HarperCollins, 2001.

Mosse, George L. *Fallen Soldiers: Reshaping the Memory of the World Wars.* New York and Oxford: Oxford University Press, 1990.

Nadelson, Theodore. *Trained to Kill: Soldiers at War.* Baltimore and London: Johns Hopkins University Press, 2005.

Nadler, John. *A Perfect Hell: The Forgotten Story of the Canadian Commandos of the Second World War.* Toronto: Anchor Canada, 2006.

Neiberg, Michael S. *Making Citizen Soldiers: ROTC and the Ideology of American Military Service.* Cambridge: Harvard University Press, 2000.

Neillands, Robin. *The Bomber War: The Allied Air Offensive Against Nazi Germany.* Woodstock and New York: Overlook Press, 2003.

Nicholson, G.W.L. *Official History of the Canadian Army in the Second World War, Volume II: The Canadians in Italy 1943–1945.* Ottawa: Queen's Printer, 1956.

Oppenheim, A.N. *Questionnaire Design, Interviewing, and Attitude Assessment.* London and New York: Printer Publishers, 1992.

Orpen, Neil. *South African Forces, World War II: East African and Abyssinian Campaigns.* Cape Town and Johannesburg: Purnell, 1968.

Overy, Richard. *Why the Allies Won.* London: Jonathan Cape, 1995.

Perrun, Jody. "Best-Laid Plans: Guy Simonds and Operation Totalize, 7–10 August 1944." *The Journal of Military History*, 67, no. 1 (January 2003), 137–73.

Pierson, David S. "Natural Killers – Turning the Tide of Battle." *Military Review* (May–June 1999).

Place, Timothy Harrison. *Military Training in the British Army: 1940-1944, From Dunkirk to D-Day.* London: Frank Cass, 2000.

Powers, Stephen T. "The Battle for Normandy: The Lingering Controversy." *Journal of Military History*, 56, no. 3 (July 1992).

Preston, Richard Arthur. *Canada's RMC: A History of the Royal Military College.* Toronto: University of Toronto Press, 1969.

Rawling, Bill. "Fire or Movement?: Canadian Tactical Doctrine, Sicily – 1943." *Military Affairs*, 51, no. 3 (July 1987), 140–5.

– *Surviving Trench Warfare: Technology and the Canadian Corps 1914–1918.* Toronto: University of Toronto Press, 1992.

Razack, Sherene H. *Dark Threats and White Knights: The Somalia Affair, Peacekeeping, and the New Imperialism.* Toronto: University of Toronto Press, 2004.

Robinson, Daniel J. *The Measure of Democracy: Polling, Market Researching, and Public Life, 1930–1945.* Toronto: University of Toronto Press, 1999.

Saris, Willem E., and Irmtraud N. Gallhofer. *Design, Evaluation, and Analysis of Questionnaires for Survey Research.* Hoboken, New Jersey: John Wiley & Sons, 2007.

Sarkesian, Sam C. (ed.) *Combat Effectiveness: Cohesion, Stress, and the Volunteer Military.* Beverly Hills: Sage Publications, 1980.

Schivelbusch, Wolfgang. *The Culture of Defeat: On National Trauma, Mourning, and Recovery.* New York: Henry Holt and Company, 2003.

Schreiber, Shane B. *Shock Army of the British Empire: The Canadian Corps in the Last 100 Days of the Great War.* Westport: Praeger, 1997.

Shalit, Ben. *The Psychology of Conflict and Combat.* New York: Praeger, 1988.

Smelser, Ronald, and Edward J. Davies II. *The Myth of the Eastern*

Front: The Nazi-Soviet War in American Popular Culture. Cambridge: Cambridge University Press, 2007.

Smoler, Frederic. "The Secret of the Soldiers Who Didn't Shoot." *American Heritage*, 40, no. 2 (March 1989).

Socknat, Thomas. *Witness Against War: Pacifism in Canada, 1900–1945.* Toronto: University of Toronto Press, 1987.

Spiller, Roger J. "S.L.A. Marshall and the Ratio of Fire." *RUSI Journal*, no. 133, (1988).

Stacey, C.P. *A Date With History.* Ottawa: Deneau, 1983.

– *Arms, Men and Governments: The War Policies of Canada, 1939–1945.* Ottawa: Queen's Printer, 1970.

– *Official History of the Canadian Army in the Second World War: Six Years of War: The Army in Canada, Britain and the Pacific.* Ottawa: Queen's Printer, 1955.

– *The Canadian Army 1939–1945: An Official Historical Summary.* Ottawa: King's Printer, 1948.

Staub, Ervin. *The Psychology of Good and Evil: Why Children, Adults, and Groups Help and Harm Others.* Cambridge: Cambridge University Press, 2003.

Stolfi, R.H.S. *Hitler's Panzers East: World War II Reinterpreted.* Norman and London: University of Oklahoma Press, 1991.

Strachan, Hew. "Training, Morale and Modern War." *Journal of Contemporary History*, 41, no. 2 (April 2006).

Thompson, John Herd, and Allen Seager. *Canada, 1922–1939: Decades of Discord.* Toronto: McClelland & Stewart, 1985.

van Creveld, Martin. *Fighting Power: German and U.S. Army Performance, 1939–1945.* Westport, Ontario: Greenwood Press, 1982.

Vance, Jonathan. *Death So Noble: Memory, Meaning, and the First World War.* Vancouver: UBC Press, 2000.

Waiser, Bill. *All Hell Can't Stop Us: The On-to-Ottawa Trek and Regina Riot.* Calgary: Fifth House, 2003.

Wakin, Malham M. *War, Morality, and the Military Profession.* Boulder, Colorado: Westview Press, 1979.

Walsh, John E. "Inadequacy of Cost per 'Kill' as Measure of Effectiveness." *Operations Research*, 5, no. 6 (December 1957).

Walzer, Michael. *Just and Unjust War: A Moral Argument with Historical Illustrations.* New York: Basic Books, 2006.

Watson, Brent Bryan. *Far Eastern Tour: The Canadian Infantry in Korea,*

1950–1953. Montreal and Kingston: McGill-Queen's University Press, 2002.

Watson, Peter. *War on the Mind: The Military Uses and Abuses of Psychology*. New York: Basic Books, 1978.

Weigley, Russell F. *Eisenhower's Lieutenants: The Campaign of France and Germany 1944–1945*. Bloomington: Indiana University Press, 1981.

Wessely, Simon. "Twentieth-century Theories on Combat Motivation and Breakdown." *Journal of Contemporary History*, 41, no. 2 (April 2006).

Williams, F.D.G. *SLAM: The Influence of S.L.A. Marshall on the United States Army*. Fort Monroe, Virginia: United States Training and Doctrine Command, 1994.

Wilson, Theodore A. *D-Day 1944*. Abilene, Kansas: University Press of Kansas, 1994.

Winter, Jay. *Remembering War: The Great War Between Memory and History in the Twentieth Century*. New Haven and London: Yale University Press, 2006.

– *Sites of Memory, Sites of Mourning: The Great War in European Cultural History*. Cambridge: Cambridge University Press, 1995.

Zuehlke, Mark. *Holding Juno: Canada's Heroic Defence of the D-Day Beaches, June 7 12, 1944*. Vancouver: Douglas & McIntyre, 2005.

– *Ortona: Canada's Epic World War II Battle*. Vancouver and Toronto: Douglas & McIntyre, 2004.

INDEX

air power, 96–9

Allan, Major J.C., 114

Allan, Major W.C., 107, 142

aristeia, 3–4, 7

armoured vehicles, 75, 88–90, 99–100, 107, 138, 145; communication with, 94–5; co-operation with infantry, 92–6; vulnerability of, 90–3, 119. *See also* Canadian Infantry Corps.

artillery, 75, 82, 99–100, 145; creeping barrage, 77–8, 82–4, 139; friendly fire of, 86–7; inaccuracy of, 84–5; and material superiority, 81, 88; suppressive fire, 87–8, 107. *See also* Canadian Infantry Corps.

Audoin-Rouzeau, Stéphane, 13, 56, 58

Bacon, Captain R.D., 118

battle drill, 62, 109

battle experience questionnaires, 26, 28–9; administrative background to, 29–33, 38–9; collection of data, 41–2, 66; officer respondents, 66–7; of other combat arms, 31; previous analysis of by historians, 32; and questionnaire theory, 40–3; reliability of, 42–3, 45–6; representativeness of, 44–5; research methodology, 46–8

battle narratives, 11–14

Beatty, Major D.S., 114

Becker, Annette, 13, 56, 58

Bennett, Lt.-Colonel P.W., 123

Bennett, Captain William, 92, 119, 134, 136, 138

Bercuson, David, 143

bite-and-hold tactics. *See* Canadian Infantry Corps.

Blaker, Captain P.A.R., 95

BLOCKBUSTER, Operation, 118

Boucher, Major G.P., 114, 136

Brown, Ian, 77

Burdett, Captain T.H., 85

Burgess, Major John Wesley, 93